Irving Babbitt

Irving Babbitt

An Intellectual Study

by Thomas R. Nevin

The University of North Carolina Press

Chapel Hill and London

© 1984 by The University of North Carolina Press

Manufactured in the United States of America

Library of Congress Cataloging in Publication Data
Nevin, Thomas R., 1944–
 Irving Babbitt.

 Bibliography: p.
 Includes index.
 1. Babbitt, Irving, 1865–1933. 2. Humanism—20th
century. 3. Criticism—United States—History—20th
century. I. Title.
PQ67.B2N48 1984   191   83-27407
ISBN 0-8078-1595-0

For Paul MacKendrick

ἐγὼ δέ κέ τοι ἰδέω χαριν ἤματα πάντα

Contents

Preface

From 1894 to 1933, Irving Babbitt taught French and comparative literature at Harvard University. In that time and long after his death he was reputed to be a reactionary defender of genteel morality and taste. Although Babbitt had mentors in the Victorian age, notably Charles Eliot Norton and Matthew Arnold, the tradition he represented was not one of class mores but of a transcultural assumption that literature had to embody and inculcate disciplinary values. This humanism, as Babbitt understood it, stood directly contrary to the ascendance of utilitarian science at the turn of the century, for the sciences, however legitimate in the area of phenomenal inquiry, had become a secular faith that supplanted the traditional strength and appeal of cultural and religious standards. With the rise of this naturalism, literature itself had become either a reflection of mechanized, demoralized society or an aesthetic escape from its ugliness.

This study examines Babbitt's formulation of humanism according to the themes of his five books and two collections of essays. Following in rough chronology from 1908 to 1932, the topics include Babbitt's attacks upon collegiate educational reform; his literary and aesthetic criticism; his political philosophy of "aristocratic democracy"; and his fusion of humanism with early Buddhism as a tentative proposal for an internationally based cultural decorum. One chapter is devoted to Babbitt's work in French letters and its relation to his conception of humanist culture.

This study is not a biography. Rather, it is a history of Babbitt's mind, his allegiances, the sources of his values and his language, and their part in his highly polemical assault upon his era and indeed upon the direction of twentieth-century society. Closely complementing his published works are his forty years of correspondence with fellow humanist, Paul Elmer More, and his extensive files of notes. I have drawn heavily upon both collections so as to allow Babbitt to speak for himself but also to qualify or amplify points he made in his books.

Babbitt deserves more attention than he has been given as a major figure in America's intellectual history. He was a highly erudite, forceful teacher who influenced the thought of some of America's foremost men of letters, including T. S. Eliot, Van Wyck Brooks, Walter Lippmann, and many others. Babbitt had strong, intensely felt biases that set him against virtually every predominant intellectual, social, and political trend of his time. Perhaps for the very reasons that he was at one time or other labeled an obscurant and a dogmatist, he may now be recognized as a pertinent critic of our own time. Although he argued largely negatively, there are positive inferences to be made from his works. Perhaps the most sophisticated of these was his attempt to reconcile Western and Eastern thought by claiming close analogies between European humanism and its counterparts in the traditions of Buddha and Confucius. This aspect of his thought has been generally ignored by critics and admirers alike and may well serve as a starting point for a revaluation of Babbitt's stature.

It is a pleasure to acknowledge the many debts I have incurred in preparing this book. The first and greatest I owe to Mrs. Esther Babbitt Howe and to her husband, Professor George Howe, for generously granting me access to the papers of Irving Babbitt, and for their gracious hospitality during my visits with them in Washington, D.C., and New Hampshire. For permission to use the correspondence of Paul Elmer More, I wish to thank Arthur H. Dakin. For permission to use the papers of Harry Hayden Clark, I wish to thank his daughter, Mrs. Walter Marshall.

I am grateful to the staff of the Harvard University Archives for its assistance while I made my way through the clutter of Babbitt's notes. I am similarly indebted to the staff of the Houghton Library, Harvard University, for the Charles Eliot Norton Papers; to the staff of the University of Illinois Archives, for the Stuart Sherman Papers; to the staff of the University of Wisconsin Archives, for the Harry Hayden Clark Papers; and to the librarians of the American Academy of Arts and Letters, for its collection of Babbitt's correspondence.

Harry Levin offered me advice and encouragement at crucial times in the course of this study. Stuart Curran gave many hours and much astute criticism to each chapter; improvements in the first revisions I owe substantially to him. Paul MacKendrick was no less exacting a reader; some measure of my debt to him I have tried to indicate elsewhere in this book. Other helpful readers of individual chapters include Joseph Anthony Wittreich, Jr., R. Jackson Wilson, and John M. Cooper. Timothy Gall provided indispensable technical assistance in preparing the final draft of the manuscript. I must express particular gratitude to my readers at the University of North Carolina Press for contributing many valuable insights and suggestions. They admirably balanced the justice of their criticism with the mercy of their enthusiasm.

For generous financial assistance toward the publication of this book, I am pleased to thank the Marguerite Eyer Wilbur Foundation and its president, Russell Kirk.

Finally, I am deeply obliged to the editorial staff of the University of North Carolina Press, and especially to Sandra Eisdorfer, for consistent efficiency, courtesy, and high professional standards.

Irving Babbitt

1. An American Cato

Und wenn ihr nach Biographien
verlangt, dann nicht nach jenen
mit dem Refrain "Herr Soundso und
seine Zeit", sondern nach solchen,
auf deren Titelblatte es heissen
müsste "ein Kämpfer gegen seine Zeit."

      Friedrich Nietzsche,
      "Vom Nutzen und Nachteil
      der Historie für das Leben"

When James Russell Lowell recalled a lecture by Emerson, it was not the theme but the hypnotic delivery that quickened his recollection. Yet, having ascribed to the lecturer the "masculine faculty of fecundating other minds," Lowell went on to disregard any seeds of thought that Emerson might have sown among his listeners. "There is keen excitement, though there be no ponderable acquisition. If we carry nothing home in our baskets, there is ample gain in dilated lungs and stimulated blood." Then Lowell returned to Emerson's "manhood" and "the masculine fibre of his will" to conclude that Emerson's power resided not in his thought but in a voice that "sweeps our minds from their foothold into deeper waters with a drift we cannot and would not resist."[1] That Lowell had left to one's inference a recumbent femininity in himself that was borne along by the Emersonian drift seemed to bother him not a whit. Nor did he care that there came from Emerson no issue of certainty of direction for the sake of Americans heady with lyceum rhetoric.

Emerson had a bland way of assuring his audiences that a divine afflatus hung over their designs and desires if they would but trust their individual convictions. His lyric appeals boded not only subtle but clear and unmistakable frontal assaults upon the smug dry rot of sterile Unitarian society. He was preaching that the societal parts were greater than their whole, were indeed themselves wholes, no longer Locke's wax tablets upon which convention might write its formulas, but molds into which the world itself, wax-like, would be poured and shaped. By inexplicable transmutation, any man's "latent conviction," privately sustained, would become "the universal sense."[2]

Not even in the comparatively sober fabric of his essay on fate, the weaving of which indelibly bears the thread of Montaigne's humanism, did Emerson relinquish a vigorous confidence in the individual's potential for a lofty fruition. That potential became a new teleology: "Liberation of the will from the sheaths and clogs of organization which he has outgrown, is the end and aim of this world."[3]

Following Emerson, transcendental idealists in America shared, despite important differences in emphasis, a vague belief that people had within their own consciousness rational and intuitive means by which to attain a kind of divinity of self. Whether upon individualistic or communitarian premises, they claimed to have brought deity into American life and made it integral to human activity. Emerson's private law, the public conscience of Henry James, Sr., Theodore Parker's appeal to human rights and Josiah Royce's to duties—all were variants of a common political aim: the assertion of one's control over one's spiritual life by resistance to the encroachments of inhumane, unethical societal processes. The degree to which their assumption of self-perfectibility played a covert part in this resistance seemed directly proportional to their perception of conventional society's imperfections.

The peculiarity that crippled transcendental idealism was the disparity between its views of human nature and the mundane reality of how people actually lived. In giving human beings moral incentives that would allow them to transcend or transform their situations and characters, the idealists presumed that people would become creatures wholly different from what they had been. A divinity imputed to humankind lay abstractedly apart from the modes of one's practical existence.

The ethically incalculable power of national industrialization, already in sway a generation before the Civil War, gradually rendered uncertain, if not precarious, the moral cohesion of society to which the idealists variously appealed. Political, financial, and industrial agglomerates became to Josiah Royce the emblems of what Hegel called "the self-estranged spirit" of a nation.[4] Societal norms became fragmented and dangerously partisan as they had been before the war, and class antagonisms kept alive the foreboding of another civil war or revolution.

The ambiguous transformation of transcendentalist idealism by radical empiricism in the late nineteenth century received a vigorous challenge from humanism. Having no certain metaphysic and being antipathetic to societal reform, humanism was essentially a temperamental revolt against the traditional humanitarian values of self and society that the transcendentalists had espoused. It had no formal antecedents before the Civil War, though it paid high psychological homage to first-generation Puritanism; and after the war it had only tacit allies in an urban gentility complacently dedicated to class values. Its most spirited proponent was Irving Babbitt.

Babbitt was born in Dayton, Ohio, in 1865, four months after the end of the Civil War. His father, Edwin Babbitt, was a businessman, a parlor socialist, and an advocate of "physical culture." After moving his family to New York City, the elder Babbitt founded the New York College of Magnetics and as its dean wrote *The Principles of Light and Color*, *Human Culture and Cure*, and *Social Upbuilding*. He also sold "chromopathic instruments" including a solar sweat bath or thermolume, which, he claimed, would cure one of tuberculosis, rheumatism, dropsy, or neuralgia.

Meanwhile, Irving sold newspapers in rough sections of New York City. Years later he was proud to recall that he had had to develop what he called a tough skin early in life. When his mother died in 1876, his father sent him with his brother and sister back to Ohio to live among relatives. In adolescence he worked as a reporter and a writer of jokes for a Cincinnati newspaper. Far more adventuresome was a summer in Wyoming where he herded cattle for an uncle. A friend recalled that Babbitt's recollections of his early years left the impression of "a strange and mixed experience."[5] However fanciful his tales might have seemed, he did enjoy telling them. If he was proud that he had been hardened in his youth, he was pained that that time held few fond memories. Much of his later contempt for shows of emotion came from his having experienced little emotive feeling in the often harsh circumstances of his youth. Edwin Babbitt, eager to promote "Cooperative Systems and the Happiness and Ennoblement of Humanity" (the subtitle of one of his books) perhaps forgot the charity that began at home.

Irving was the valedictorian at his high school graduation in Cincinnati. Shortly afterward, at sixteen, he passed an examination that qualified him to teach in a district school. But he returned to high school to study science and engineering. Not until he was twenty did he manage to get enough financial support to go to college. Although he had no relatives or acquaintances in New England, he went to Harvard. Quite soon he concentrated his study on European languages and literature: French, German, Italian, Spanish, Greek, and Latin. It was at that time that Babbitt first encountered the "genteel tradition," from which by temperament and background he was forever excluded. Even though Professor Charles Eliot Norton was a member of this tradition, it was to his cultural values and paternal image that Babbitt responded enthusiastically.

Most of Babbitt's intellectual convictions, prejudices, and preferences were formed in his undergraduate years at Harvard, where his earnest application earned him the tag of "professor" from less serious students. He was a conspicuous exception to classmate George Santayana's Harvard of the 1880s, where "life, for the undergraduates, was full of droll incidents and broad farce; it drifted good-naturedly from one commonplace thing to another."[6] Babbitt early displayed a character that distinguished him to the end of his life: a taste for epigrammatic truths, wry humor, and inexhaustible talk of a high cerebral order. A fellow sophomore recalled many years later that

> Whole evenings would go to Apollonius of Tyana, to Plotinus or to Porphyry . . . or deserting his specially favored fields, he would discourse with equal zest and readiness on Japanese art, or Greek tragedy, or Goethe's *Faust* or Arnold's *Literature and Dogma*, or, digressing yet farther, he would hold forth for an hour or two on a volume of Eliphas Levi [a French mystic] and move on from this to modern scientific orthodoxy or from the analysis of such a book as Walt Whitman's *Democratic Vistas* to an excursion on the psychology of the latter day American.[7]

Babbitt was already establishing the bearings of philosophy and literature upon life, the inexhaustible correlations between ideas and conduct.

Soon after his graduation from Harvard in 1889, he returned to the still very wild West, this time not as a cowboy but as sole professor of Greek and Latin at the College of Montana in Deer Lodge. Two years at this small Presbyterian school provided his initiation into the self-mortifying role of pedagogue. It was the first and last time that he taught classical languages.

With his earnings, he went to Paris to study Sanskrit and Pali under Sylvain Levi, an orientalist only a few years his senior. Levi welcomed with surprise Babbitt's avidity for obscure and difficult Pali texts and the untiring exuberance that was part of his passion for ideas. After his year abroad, he continued oriental studies at Harvard with Charles Rockwell Lanman. The class was composed of himself and another graduate, also a midwesterner, Paul Elmer More. So began a friendship that was to last until Babbitt's death forty years later. It was More who became his one constant supporter and ally.

Another important friendship began in 1893 at Williams College where Babbitt taught romance languages. By that time graduate research in philology had become a conventional preparation for instructing languages. Frank Mather, who had studied philology in Berlin and had taken his doctorate at Johns Hopkins, was an English instructor at Williams. Babbitt, eschewing this route and seeing its pitfalls, persuaded Mather to join him in looking to French rather than Teutonic standards of instruction. His intent was to vindicate the critical examination of ideas in literature rather than practice increasingly specialized analysis of language structure.

Many years after serving as "cub instructor" at Williams, Babbitt recalled the importance of its tradition: "This tradition like that of other American colleges of its general type rested on the assumption that there is a body of selected experience, religious and humanistic, that lies at the very basis of civilization and that therefore needs to be transmitted through education by each generation to the next."[8] But at the time he was not careful to define or characterize this tradition. The urgent business was to defend it.

Babbitt was nearly thirty when he returned to Harvard in 1894. Up to that time he had exemplified some commonplace American traits. His extensive travels had bred a stout, practical self-reliance and a disposition to an experimental individualism. He had come to maturity in urban, agrarian, and frontier communities, from the Eastern seaboard to the Rocky Mountains, a witness to America's rapid economic transformations; he enjoyed the rough egalitarianism of the plains but was no less familiar with an urban society as stratified as any European duchy.

Having mastered the arts of survival and sufficiency, he had developed a keen, realistic sense of what was practicable and sensible. But this sense was perhaps too keen in that it carried an implacable resistance to standards and values other than those he had tested for himself. Babbitt lived in an epoch that adversely challenged the worth of the individual, whether the transcendentalist of an idyll or the pragmatist of a laboratory. Material growth and prosperity, a largesse of mechanical power, and technological skills somehow worked an increasing chaos in secular and spiritual values.

Babbitt was not the first to contend that "there is likely to exist in the individual of today the same confused conflict of tendencies that we see in the larger world,"[9] but he did not take account of his own confusion. Although he wrote and spoke in plain, aggressively blunt English, his training and his livelihood were spent in foreign languages. In a profound sense, his competence became his incapacity. The languages he loved most were ancient and remote, and though civilized values may have attained their acme in the tongues of Socrates and Cicero, and spiritual truths in the tongues of Buddha and Confucius, neither had much to say to Babbitt's America. But he insisted that they had everything to say and, by the transposition of key terms from alien cultures, he began to say it. Thus he diagnosed the ills of his age in austere accordance with "the wisdom of the ages." The syndrome of the disease had been apparent for more than a century, and effects were so pervasive in both Europe and America that any cure was, in a collective sense, probably impossible. Instead, he thought it would be found in a familiarly American antidote, a quality of individualism. But, contrary to the libertarian implications of this rubric, Babbitt meant by it an unremitting spiritual discipline.

He never uttered a Christian sentiment, but he harkened on occasion to the example of the early Christians, models of a militant few who against almost universal opposition had been able to withstand the world, if not redeem it. And, like the most anguished and zealous of American Christians, Jonathan Edwards, Babbitt devised his own dire strictures to try to convince men no longer convincible of psychological truths no longer comprehensible. He did not enjoy with Edwards a certainty of God's existence; he had to improvise an almost divine image of man, one proximate to mortal experience yet unexplicit in its mystical capacities. In short, he became a legatee, one of the last, of American transcendentalism.

He was also its hostile critic. He acquiesced in its burial of the Puritan's god and welcomed its transformation of "salvation" from a theistic to a human sense, but he wanted to retain the arduous, inhibitive properties of belief so essential to a Mather or a Winthrop. To this end he weighed everything on the scales of volition. Divine will was demoted to an ambiguous "higher will"; the inner light of radical Protestantism became the "inner check."

Babbitt looked over the span of so many other cultures and ages that he never bothered to place himself within a native tradition even though he was at once an exemplar and an opponent of its principal intellectual direction in the nineteenth century. As the most important revolution, he remarked, takes place in the dictionary, so the transcendentalists once stormed the Bastille of convention with "soul," "self," "instinct," "rights," "nature," and "humanity." The pragmatists followed them with terms less human and more technical but equally subversive. Babbitt's lone, one might say Thermidorian, reactions came after two generations of Americans, fired by excesses of sentiment and a new faith in science, had abolished the old constraints.

A stolid reactionary would have been content to restore those constraints in any way and at any price. Babbitt, perceiving the psychological power in the transcendentalist's appeal to intuition and the pragmatist's to experience, wanted what he called an "imaginative reaction," one that would leave the will its integrity, its power to act. An active individualism based on a common sense would prove far more efficacious than any outward convention.

It would not do, then, to fill the air with jeremiads. Dismal prophet though he might have seemed, Babbitt discovered early in his teaching that his forceful personality, conveyed in extremes of self-dramatization even to the point of self-caricature, evoked some response from students, even those (a probable majority) unsympathetic to or appalled by his disposition. He would make himself the personification of the power of will to which he appealed. Some of the inelegance of the cowboy and the city reporter came into his style, tempered by a massive erudition that made any outward crudity or bluster seem superficial. Babbitt knew how to be a showman.

It was true, however, that in an age occupied, like any other, almost entirely with itself, Babbitt ran a double jeopardy. He knew that an appeal to the common sense of mankind was not necessarily an appeal to an American sense; there was the hazard of a kind of exoticism in his preferences. Teaching at Harvard itself was an isolating experience, as he was soon to realize. But his forensic manner, unrelenting and uningratiating, threatened to preclude any affirmation of the sort he wanted to elicit. Histrionics were one thing; conversion, another.

Although he was never reconciled to his time, Babbitt as teacher was more successful than he realized: "I have had to live at a time when all the ideas which I know to be most vital for man have more and more declined."[10] That more than his own vitality would compensate for this decline was suggested in remarks from T. S. Eliot, who better than any other student testified to Babbitt's authoritative impact:

> To have been once a pupil of Babbitt's was to remain always in
> that position. . . . I do not believe that any pupil who was ever
> deeply impressed by Babbitt, can ever speak of him with that
> mild tenderness one feels toward something one has outgrown
> or grown out of. If one has once had that relationship with Bab-

bitt, he remains permanently an active influence; his ideas are permanently with one, as a measurement and a test of one's own.[11]

Eliot's testimony came, of course, from personal contact. Babbitt invariably made his strongest impressions in this way, far more effectively than in his printed arguments. Yet, fifty years after his death, Babbitt still elicits so many reactions similar to those from students and others in his day that he cannot be dismissed as merely a historic figure.

Babbitt's writings in education, aesthetics, literary criticism, political theory, and, perhaps most important, religion, were the topical fields for standards of a humanistic imperative still applicable, in some instances prophetically so, to the present age. How he came to formulate these standards is the subject of this book. According to them the extent to which he is an abiding critical force may be judged. It is almost certainly true that Babbitt would not alter his arguments if he were reiterating them today. He would have identified the present time as very much his own, if indeed more drastic in the aberrations he attacked earlier in this century.

2. Babbitt at Harvard

"Niebuhr hat recht, sagte Goethe, wenn er eine barbarische
Zeit kommen sah. Sie ist schon da, wir sind schon mitten
darinne; denn worin besteht die Barbarei anders als darin,
dass man das Vortreffliche nicht anerkennt?"

Johann Peter Eckermann, *Gespräche mit Goethe*, 1831

I have often been forced in these essays to tread on burning
ground, at the risk of giving offense to some of my readers.
I may at least say that my aim has been to define types and
tendencies, and not to satirize or even label individuals. . . .
but there is likely to exist in the individual of today the same
confused conflict of tendencies that we see in the larger
world.

Irving Babbitt, Preface to *Literature and
the American College*

When Irving Babbitt returned to Harvard from Williams
College in 1894, he hoped to join the Department of
Classics, from which he had been graduated with honors
in 1889. But the chairman, William Goodwin, had no position to
offer and Babbitt was obliged to turn to romance languages. His
disappointment was undoubtedly part of the chagrin he felt as a
French instructor. His closest friend, Paul Elmer More, who had an
overcultivated love of paradox, once claimed that Babbitt ap-
proached French letters as an adversary: "What might have hap-
pened," More once mused after Babbitt's death, "if he had spent his
energies on expounding a literature to which he could have given his
positive allegiance instead of one which he studied chiefly to annihilate?"[1]

Indeed, Babbitt privately condemned French as a "cheap and nasty
substitute for Latin,"[2] and neither Boileau nor Sainte-Beuve would
ever attain for him the measure of Horace. But teaching French literature forced him to grapple with the unsavory present, to analyze,
assault, and "annihilate," if possible, the modes of those men of letters whom he soon learned to suspect or despise. While More, an elegiac classicist, confessed himself to Charles Eliot Norton "ready to

bow my head and veil my face in the presence of ruin overtaking ruthlessly what is fairest to me in all the world," Babbitt was "now devoting himself so exclusively to French" that they seldom discussed the ancients.[3]

But Babbitt's devotion to French was troubled. He complained in letters to More, who was teaching Greek at Bryn Mawr, that his classes were overlarge; correcting examinations was "an entirely distasteful task"; and the readings were unworthy: "I might be willing to sacrifice myself for Greek but I am not going to turn myself into a teaching automaton in order that Harvard sophomores may read French novels of the decadence in the original."[4]

Early in 1896, he began to inquire surreptitiously through More about vacancies in the Classics Department at Bryn Mawr while making similar inquiries through a former classmate, William Giese, at the University of Wisconsin. His motivations, as he made clear to More, were not exclusively based upon a preference of classical over modern language and literature: "Even though I were not to accept an outside offer, it might be extremely useful for me to get one for the way in which I might use it to strengthen my position at Harvard: so that I think it might be well for you to suggest my name . . . should there be a vacancy at Bryn Mawr. . . . In the meanwhile I should like to get fuller information about the place—hours and kind of work, probable salary and chances of promotion."[5] It is not clear whether Babbitt intended to employ the leverage of proffered appointments at other colleges to obtain a promotion within his department relieving him of the obligations about which he complained, or whether he nourished hope of securing a post among Harvard's classicists. Appreciating the political delicacy of his position, he conferred with President Eliot, rather than the chairmen of the departments, "to arrive at a clearer notion of my present situation."[6]

Babbitt's decision to discuss his predicament with Eliot made sense. Nominally, Harvard's president was the head of every faculty and appointed all faculty committees; he headed the two governing bodies of the college, the Corporation and the Board of Overseers. Charles William Eliot's imagination and initiative had made the presidential powers elastic. He preferred an informal to a strictly procedural exercise of authority, and his congenial personality was potent in forwarding his reforms. When Babbitt was appointed in 1894, Eliot had served as president for a quarter of a century, during which he had extended the elective system, begun in 1825, through all undergraduate levels. He had improved the coordination of functions between his office and the professional schools, leaving them more autonomous. In his early years, Eliot consulted professors within departments regarding appointments and promotions, but by the 1890s departmental committees handled such matters. Their recommendations went through a hierarchic chain that included the dean of the college and the governing boards as well as the president. By his own forfeit, Eliot was far less the paterfamilias he had been in an earlier, less complicated age. Babbitt was fully aware of the decentralization of power and did not attempt to enlist Eliot's still formidable influence against recalcitrant members of his own department. Instead, he took advantage of Eliot's receptivity and his seasoned knowledge of the vagaries of collegiate politics.

It was probably through Eliot's intervention that Babbitt was relieved from instructing elementary French in the first semester of 1896–97. He was now free to plan what were called "advanced half-courses" given for upperclassmen and graduates. Concurrently he was teaching at Radcliffe College. Although he undertook instructorship there largely for financial reasons, he quickly came to look upon Radcliffe as a testing ground for the advanced course work he hoped to secure at Harvard.

In 1900, he married one of his former Radcliffe students, Dora Drew, the daughter of a Protestant missionary to China. Babbitt was thirty-five years old; his wife, a small, handsome woman, was only twenty-three. A daughter, Esther, was born in 1902; a son, Edward, in 1905. For the rest of his life, Babbitt rented a three-story house on Kirkland Road in Cambridge, only a few minutes from the homes of colleagues William James, Charles Rockwell Lanman, and Josiah Royce. Babbitt never felt that he earned enough to buy a home, and his continual financial worries were no small part of the exasperations he expressed early in his career. Small relief came with his promotion to assistant professor in 1902.

Late in 1896, Babbitt submitted an outline for a half-course entitled "Literary Schools in France during the xixth Century, with special reference to the Origins of the Romantic Movement." He was already planning to revise some lectures for this course into a book. When the outline was rejected, Babbitt lost no time in identifying and indicting his foes. Rather than construing his immobility and lack of power as conditions normally the lot of a subordinate, and one without a doctoral degree, he imputed willful opposition to those of the faculty with whom he felt no agreement upon educational principles.

From his first years as an instructor, Babbitt had defended the humanities against what he felt to be undue applications of scientific method to literature and education. He had a precedent in what was long known among literary critics as the battle of the books, a contest between ancient and modern languages for the determination of cultural values. Antiquity invariably lost ground. Now the contest was not so much between languages but in the approaches to them. By the late Victorian age, an era entranced with the efficiency of scientific techniques, the traditional cultural emphases of education were superseded. In his defense of tradition, Babbitt was renewing the struggle that Matthew Arnold had made against the Darwinists in an earlier generation. He was also providing himself with an aggressive stance that he found lacking in his genteel mentor, Charles Eliot Norton, but amply present in the militantly modern humanism of Arnold.

As Arnold's foes had been the philistines, Babbitt's were the philologists. What the philologists had in common was an increasingly fashionable approach to literature and language that Babbitt had first noted at Williams. Philology was the application of German positivism to letters, a laboratorial reduction of literature to its historical and mechanical parts. The leading philologist at Harvard had been Francis J. Child, a professor of rhetoric, who introduced philology to the study of ballads. In his path came George Lyman Kittredge in English, Ferdinand Bôcher in French, Charles Grandgent in Italian, Jeremiah Ford in Spanish, E. S. Sheldon in comparative linguistics, and a host of others. Some were trained in Germany; others had come from Johns Hopkins, the first graduate school in America. By Babbitt's time, Harvard itself had become a philological laboratory. The Department of Comparative Literature was considered an "off-shoot" of romance philology.[7]

Babbitt was not the first critic of this science of literature. William Peterfield Trent, founder of the *Sewanee Review* (1892), and the classicist Basil Gildersleeve had attacked it in journals in the 1890s. Harvard's Barrett Wendell scoffed at Germanic method as "the alien tyranny."[8] Essayist and poet John Jay Chapman, a Harvard alumnus, soon followed Babbitt in seeing philology as the triumph of quantitative measure over literary and moral values. But although Babbitt was not alone, he felt that he was, and the vulnerability to which he exposed himself by criticizing philological method partly justified that feeling. Courageous or foolhardy or both, Babbitt, still an assistant professor as he entered his forties, continued to publish articles that the faculty in his own department could construe as assaults upon them.

Against the scientism of philology Babbitt posed what he called humanism. Noting its common usage among men of different biases, he ironically subjected the term to a philological scrutiny. It came from the Latin *humanitas* and implied a doctrine shared among an aristocratic few. Cicero, for instance, was the model master of its "disciplined and selective sympathy." By contrast to the humanitarian, with whom he was often confused, the modern humanist was "interested in the perfecting of the individual rather than in schemes for the elevation of mankind as a whole."[9] This "perfecting" was actually nothing more than a cultivated sense of proportion.

Central to this proportion was the notion, derived from Greek rationalism, that there exists in human nature an ineradicable dualism, the contrary claims of the One and the Many. On the one hand, the One is that which transcends circumstance and abides as the source of all moral effort or religious need. On the other, the Many represents the impermanent, the indeterminable flux to which human beings as creatures of nature, with all their attendant urges, are subject. In defending the claims of conscience and, implicitly, those of faith as essential rather than historically accidental, Babbitt set his humanism against the upsurgent intellectual revolutions of his time, those of Marx, Darwin, and Freud, all of which gravely imperiled—if they did not destroy—the traditional assumptions of dualism.

It must be noted, however, that Babbitt's appeal to fixed standards was and remained primarily secular rather than spiritual. Indeed, according to him, early Renaissance humanism had served to encourage revolt against the shackles of medieval theology; it rightly celebrated the claims of the intellect to freedom of inquiry. But a conventional discipline and decorum became necessary when intellectual freedom grew anarchic and questioned all authority. Babbitt used this late Renaissance humanism as a corrective model for the directionless scientific and sentimental or humanitarian trends of his time. A law of measure; a sense that a human being is not wholly animal and must acknowledge standards above private temperament; a recognition of disciplinary values for the health of society—such props, used against excessive attention to "nature," whether Darwin's nature or Rousseau's, would perhaps keep men from dissolving their values into a relativistic chaos.

But educational norms in the late nineteenth century were going in that direction. A science of literature, for example, translated what Emerson called "law for man" into "law for thing."[10] Babbitt's humanism was less a dogmatic than a dispositional insistence upon keeping the first above and distinct from the second.

It is important to note that Babbitt's criticisms of specialized research, including the scientific methods used in graduate theses, were not intended to condemn such trends. Training in methodology and the mastery of detail were fundamental to scholarship; they served to eliminate dilettantes, who looked upon literature as a source of exquisite sensations. But an emphasis upon skills used to explore often obscure and meaningless facts was an affront to students capable of mastering ideas. What Babbitt wanted was an assimilative rather than an entirely accumulative approach; he stressed the student's capacity to use ideas and relate them to general standards.

Babbitt presumed that while the emergent university system would further programs of graduate research and specialization, the college might remain the harbinger of traditional emphases upon a general education. It was indispensable, therefore, that the college not emulate the utilitarian character of the university but keep strong the bonds holding the present to a culturally edifying past. Thus, his argument that modern-language teachers should be familiar with Greek and Latin was based on the belief that those languages were unsurpassed treasuries of disciplinary values from which modern cultures could not afford to depart. Such values would make more than erudite scholars; they would create men of character and general intelligence, "the future citizens of a republic."[11]

Babbitt was not reticent in employing his mordant satiric sense of a situation so lamentably opposite to the standards he was defending:

> There are persons at present who do not believe that a man is fitted to fill a chair of French literature in an American college simply because he has made a critical study of the text of a dozen medieval beast fables and written a thesis on the Picard dialect, and who deny that a man is necessarily qualified to interpret the humanities to American undergraduates because he has composed a dissertation on the use of the present participle in Ammianus Marcellinus.[12]

Babbitt printed these barbs in more than jest and knew that they carried a high price for him professionally.

It is not difficult to interpret as patently autobiographical his view that the humanistic educator "will be more or less out of touch with his colleagues."[13] Frank recognition of coolness between him and his departmental chairman, Frederic-Cesar Sumichrast, kept Babbitt willingly "out of touch." Babbitt assumed that because, as he believed, the philologists controlled the romance languages, the only way to secure promotion would be to endorse their methodology. He acknowledged that the philologist's use of historical method in tracing origins and influences in literature was legitimate, but he protested that too often such methods usurped the primary consideration of studying literature as a source of values and for "the application of real standards of taste and judgment."[14]

A provocative instance reflecting the hegemony of the philologists came while Babbitt was preparing to publish his essays on collegiate education. William H. Schofield, an English instructor since 1897, was appointed professor in the spring of 1906. His dissertation had been a philological comparison of medieval French, English, and German poetry. Babbitt was shocked that a philologist had been appointed to a full professorship in literature. Not only did Schofield's advancement reflect what Babbitt perceived to be a national trend in collegiate offices, but it seemed to carry a threat to himself, for "the standards insisted on by these very philologists are such as to eliminate almost automatically the opposite type of scholar."[15]

Babbitt's alarm was not wholly justified. Schofield, who created *Harvard Studies in Comparative Literature*, actually shared some of Babbitt's views on the decline of undergraduate standards at Harvard and the need for rigorous discipline to restore them. In the year of his promotion, with professors Lowell, Haskins, and Wendell, he created a field of concentration known as "History and Literature" that encouraged supradepartmental, integrated studies upon which the student would compose a thesis and take an oral examination. But Babbitt, feeling he stood virtually alone before the "opposite type of scholar" that Schofield represented, had so long held his distinction between philological and humanistic disciplines that he was unable to conceive that one individual could practice both. And yet he argued adroitly that the utilitarian and sentimental tempers, outwardly antagonistic, often complemented one another in a single personality, each being extremes against humanistic proportion and balance.

In spite of his aloneness, Babbitt dutifully observed the often painful amenities of professorial life. In the early days, as Mrs. Babbitt recalled,[16] social gatherings of the faculty were dismal affairs. Colleagues and their wives sat staring at one another across the parlor in a chilling silence, infrequently broken. Babbitt's fame as a convivial host and guest came only in the later, securer years. For the while he preferred a brisk walk along the Charles River or a hard game of tennis to the dullness of departmental proprieties.

Babbitt's friends were few but close. Foremost among them was Charles Eliot Norton, professor of fine arts, who, already in his sixties when Babbitt and More were undergraduates, had become a kind of Nestor to them. Babbitt, wanting to be convinced that hu-

manistic studies would withstand the tide of scientism, turned to
Norton as his mentor. During a sabbatical in 1907, while preparing
his first book, he confided to Norton: "I note signs of late of a reaction against certain excesses of the scientific spirit in literary study.
Your own work will have helped me largely to bring this reaction
about."[17] But the purpose in composing *Literature and the American
College* links Babbitt not so obviously to Norton as to Matthew Arnold.

Babbitt had long been familiar with Arnold; he knew his works
thoroughly and quoted from them frequently as an undergraduate.
This attentiveness was not an unalloyed enthusiasm. Arnold always
remained somewhat suspect to Babbitt because he had, like Emerson,
an accommodating fluidity of principle, a "romantic fear of precise
analysis" that the sobriety of age never fully overcame.[18] Despite that
critical shortcoming, Arnold did propound an Aristotelian emphasis
upon a "rounded human nature."[19] He had foreseen dangers in
American democracy, notably the undisciplined materialistic obses-
sion with quantity and the exaltation of the common. Babbitt
concurred with Arnold that the pressing need of Anglo-American
society was for high standards and trained leaders, though he remained skeptical of Arnold's assumption, in *Culture and Anarchy*
(1868), that all socioeconomic classes should contribute qualitative
leadership. As for education, Arnold anticipated Babbitt's alarm over
the degeneration of humanistic and religious norms with the advent
of curricular utilitarianism. In sum, Arnold served Babbitt in the
manner of Norton as a worthy exemplar of the classically critical
temper. The pertinence of that temper to the age Babbitt attempted
to explain in *Literature and the American College*.

The tone of the book, much like that of *Culture and Anarchy*, was
restrained and the reasoning, like Arnold's, straightforward and with
a close attention to contemporary events. From its ad hominem gravity one might have inferred that Babbitt was addressing an audience
limited to a collegiate circle. Babbitt did make his appeals principally
to discriminating traditionalists who would recognize that the breakdown of some outmoded educational norms was inevitable yet could
be met, not with a crabbed hostility to the new, but by an imaginative
reaffirmation of what was lastingly valuable in the old. Seeking to
face facts free of illusion, Babbitt suggested that "if the humane ideal
appear at all in the future, it must be in the very nature of things
more a matter of individual insight and less a matter of tradition
than heretofore."[20] Such was the precept that he had derived from
what he called the humanist's bible, Aristotle's *Nicomachean Ethics*; it

was, in his own terms, an ethical positivism by which the individual was obliged to conform moral judgments to the facts of actual life.

Babbitt kept an American faith in individuality but stressed its need of a discipline foreign to the atomistic temperament of most Americans. One of his central definitions of humanism indicated the nature of this discipline and Babbitt's close affinity with the ancients:

> The true humanist maintains a just balance between sympathy and selection. We moderns . . . tend to lay an undue stress on the element of sympathy. On the other hand, the ancients in general, both Greek and Roman, inclined to sacrifice sympathy to selection. . . . Ancient humanism is as a whole intensely aristocratic in temper; its sympathies run in what would seem to us narrow channels; it is naturally disdainful of the humble and lowly who have not been indoctrinated and disciplined.[21]

What little "sympathy" Babbitt himself evinced was for precisely the austerely selective pagan humanism that was by his own definition one-sided. And the channels of his sympathies grew narrower as he perceived that collegiate indoctrination and discipline were being directed to ends other than the disciplinary ideal of humanism.

But humanism as a training in standards of taste and conduct implied more than individual insight; an aristocratic ideal presupposed collective expression. "The need of discipline and community of ideal enters into human nature no less than the craving for a free play of one's individual faculties. . . . So many of the very forces that make for material union would seem at the same time to tend toward spiritual isolation."[22] Just as the pragmatist Charles Peirce hypothesized a community of scientific inquiry and the idealist Josiah Royce one of spirituality, Babbitt conceived of a community of culture as disciplined as any science but as ethically demanding as any religion.

To Emerson's distinction between "law for man" and "law for thing," Babbitt added the dualistic corollary central to all his subsequent pleas for humanism: prone to temperamental extremes, human nature can maintain its humane self only by cultivating equanimity, by continually striving to observe the claims of the One as well as the Many. At the same time, a person's rootedness in nature enforces awareness of an enduring subjection to its relativity and flux. Babbitt believed that his humanism was Aristotelian in seeking not an ascetic's uprooting of passion or desire but their subordination to the rational purposes that, according to Aristotle, they foreshadow. "Solve the problem of the ethical will and intellect in relation to it and feelings will almost take care of themselves—they become virtues only when they become the servants of the will."[23] As thoroughly as William James, Babbitt insisted on the wholeness of the individual, but with the crucial difference that he perceived a symptomatic disintegration of that wholeness under the pressure of multiple delusions and untested philosophies.

Babbitt traced the history of this disintegration back to the Renaissance and Francis Bacon. He ascribed to Bacon the modern impetus for *libido sciendi*, the passion for knowledge as gathered data, pursued on the premise that scientific investigation determines the progress of humanity. Complementary to this scientific naturalism was a sentimental naturalism, or *libido sentiendi*, a passion for feeling at the expense of self-discipline and restraint, for moral impressionism in lieu of conscience. The archetypal intellect of this aberration was Jean-Jacques Rousseau, who had been calumniated so long by so many French critics that Babbitt was far from original in his charge. The Renaissance and the Enlightenment had furthered these two naturalistic or humanitarian tendencies while eroding the authority of institutional Christianity. The psychological consequence of our loss of a transcendent spirituality was our arrogation of divinity to ourselves in relation to nature and society: science became a quasi-religion while romantic sentiment divorced head from heart. Humanistic decorum indirectly abetted both processes whenever it became mere hollow formalism, a dogma of rules without imaginative direction. Babbitt saw a confluence between scientism and sentimentalism in that both were naturalistic drives for power under the guise or illusion of service to humankind. By the turn of the nineteenth century, the progeny of Bacon had become positivistic specialists, so many "serviceable fragments" that had surrendered their inner sense of self upon the altars of material progress.[24] The Rousseauists, in turn, were to be found among "progressive" reformers, among the most dangerous of whom Babbitt numbered educators like John Dewey.

A tendency to make blanket indictments, while typical of Babbitt's stylistic tactics, was partly attributable to his resentment of the very immediacy of the problem he had analyzed, since Harvard itself had become a leading promulgator of positivist methods and related heresies. In fact, Babbitt laid much of the responsibility directly at the door of President Eliot.

Shortly before assuming the presidency in 1869, Eliot had outlined the purposes of the elective system. Primarily, he was defending the worth of the "scientific school" then struggling to win financial support and popular acceptance. The orthodox, theologically grounded colleges of "classical" education were unfairly resisting the academic recognition he felt the sciences deserved: "The foundling has suffered by comparison with the children of the house," sighed Eliot.[25] Enforcing against tradition a broad availability of studies in language, science, and mathematics would, he claimed, encourage scholarship "because it gives free play to natural preferences and inborn aptitudes, makes possible enthusiasm for a chosen work."[26] In Eliot, then, a Baconian ethic of utility fused with the Rousseauist assumption of individual spontaneity. Eliot's "department store conception of education" was only figuratively his handiwork because, as Babbitt concluded not long after the president's death, "Eliot did little more than reflect the time in its main tendency. . . . His whole career, indeed, illustrates the advantages of going with one's age quite apart from the question whither it is going."[27] Not merely the exigencies of an industrialized nation but the dogma of its egalitarian democracy required that education be "something of everything for everybody."[28]

Occasional lapses into a caustic manner betrayed Babbitt's anxiety that the "common sense" to which he felt he was appealing might not be sufficient to restore a corrective balance between present knowledge and past wisdom. Sentimentalists like Eliot, in the tradition of Rousseau, baited the capricious inclinations of sophomores and transformed the Socratic grove into a curricular fairground. The philologists especially had degraded the advanced degree by placing proficiency in research above mature appreciation of literature and philosophy. But above these particular perversions there was perhaps an ineffable circumstantial force confounding will itself. As Babbitt was obliged to concede, "the very conditions of modern life require us nearly all to be experts and specialists."[29]

One senses behind each of Babbitt's often persuasively argued essays in *Literature and the American College* his dread that perhaps time had subverted the value of an idea or at least its power; that he and others of the would-be vanguard of a revivified humanism were being pushed to the margins of society; that the realism he was pleading for, the balanced life, was being overshadowed by the mundane realism of experimentation; that to refute naturalism in its dualistic forms would be tantamount to sentencing oneself to the romanticists' isle of private fantasy. Against these tentative grounds for despair, Babbitt insisted that the humanist's aim was "not to deny the age but to complete it" and that the humanism of classical literature, especially of the Greeks, afforded

> an avenue of escape from ourselves, enabling us to become participants in the universal life. It is thus truly educative in that it leads him who studies it out and away from himself. The classical

spirit, in its purest form, feels itself consecrated to the service of a high, impersonal reason. Hence its sentiment of restraint and discipline, its sense of proportion and pervading law.[30]

This formulation of what was literally an ecstatic experience was Babbitt's closest proximation to the genteel religion of letters but his emphasis was not, like it, aesthetic; it was moral and depended on a continuation of the classical influence. In his chapter, "The Rational Study of the Classics," Babbitt frankly perceived the consequence of their decline: "Those who can receive the higher initiation into the Hellenic spirit will doubtless remain few in number, but these few will wield a potent influence for good, each in *his own* circle, *if only* from the ability they will thereby have acquired to escape from contemporary illusions."[31]

Perhaps Babbitt was simply formulating a variant to the characteristic problem of the sensitively educated mind seeking to "enter into life" in the hope of finding some self-justification. There was at least a scarcely veiled self-commiseration in his advice to the hypothetical humanist aspiring to become an educator: "Under these circumstances the humanist will have to undertake the task that Wordsworth so modestly proposed to himself, that of creating the taste by which he is to be enjoyed. . . . And, though he will attract some students of the more serious sort, he will not necessarily win wide and sudden popularity."[32]

Babbitt was dismayed when his book was reviewed in the *Nation* in April 1908. More, the literary editor of that organ, sent the book to Paul Shorey, professor of classics at the University of Chicago. Babbitt was piqued that Shorey ignored his assessment of Rousseau's influence as the father of humanitarianism, but even more galling, Shorey dismissed his criticism of collegiate philologists as "not quite fair or generous" while taking Babbitt's characterization of them as a syndicate as "surely an exaggeration." Wrote Shorey, they had tastes worthy of "an indwelling humanistic spirit"; besides, many were "enthusiastic and intelligently appreciative readers of the classics."[33]

It was frustrating not merely that Shorey had inflated a minor point at the expense of more important ones, but that, as Babbitt complained to More, "my one chance of getting a serious review of my book has thus failed me. . . . From a purely tactical point of view, as an incident in the warfare we are both carrying on against certain tendencies in contemporary life and education, a review of this kind is a serious error." Nor did Shorey's concurrence with Babbitt on certain points mollify him: "It is the kind of tepid stuff that will help a book on its way to oblivion."[34]

Babbitt could not have hoped that his first book would aid his hopes for promotion; he had offended too many of his colleagues. He was acutely concerned that the book's public reception would make him appear "a clever person but rather unbalanced." "The review is a small thing in itself, but it comes at a very critical moment both for me personally and for the ideas I have been trying to defend for years, and so has produced in me a mood of lassitude and discouragement."[35] He knew that no review, favorable or not, would affect the response of colleagues such as Schofield and Sumichrast, who could be expected to take the book as an offensive against them. Indeed, as a series of polemics, the book was exactly that.

Convinced, reasonably enough, that *Literature and the American College* stalled his promotion to full professorship, Babbitt may even have realized at the time what he rationalized many years later: "It would be too much to expect from human nature that they should promote you, when you are undermining their influence."[36] In 1908 he was forty-three years old and still an assistant professor. Younger members of his department, notably Ford, with whom he was never on cordial terms, won promotion, as it seemed, over his head. He could only believe that in accord with the philological emphasis upon research and publication, a quantitative measure figured in advancements: "It would seem to be necessary not only to have quality but to pile up large numbers of volumes."[37] By that criterion he had scant hope for recognition. Composing in longhand—he never reconciled himself to the typewriter—he would spend weeks upon individual essays and chapters, fastidiously revising their organization and weighing More's judicious criticisms.

Another factor delaying his promotion was A. Lawrence Lowell's assumption of Harvard's presidency in 1908. With Charles William Eliot's retirement and the death of Charles Eliot Norton, Babbitt marked the end of the genteel era. He urged More at the *Nation* to use his editorial power to influence the selection of a new president. Eliot had made legendary his own uses of the office's powers and Babbitt recognized the political importance of a successor. Initially favoring Lowell, he soon found that Lowell's administration did not satisfy his expectations. In 1910–11, with large advanced courses, he protested privately to More that Harvard still failed to accord recognition commensurate with responsibilities, and he quietly resumed his search for a position elsewhere.

Correspondence with a dean at the University of Illinois over an opening there indicated to Babbitt that he had little to gain by leaving Harvard. Publication pressures were similar to those at Harvard, and the dean defended the philologists at Urbana on the ground of a "symmetrically developed" departmental structure.[38] Babbitt was promised a sabbatical only after the usual seven years of instruction. Distasteful though the terms were, he used the offer from Illinois to sound out his chances at Harvard. Lowell, after consulting the Corporation, declined to pledge a full professorship though he emphasized indirectly through More that no doors had been permanently closed.

Babbitt knew well enough that worry over securing tenure was part of a generalized anxiety. When his friend Josiah Royce collapsed from an apoplectic seizure, he cited "an atmosphere of strain and high pressure here during the latter part of Eliot's administration; and things have not been much improved by the advent of Lowell."[39] Within a month of this remark, in February 1912, he learned that his promotion was certain, but he did not relax his criticism of Lowell. Advancements would be few since Lowell believed "his faculty so far as full professors are concerned should be a collection of jewels. The problem will be to find the jewels and especially to make sure they are not paste imitations."[40]

In a letter to More, years before he won tenure, Babbitt attempted a frank self-estimation that seemed to suggest why he was becoming increasingly popular as a lecturer and yet without appreciable success as a writer:

> A friend like yourself, who knows how ready I am to deliver myself of crude and rash generalizations in conversation, will possibly be somewhat surprised at this commendable slowness on my part to put my theories in print and may regard as indolence what is really caution. I am not, however, so subject to violent *parti-pris* as would appear from my talk. A certain cold judicial habit of mind is I fancy much more essential in me than my vehemence of expression which comes in part from humorous exaggeration and partly from a mere impatience of the blood joined to my natural combative instincts in the face of contradiction.[41]

At least by implication, then, Babbitt conceded that an emotional excess readily distorted the views he expounded. It was as though the improvisational nature of talk disallowed or hindered the "cold judicial habit" he found necessary to a proper articulation of his thought. His awareness that exaggeration shaped his speech was not so thorough that he would have recognized it as a tactic or "combative instinct." Caricature, rather than characterization, served his confessed impatience too easily as a rhetorical means by which to distort or ridicule points of opposition. Babbitt's vehement manner no doubt offended many of his colleagues and played a great part in his political difficulties in the years before he won tenure. But in later years that same manner made him a celebrity among students.

The self-consciousness of aloneness usually induces reserve or withdrawal, or, in undaunted people, a defensive pugnacity. The latter shaped Babbitt's pedagogical style. He put an ease of articulation and a capacious memory to dramatic use. His personal convictions, which he would never have thought to withhold from his lectures, hardly catered to the penchants of most undergraduates. Electing a course on French romanticism, devotees of Musset or Baudelaire expecting to hear them extolled would hear them execrated.

In his autobiography, Van Wyck Brooks has left a vivid recollection of one of Babbitt's classes in about 1905: "Babbitt, tossing and goring the writers he disliked, seemed to be acting the part of Boswell's hero. Babbitt was another Dr. Johnson in his grunts, blowings and gurgitations, roaring his opponents down, harsh and abrupt in manner and voice, repeating, 'There are tastes that deserve the cudgel.'"[42] The comparison with Johnson, one that would have flattered Babbitt, had by then become obvious. Brooks offered a depiction perhaps more derisive than accurate, but he described fairly enough Babbitt's energetic outpouring that made every lecture a tour de force, holding the student by fascination, whether attractive or repelling. Even those who disliked him, including Brooks, were constrained to a grudging respect and to the acknowledgment that Babbitt's exemplary force of mind may have activated something in their own.

As to Babbitt himself, his claim that people are too disposed to one-sidedness, to "sympathy" or "selection," was documented in his own excess, his own violently exuberant selectivity. It was a prescription for himself that Babbitt may have had in mind when he appended to his definition of humanism Julius Caesar Scaliger's *fastidium sui*, the severe discipline imposed from within. But if he strove to maintain a *fastidium sui* for his written style, it was contrary to that which he employed in lecturing.

More testimony is needed to explain why Babbitt, as friends and students testified, was far more effective in lecture and conversation than in print. From reminiscences, a physical impression of Babbitt emerges. Typically, he entered a lecture room, usually at Sever Hall, carrying a large green bag that bulged with papers and books. His large bulky frame stooped increasingly with age, but he compensated for apparent clumsiness by untiring animation in talk. What Babbitt presented to his classes was not so many points of argument but his own personality, fired by what sympathetic students believed to be convictions and unsympathetic students accepted as prejudices. T. S. Eliot, one of his most admiring students, found that the unifying power behind Babbitt's deliveries was "intellectual passion, one might say intellectual fury . . . the constant recurrence of his dominant ideas; what gave them delight was their informality, the demand which they made upon one's mental agility and the frankness with which he discussed the things which he disliked."[43] Babbitt employed, consciously or not, the Ciceronian device of censure in his persuasion—and persuasion was as much a part of his pedagogic intent as was mere instruction. He probably never considered them separately. William Blake's maxim, "Damn braces, bless relaxes" hints at the effectiveness that even unfriendly students recognized in his belligerent method.

Homiletic rather than dispassionate or detached, Babbitt's lectures were covertly aimed to convert recalcitrant, often romantically disposed students to the austerities of humanism. "The whole of life," he once wrote in one of his pithy generalizations, "may, indeed, be summed up in the words diversion and conversion."[44] In that same insistent and unyielding either/or tone, he contended: "No more essential question can be asked regarding any man than whether he regards liberty primarily as a taking on or as a throwing off of limitations."[45] His emotive vehemence as a lecturer provided not only the Johnsonian bluster that entertained or horrified students; it was the fuel that propelled his dualistic reduction of the philosophic values in literature.

In disregarding analysis of literary technique, Babbitt revealed a seeming insensitivity to literature as an art. He was perhaps never fully aware of this insensitivity as a factor in limiting the number of students whom he could convert. He was a zealot for a humanism of decorum and discipline who compelled himself to violate those standards because he felt they were a twilight cause that only the most vigorous personal dedication could sustain. Austin Warren recalled that Babbitt's lectures were challenges that students either received or denied. But whether one felt elect or damned in one's philosophy was not germane to an exposure in which the student "learned to test life by books and books by life, was compelled to define one's terms, articulate and defend one's concepts."[46]

Particular aspects of Babbitt's lecturing style reflect his manner of thinking. Frequent repetition of favorite maxims or epigrams, a technique evident in his published works, aided the student's memory and gave a kind of catchword unity to Babbitt's notions and attitudes. Reiteration, a commonplace rhetorical device, became a prop to his otherwise loose organization. His delight in terse, epigrammatic statements, usually French, reflecting an inclusive insight that would capture both imagination and reason, indicated his lack of closely developed propositional thinking.

Babbitt worked from the encompassing truths within generalizations and supported or attacked them by deductive reference to specific, telltale literary passages. "I choose an illustration at random" was a frequent aside during lectures as he selected from his cluttered desk one book or another distended with noteslips. He had a firm control of his evidence but seemed to depend upon it to speak for itself. To conceptualize general ideas, periods, and doctrines; to collate citations; or to characterize personalities whose lives exemplified these citations—such were his tasks as lecturer, but it was his earnest extolment or no less earnest censure pronounced upon ideas and their makers that gave his lectures impetus.

Student notes reflect Babbitt's penchant for definitions. For example, he defined eighteenth-century deism as "a sort of intermediary stage between pure supernaturalism and pure naturalism" that "denies the total depravity of man." He divided deists into two classes as they exalted either reason or emotion against traditional views of society, the individual, and God. From that base he analyzed the influence of the third earl of Shaftesbury, who expanded the optimistic humanitarianism implicit in deism: "love of man was substituted for love of God."[47]

Often Babbitt reverted to classical antecedents of modern ideas. The Romans were particularly serviceable fellows. Babbitt found Shaftesbury's doctrine of ethical pity an echo of Roman stoicism and of Seneca's belief that it is natural to serve others. Likewise, to Shaftesbury's view that people are born harmonious with nature and God, he opposed Ovid's that a person's very idea of God was created from fear. Such comparisons and cross-references transcended temporal or national differences and underscored Babbitt's belief in the recurrent potence and pertinence of basic ideas and appeals. Although his lectures had a format of linear, historical progressions, he gave no prominence to historical perspective or method; ideas and dogmas had a vivid immediacy of which their representatives, ancient or modern, partook. Like Montaigne, foremost of humanists, Babbitt crowded the moment.

In that suprahistorical immediacy Babbitt was fond of posing antitheses. The diametric counter to Shaftesbury's gospel of benevolence was what Babbitt, borrowing from Friedrich Nietzsche, called Hobbes's "will to power." What Hobbes shared with Shaftesbury—and Babbitt enjoyed making alliances between seeming foes—was a suppression of the dualism that supernatural Christianity propounded as good versus evil. Within a lecture hour Babbitt would introduce numerous humanistic and religious exponents of this dualism and, as though the wisdom of the ages could be proclaimed in an arena, they fought and invariably routed their naturalistic adversaries. Students too listless to be partisan used to hold lotteries on how many contestants Babbitt would enlist during the hour. (The winning number was usually around seventy.)

Babbitt's concise definitions and characterizations had a sureness that appeared arbitrary, and his blanket judgments often incited students to charge him with unfairness toward a condemned author. "One doesn't have to eat all the apples in a barrel to pronounce them all rotten," he rejoined in what was hardly the stance of balanced criticism.[48] But that shortsightedness which caused him to distort or misjudge was a part of his restless intent to extract the ethical bases underlying expression, whether poetic or discursive. Perhaps consciously, Babbitt sacrificed discriminating, qualified assessment to the determination of where a writer ultimately stood in his values. He even dismissed appreciation of literature as a goal for students because it threatened to obscure standards and foster dilettantism: "The true point at issue," he remarked in reference to Harvard's philologists, "is not whether a man has a love of literature but whether he believes that there are any standards or discipline in life apart from the discipline of the scientific fact. If the basis of a sound humanistic discipline is once established, the 'love' will take care of itself."[49]

The common denominator of the lectures, as of his books, was the estimation of values; it was the hallmark of what Babbitt called "a general critical intelligence."[50] Convinced that the dilettante's separation of literature from life debased and impoverished both, Babbitt upheld what he called the "masculine" virtues of literature—"design," "informing purpose," and "symmetry"—over the "feminine" ones of "color," "illusion," and "suggestiveness." The ultimate quality of a writer's imagination would be determined by his capacity to subordinate the latter to the former. It was the absence in Rousseau's personality and works of what Babbitt presumed to be masculinity that prompted him to suggest, "There is indeed much in his makeup that reminds one less of a man than of a high-strung impressionable woman."[51] Lessing—Babbitt's model critic—was by contrast a figure rivaling Luther in this imputed virility of character.[52]

A lecture on eighteenth-century primitivism illustrates the humanistic point of this masculine/feminine dualism of imagination. Babbitt noted that the cult of the ballad emerged from the exaltation of impulse whereby poetry "poured forth unconsciously, simply and spontaneously."[53] But the master of this form, Robert Burns, was at the farthest remove from such "feminine" qualities. Rather, as an educated poet, he labored to develop a conscious artistic technique that employed those qualities to purge traditional artificial diction. Even more important, Burns was not, like Wordsworth, a primitivist in his attitude to life.

Although Babbitt's readings of poetry in lecture were deliberately flat and uninspired in proportion to his dislike of the emotions conveyed in the verse, he did not share the genteel critic's hostility to shows of feeling. But he was more likely to alternate his fulminations with a burlesque of the romantic sensibility; he never underestimated laughter-provoking ridicule as a potent antidote. Yet, the poetry that he revered (the word is not too strong), that which balanced what he believed to be ethical insight and imaginative beauty, elicited from him an almost mystical view of poetry that kept him from a desiccating neoclassical adherence to formulae: "You can't explain poetic magic. There is something there that eludes you. When you have got all your rules, you will find that the spirit has escaped. Mere mechanical regularity is a poor substitute for the *je ne sais quoi* in poetry."[54] Seldom, however, did he afford his students a display of his joy in that peculiar magic. For him it was akin to a religious experience, as his high rating of Dante and Milton suggests.

The Johnsonian roar that Van Wyck Brooks and generations of students heard reverberating through Sever Hall was not simply a showman's flamboyance but the echo of a species of intellectual loneliness; short of total despair, it was spirited by Babbitt's intuited certainty of imminent battle with people and ideas that would give no quarter. It was subdued but present even in informal talk, transmuted into what acquaintances characterized as spontaneity ("feminine"?, one wonders) and wit (gender uncertain). Babbitt was sometimes known to give praise to insights and virtues in men like Rousseau whom he assailed in print or from behind the lectern. Thus, by contrast to his written style with its tendentious hardening into a dogmatic generality, his spoken style was often relaxed. Many shared Paul Elmer More's preference for Babbitt's promptness and vim in conversation over his printed arguments, where those qualities were obscured or wholly absent. Talk had the obvious advantage lacking in books, one that Socrates held up to Phaedrus as definitive: the opportunity to persuade, dissuade, or refute.

Babbitt was temperamentally incapable of resisting a didactic urge. It was not unusual for him to breach the etiquette of Harvard's social life, so insufferable in his early years, by directing to host or hostess the query, "How would you define the difference between humanism and humanitarianism?" with as much concern for an accurate answer—as preexisted in his mind—as Kittredge had when he fired out before timid undergraduates, "Where does a play begin?"[55] Babbitt made no distinctions among his company, in or out of the classroom, for the problems and ideas he believed to need combating were not, in his view, academic but life-suffusing.

He was dismayed at the incapacity or unwillingness of his colleagues to share this supra-academic stance. Although, as he told More, his attack upon Harvard's specialists, the positivists and dilettantes, was "a warfare of principles" in which he attempted to "abstain as far as possible from personalities and ill-nature,"[56] he could not refrain from setting in print his contempt for what he considered the superficialities of academic life: "When it comes to the deeper things in life, the members of a modern college sometimes strike one, in Emersonian phrase, as a collection of 'infinitely repellent particles.'"[57]

Babbitt, though isolated and apart from most other faculty, resisted the expedient of enlisting students as allies. Against a student's harsh attack upon the literary theory of John Livingston Lowes, whom Babbitt had engaged in public debate, Babbitt made an unexpected defense of Lowes and reminded the upstart that he was assailing a reputable scholar. Sometimes enjoying contrariety for its own sake, he would surprise a would-be devotee who echoed his prejudices by coming to a sudden defense of the Shelley or Chateaubriand he had flayed in lecture. Yet, his writings on education amply allow the inference that he knew he was dispositionally *à rebours* to the greater number of his students. On the other hand, he was not an insensate dogmatist who would react hostilely to this algebraic fact. He relished it as a challenge.

It is, nonetheless, difficult to determine how satisfied Babbitt was merely to challenge his students, to oblige them to understand concepts and values contrary to their own. He once confessed, "When one fights single-handedly, it's lonely," and his hope for some affirmation from his students probably concealed a need not only for support of humanistic standards but for some unspoken personal encouragement.[58] Enabling young men to comprehend the quality of disciplined will through literature was Babbitt's conscious goal, but he could appreciate their comprehension only through an intimation of support. He was the necessary reagent or catalyst needed to form a compound from youth's active intellectual potential and from humanist tradition. As his most illustrious student wrote, tradition required "a perception, not only of the pastness of the past, but of its presence . . . a sense of the timeless as well as of the temporal and of the timeless and the temporal together."[59] Babbitt, who may be viewed as one of the godfathers of T. S. Eliot's "Tradition and the Individual Talent," held as a supremely imaginative and ethical act the individual's affirmation and renewal of the letters of tradition: "it is what a man is imaginatively and not what he preaches that really counts."[60] His own imaginative task was to evoke from students the sense of humanistic values to which he felt all great and enduring literature in some way appealed.

As early as his own student days, Babbitt was convinced that a nations's fate depended upon the quality of its best minds rather than upon impersonal forces or putatively cosmic laws, as it was fashionable to believe at the turn of the century. And as Harvard was the nation's foremost institution for training these best minds, he felt his position entirely fitting, perhaps even fateful. At the time he published his first book, when his advanced classes were still small, he anticipated attracting only "some students of the more serious sort," but even with increasing popularity as a lecturer after he became full professor in 1912, Babbitt never entertained assurance that he was a successful teacher. His distance from his colleagues was matched by occasional despair about students and their seeming inability to react to ideas.

At the same time, aware that youthful enthusiasms are commonly as short-lived as they are ardent, he dreaded the degradation of his strictures into passing fashion or fad, especially during the fetishistic years following World War I. Even more, he feared becoming himself an object of cultism. He preferred the good-natured mockery of a joke that was common around Harvard in the 1920s: Babbitt's fame was spreading around the world and had in fact already left Cambridge.

It remained difficult for him to distinguish genuine responsiveness to humanist thought from fleeting, superficial advocacy; he could only discourage students who sought to lionize him or sloganize his ideas. Some few, like Eliot, Stuart Sherman, and Norman Foerster, were constitutionally able to embrace, at least partially, the humanistic bias and to emulate Babbitt in their careers as men of letters. Apart from this thin minority was a larger group that responded to Babbitt appreciatively and critically, those that Austin Warren claimed Babbitt had taught to think for themselves. Brooks, Lippmann, Theodore Spencer, Harry Levin, and several other distinguished critics are to be counted in this rank. As we will note in subsequent chapters, it was Babbitt's peculiar fate that some of his most competent admirers became his most telling critics; as a teacher he had aroused and for a time retained intelligent supporters but was unable to keep their company. Ultimately, the moralist in him was alone. Perhaps in no other way was he so like the Augustan sage to whom his students most often likened him, Samuel Johnson.

3. The Lessing Persuasion
Babbitt as a Literary Critic

εἰ μὲν οὖν ἕκαστος ἑαυτῷ τῆς ἕξεώς εστί πως αἴτιος, καὶ τῆς
φαντασίας ἔσται πως αὐτος αἴτιος.

Aristotle, *Nicomachean Ethics*

Till America has learned to love art, not as an amusement,
not as the mere ornament of her cities, not as a superstition
of what is *comme il faut* for a great nation, but for its human-
izing and ennobling energy, for its power of making men
better by arousing in them a perception of their own instincts for what is beautiful, and therefore sacred and religious, and an eternal rebuke of what is base and worldly, she
will not have succeeded in that high sense which alone
makes a nation out of a people.

James Russell Lowell, "The Function of the Poet"

By the late nineteenth century, the New England generation
that formed what George Santayana called "the genteel tradition" was able to sustain its gospel of taste only by retreating
before the ascendancy of the industrial age. Unable to accommodate
urbanization, immigration, and the problems of a rapidly changing
economy, and equally unable to embrace the bureaucratic and scientific progressivism that attacked such problems, genteel men of
letters—Charles Eliot Norton, E. C. Stedman, Richard Stoddard, Ba-
yard Taylor, and other Brahmins—were left with an outdated romantic optimism. Their assumption that art exists for its own sake rested
upon their belief in transcendent moral laws that art was supposed to
express. By the 1890s, the decadence of that aesthetic was already
subverting the gentlemanly code it had once sustained.

The breach between ethics and aesthetics grew wider in the first
decades of the twentieth century. Literature reflected the relativism
of the sciences through experimental modes that confounded moral
and social convention. Language itself became a weapon in the assault upon orthodoxies; its transparent psychological properties were
revealed in poetry, plays, and novels celebrating the incalculable, irrational, and primitive urges of humankind.

Sharing the dismay of his Brahmin predecessors over the apparently fallen state of literature, Irving Babbitt argued for the restoration of art and morals. Hostile as he was to his age yet insisting that he was a modern, Babbitt could formulate his aesthetic views only by using a historical perspective, and even so he was unable to escape a predominance of negations in his argument that overshadowed what he positively upheld.

For Babbitt, the creation or experience of art, like moral endeavor, required a balance of temperament. To be worthwhile it had to be difficult to express or feel. Art was almost a religious event; ideally, it not only reflected but somehow transcended the temperament of the artist. This transcendence of the creator's particular sensibility was what Babbitt understood as classicism; romanticism, in sharp contrast, directly revealed that sensibility and offered no escape from it.

One of Babbitt's few definitions of a humanistic aesthetic indicated the delicate nature of its experience:

> For me the sense of beauty admits all manner of excitement but always an excitement within an unfolding serenity. Within limits many degrees of keen emotional experience are possible. But the moment the sheer excitement perturbs the serenity, the impression of art is tottering. Contrariwise when the excitement departs, the serenity becomes void of content, a complacency splendidly null. If this be true the sense of beauty is akin to the feelings we have at moments of greatest physical and mental efficiency. . . . Every impression of art must end within this sense of leaving becalmed and fortified—the meaning, I take it, of Aristotelian katharsis.[1]

Failing or disdaining to clothe these abstractions with references to contemporary arts, Babbitt repeated the error he ascribed to Samuel Johnson's neoclassicism and "put himself out of touch with the creative forces of his own age."[2]

Babbitt once concluded that aesthetics were something of a nightmare but he wrote a book and several essays on the subject. In spite of his prodigious efforts to clarify, aesthetics remained the most elusive aspect of his polemics. He was fully cognizant of the influence that English and French impressionists of the fin-de-siècle (Pater, Wilde, Anatole France, Gourmont) were exerting upon American critics like James Gibbons Huneker, Carl Van Vechten, and H. L. Mencken, but he maintained a determined and retrograde view of criticism, convinced that impressionism meant the abandonment of all standards. He even failed, perhaps purposely, to recognize that

Matthew Arnold, the stoutest pleader for critical standards, was an impressionistic critic who kept his romantic proclivities long after he ceased to write poetry. It was not strange, then, that Babbitt had to look as far back as the eighteenth century to find an acceptable proponent of aesthetic criticism.

During his sabbatical of 1907–8, Babbitt read musty tomes of Renaissance criticism in the Bibliothèque Nationale and the Bibliothèque Ste. Geneviève in Paris. With previously gathered materials he hoped, following Lessing's *Laokoon* (1766), "to make a contrast between the pseudo-classic and the romantic melange de genres." He asked More, "Would it be presumptuous to call my volume *The New Laokoon* (with subtitle) *An Essay on the Confusion of the Arts*, provided that my title expresses what I think needs doing rather than what I myself would claim to have done?"[3]

Babbitt took the father of the German Enlightenment as his mentor because he found that he shared Lessing's position in time, standing at the close of a movement the decadent aspects of which were in need of assault. Both men looked to France as the battleground of standards—Lessing, contemporaneously, Babbitt, historically—and wrote, as perhaps only a Frenchman or a Francophile would, with an acutely polemicized audience in mind even though both were aware that no such audience existed on home ground.

Lessing had an advantage over Babbitt in a literate, learned, and sophisticated European public. Even in Germany there were minds other than the pygmies whose heads, said Heine, Lessing lopped off with his shafts of wit. There was Winckelmann, fired to brilliance in a compulsive love for antiquity. His works were in a great way the occasion for Lessing's *Laokoon*. Babbitt's public was at best a composite of academicians and journalists.

What Babbitt felt with the German classicist was a concern for the intent of the artist within his expression. He imputed to Lessing what was his own business as a critic: "It is the goal of art that interests him rather than any pleasant vagabondage of fancy or sensibility on the way thither."[4] It was this "tremendous purposefulness" that Babbitt praised in Dante and the Greek tragedians and that he confessed he found lacking in Shakespeare's occasional "wanton luxuriating in imagination for its own sake," but the point was not only aesthetic but ethical and spiritual in implying that "one should at least have a philosophy of life and when the idea of purpose is sufficiently developed, a religion."[5] Lessing was the model of a critic who extended aesthetics and literary criticism into issues of philosophy and faith.

Lessing had sought a median between a German neoclassicism

made decadent by French influences and the romantic antinomianism of the Storm and Stress movement. Following his example, Babbitt attempted to make clear that hostility to excesses of romanticism in the arts did not necessarily signify allegiance to the brittle rulemongering of reactionary pseudoclassicism. He knew that Lessing's penetrating criticisms, though winning him attention and notoriety in his own time, did not stay the floodtides of reaction against formalized prescriptions in the arts and in society itself. In the end, Lessing became the kind of sage who is "recognizable through the infinitely diverse accidents of time and space" and yet without effectual influence upon his own age.[6] It was the fate of other humanists.

Babbitt regarded his published works as complementary parts of a single argument and as he felt those parts cohere, he became aware of a need for a national audience. Conventional journalistic channels were open and there was More's influential editorship at the *Nation*, but Babbitt was skeptical of the quality of even that prestigious organ's patronage. He posed to More what he believed to be "the chief problem of all" in responsible journalism: "[H]ow is it going to be possible in this country under present conditions to run a paper with a serious intellectual purpose and at the same time make it commercially profitable. I hope you are conscious of an audience outside of the specialists, women and dilettantes who read anything besides the daily newspapers and cheap magazines."[7] The golden age of journalism, of E. L. Godkin, Charles Dana, and Charles Eliot Norton, was irretrievably gone; the brass age of Hearst and Pulitzer was in full sway.

Babbitt's fretting over the quality of American journalism was far from impersonal. He realized that the journals were a vital factor in propagating his humanism beyond the collegiate community. His first book was partly a collation of essays he had published in the *Nation* and the *Atlantic Monthly*. Once, having submitted an eight-thousand-word article to the *Atlantic Monthly*, he was obliged to reduce it to five thousand words. He found that in "mutilating" his work, the argument "suffered seriously both in form and substance."[8] But rather than remain aloof and apart, he made distasteful compromises. Several years after he performed his first painful excisions, he told More, "I never dare to put my most serious thought into the *Atlantic*."[9] Yet that journal was one of the few that he recognized to have any merit.

Even before his first book was issued, Babbitt had become suspicious of journalists, whose profession "seems about as conducive to slimy diplomacy as that of college presidents." But he also sensed his own stylistic shortcomings in appealing to a broad readership: he had none of the "distinctly romantic quality" of gusto that seemed to be fashionable in journalism.[10] Babbitt confessed envy of More's ability to overcome the deadening routine of an editor to write essays that were of a consistently high quality. Yet the meager sales of More's serial *Shelburne Essays* (seven volumes appeared between 1904 and 1910) indicated to Babbitt "in discouraging concrete form how little audience there is for real criticism in this country. All this would change fast enough if there were college teachers capable of inspiring in their students a taste for intelligent reading."[11]

Babbitt evidently felt that there was a collusion of incompetence between academic and journalistic practices, but what he prescribed as a tactical counter or corrective is difficult to characterize. He knew that disciplinarian humanism was scarcely current in the midst of a nationwide progressivism; further, journals like the *New Republic* and *Outlook* were emerging as ideological props of that progressivism. But Babbitt did not wish to advertise too presumptuously what humanist community there might be. More shared this caution in advising him on revisions of *Literature and the American College*: "Certainly you should not bring in my name more than once, if once in the notes. We shall get the name of mutual puffing, which will aid neither of us."[12]

Although eminent journals were the ideal medium for exchanging views, More's mishandling of a review of Babbitt's first book indicated how potentially damaging the press might be even to the most closely reasoned arguments. Babbitt objected again when More inadvertently selected an unsympathetic reviewer for their friend Prosser Frye's *Literary Reviews and Criticism*: "There are several of us who stand for somewhat similar ideas in education and literature at the present time but I fear that we are not showing much practical shrewdness in our team play."[13]

Far afield, the "team" to which Babbitt referred included, besides Frye at the University of Nebraska; William Giese at Wisconsin; Frank Mather at Princeton; the critic and editor, William Crary Brownell; and Babbitt's own protégé, Stuart Sherman at the University of Illinois. But those men were not of the sort to form a cabal or literary clique. Indeed, Babbitt saw that far more likely and far worse than a public recognition that would group them into a cabal would be no recognition at all.

Babbitt puzzled over the problem in rather amusing ways. He chose to write almost exclusively for the *Nation* because it was one of the few periodicals "to get out before a very large number of the people I am trying to reach."[14] If More and he were too furtive, they would be unable to create any audience nor would they be able to maintain ties with others propounding their own or similar views. There was at times a strange make-believe in both men's efforts to elicit a public response. Babbitt was surprised to read in one of More's articles of certain anonymous persons who were attacking the Rousseauist, currently Deweyan, postulates of education. He asked More, "Who are these certain persons besides myself? There has been a curious absence thus far of this kind of attack in either English, German or French."[15] Yet, in a note to Norton less than a year before, Babbitt had been equally obscure in noting "a reaction of late against certain excesses of the scientific spirit in literary study."[16] Babbitt would have been inclined to an unwonted optimism had such a "reaction" proven as substantial as Norton, himself no optimist, might have inferred from Babbitt's own statement.

The foreboding note that Babbitt recurrently sounded was fear of public indifference. He admitted hesitation in writing on religious or philosophical issues because of "the discouraging feeling of being without an audience. Someone has to make a beginning though it is disheartening to stand out almost alone against the main drift of one's time."[17] Wishing perhaps to preclude any delusions of success, he advised More that even as an editor of the *Nation* he might "turn out to be a general without troops. That is the way I have felt about a good deal of my own writing."[18]

Babbitt was further apprehensive lest the values that he espoused with More might seem esoteric or obscurantist. More's wistful love of ancient India and Greece, combined with his austere style and disdain for the twentieth century, could hardly prove palatable to most readers. Babbitt objected to a tendentious, reclusive gloom in his friend that actually foreshadowed More's ultimate break with humanism and his affirmation of Anglican Christianity. His "Delphi and Greek Literature" left Babbitt with "the melancholy feeling that after all the human spirit may be fatally condemned to be blighted by some unfriendly excess and indeed become the victim of its own virtues."[19] It was a subtlety that More labored[20] but which Babbitt never cared to probe deeply, least of all as it might have applied to himself. He feared in More a valetudinarian withdrawal from life in the manner of Norton, but he saw very few alternatives to that withdrawal.[21]

For himself Babbitt could see no other alternative than to have what he called "something of Lessing's virile emphasis on action."[22] In the words of his own trope, he was a general who did not wait to see if he had troops to command before engaging in what he believed to be obligatory combat. There was a seeming quixotism that he shared with Lessing.

The New Laokoon suffered from Babbitt's acute awareness of his defensive and solitary position against the "impressionistic flutter" of literature and criticism before World War I.[23] Whether he was genuinely convinced that his posture was solitary and self-isolating mattered less than the exhilaration he seemed to derive by assuming it. At the same time, his dread of inconsequence made him fight any semblance of defensiveness in his writing. He regarded himself as no traditionalist, no upholder of genteel mores. Neither was he urging slavish imitation of classical or any other models in the manner of a formalist. The Greeks, he knew, served as a warning to all cultures of the hazards in abandoning the qualities of discipline—"vital unity, vital measure, vital purpose"—that had made their artistic achievements supreme.[24] Hence the study of Greek society was of critical importance in deriving a model drama of the grandeur and misery of peoples.

What Babbitt did find most admirable in the Greeks was their genius in combining an individual spontaneity and inspiration with a disciplined reference to some standard ulterior to individuality. This balance between inspiration and control was the only legitimate aim of aesthetics. Rules when taken as all-sufficient tended to warp or deny inspiration, to become dogmas against which the artist would be compelled to react. The Greeks at their best had precluded such a reaction by balancing the claims of tradition and those of originality and so achieving what Babbitt called "creative imitation."[25] Creativity, in other words, presupposed and required a sound artistic and critical tradition.

Thus, Babbitt's rejection of strict neoclassicism was partly based on recognition of the limitations of an adherence to traditional authority beyond its time. A convention of formulas, inflexibly held, would ossify and its supporters would be left impotent in its wake. Norton, Henry Adams, and others of the genteel order had exemplified the debilitation that came in seeking a dogma by which to condemn an age they could not comprehend.

Babbitt resolved to avoid even the appearance of such a reaction. In one of his tactical discussions with More, he defined the humanist position as "positive and critical . . . as opposed to the spirit which accepts things on traditional authority; it is not identical surely with the spirit of innovation and mere intoxication with the future."[26] More rejoined that antitraditionalism brought "flimsiness of mind" so as to discredit "anything settled in the mere wantonness of change," and he proclaimed himself a reactionary in "wishing to bring people back to a proper, not a superstitious respect for sheer authority."[27] Babbitt viewed the issue not as word-gaming but in terms of what might be called public relations: "To admit at present that one is a Tory or even a reactionary is in my opinion to commit a tactical mistake of the first order. One is at once put on the defensive, and in the war of intellect as in other forms of warfare the advantage belongs with the offensive."[28] The matter was, of course, not solely "tactical" nor did Babbitt believe that he was even covertly reactionary. Indeed, he faulted Samuel Johnson, whom otherwise he held in high esteem, for having rested his literary judgments upon a formalism of tradition instead of upon an immediate insight. Babbitt wrote in terms of issues and problems rather than systems or dogmas, and so he required in his style a kind of militant offensive that was lacking in More, who, stylistically relaxed, sought a bulwark of doctrine.

Babbitt's tendency to argue circularly and his occasional failure to define terms that he insistently used left and still leaves an appearance of dogmatism. He would never concede that he was dogmatic because he regarded dogma as the sclerotic aspect of tradition and he knew himself to be without any tradition, at least as an American. Besides, there was a difference between appealing to tradition and appealing to its example. Yet, Babbitt perhaps did not realize adequately that in a relativistic age, in which subjective impressions were the only rules, any critical insight or disciplined creativity would seem no less superfluous, no less relative than the rankest impressionism.

Babbitt's analysis of the basic deficiencies of his age seemed to require some systematic or cohesive formulation precisely because he felt that people in the present "have no center, no sense of anything fixed or permanent either within or without themselves that they may oppose to the flux of phenomena."[29] But Babbitt had no praise for human nature itself that would have allowed him to suggest that the present unawareness of a fixed center was only temporary or circumstantial. He claimed that the history of ideas revealed people to be not lovers of truth but of half-truths: "Of course most men cannot be said to love in any effective sense even half-truths but are hungry above all for illusions."[30] When half-truths gained currency, they became sources of fanaticism and the effects of such extremity often lasted well beyond the primal heat. Babbitt sensed from history an unending oscillation between extremes wherein successive series of half-truths provided justifiable reaction against their opposite.

Accordingly, Babbitt had to grant a measure of justice to romantic assaults upon pseudoclassical dictates in the eighteenth century. His most concentrated critical efforts he directed against the romanticists because he saw the predominant half-truths of his own age as the fruits of their revolt over a century before.

With this background in Babbitt's attitudes and concerns at the time of *The New Laokoon*, we can now consider some of the book's central arguments. The problematic inspiration for it related directly to its predecessor:

> With the spread of impressionism literature has lost standards and discipline, and at the same time virility and seriousness; it has fallen into the hands of aesthetes and dilettantes, the last effete representatives of romanticism, who have proved utterly unequal to the task of maintaining its great traditions against the scientific positivists.[31]

In *Literature and the American College*, Babbitt had identified the aesthetes and positivists as kindred in their promotion of naturalism against the literary and philosophical legacies of humane standards. *The New Laokoon* narrowed the field of combat to the arts and the *mélange de genres* among and within them. Babbitt's prefatory remarks seemed to foretell some aesthetic theorizing to counter the breakdown of artistic standards, but he declined to give any formula for a humanist aesthetic. Instead, he made tentative statements that followed deductively from his general plea for a balanced temperament: "Any sound analysis of beauty will always recognize two elements—an element that is expansive and vital and may be summed up by the term expression, and in contrast to this an element of form that is felt rather as limiting and circumscribing law."[32] Expression and form would have to exist as "reconciled opposites" rather than as "clashing antinomies" oscillating in the ascendance of pseudoclassical and romantic extremes.[33] Babbitt found that people's aesthetic judgments are subjective—"if a thing really 'finds' us, we do not worry much about form or the dignity of the genre"—but it was precisely there that came the indolence that eroded the critical sense of balance.[34] The only corrective was an art that satisfied both imagination and understanding as equitably as possible. There, again, was the classical theme. The romanticists, according to Babbitt, tended to overstress imagination so as to justify the penchants of their private sensibility or "genius." Instead of communicating general truths about the human condition, truths that would have ultimate reference in an abiding oneness, the romanticists offered only documentation of their own fleeting emotions.

Babbitt traced modern confusions in artistic expression to a romantic misappropriation of Platonism. Romanticism and Platonism alike attacked the decadence of academic sophistries and constrictive conventions, but whereas Platonism was based upon controlled insight and concentration of will, romanticism was predicated upon emotion and the expansion of feeling through sensation. The prototypal personalities reflecting these differences were, of course, Plato and Rousseau. In *Literature and the American College*, Babbitt had paired Rousseau and Montaigne as examples of humanitarian and humanist ethics; in *The New Laokoon*, he again employed a dualism of personalities that kept his argumentation from excessive abstraction.

Babbitt's characterization of Rousseau was not a caricature. In Rousseau romanticism did not have its prime initiator (a title that Babbitt felt Shaftesbury more justly bore) but its most powerful and ingenious exponent. Babbitt made Rousseau the standard-bearer of the romantic epoch because he found him the most eloquent and sophistical champion of spontaneity. Rousseau promoted a "subliminal uprush" of emotion against pseudoclassicism's "over-analytical dryness of mind": "That such a reaction would have taken place without Rousseau is certain; but it is equally certain that he first gave powerful expression to it and profoundly influenced the forms that it assumed."[35]

Babbitt did not wish to make Rousseau a bogy against whom to foster shibboleths. (A joke among Harvard's undergraduates was that Babbitt nightly looked under his bed to see if Rousseau were there.) As though concurring with Nietzsche's injunction to choose worthy enemies, he showed no little esteem for Jean-Jacques. Besides "an incomparable freshness and charm" in Rousseau's Arcadian reveries, he found in the descriptive style a frequent sobriety and balance between sensuous and intellectual elements.[36] "Judged by any standard Rousseau is a man of intellectual power," who, in his essay on the origin of languages rightly repudiated pseudoclassical attempts to commingle the effects of different arts.[37]

In another passage Babbitt owned that some of Rousseau's writings were "at least as assured of immortality as any of Voltaire's, and are at the same time filled with color and imagery. Art can stand plenty of fresh and vivid impressions and indeed requires them, only they must be subordinated to something higher than themselves."[38] Most of Rousseau's sophisms stemmed from his refusal to make that subordination, to acknowledge any force above his own temperament and impulse. In his qualified commendation, so much in the style of Charles Augustin Sainte-Beuve but without a trace of his sarcasm,

Babbitt seemed to regard Rousseau as a schoolmaster would a pupil whom he chides for having learned some lesson too well, that is, to the neglect of others. The result of Rousseau's one-sided stress upon feeling and mere sensuousness was that writers of his lineage became automatons for recording their idiosyncratic impressions (the last two words were tautological for Babbitt) without a balancing attentiveness to "the normal, the representative, the human."[39] With an algebraic formula that recalls the artifice of Henry Adams's "rule of phase," Babbitt traced the decline of purposeful expression in French literature after Rousseau: from Chateaubriand to Lamartine, Hugo and Verlaine, the order of cerebration fell, so that fin-de-siècle literature was void of any rational purpose and expressed merely private quests for sensation.

Rousseau's errant genius so fascinated Babbitt that he tended to see the history of Western literature from the eighteenth century as largely a reaction to Rousseau. He neglected to scrutinize the aesthetic theories or intents of different literary schools or individuals; it is as though he saw romantics like Chateaubriand and Lamartine, the *parnassiens* and the *symbolistes*, as but older and younger branches of a Genevan tree. This too neatly conceived declension of corruption revealed the polemical nature of Babbitt's view. His stylistic bias necessarily neglected any correlation between historical and literary developments, such as the rise of an industrial bourgeoisie from the First to the Third French Republic and the rise of the novel.[40]

Babbitt believed that historical method, though sound when limited, too easily externalized issues and so dissipated their moral importance. To explain literature through history was, he felt, a perverse inversion of method: history was to be understood through literature just as, according to Aristotle, particulars were illumined by universals. He considered Sainte-Beuve a victim of historical method in his sometimes obsessive attention to circumstantial minutiae in the formation or reflection of a writer's character.

In addition to his scorn of historical method, Babbitt was averse to the niceties of technical analysis. A philological reduction of verse or prose to its smallest components would be the transparent equivalent of Verlaine's *le nuance toujours* and would distort the essential focus upon an aesthetic whole by which one would judge what Babbitt called "representative" aspects within it. Free from the scruples of literary technique, Babbitt extended his attack upon romanticism beyond its manifestations in belles lettres. There was some symmetrical sense, he thought, in designating a contemporary like Henri Bergson a legatee of Rousseau: both were not only discursive, unsystematic philosophers but also proponents of an aestheticism without relation to intellectual or moral intent. Babbitt claimed that the process by which "art and literature pass more and more from the domain of action into the region of revery" found logical culmination in Bergson's advocacy of art as "a sort of lotus-eating."[41]

Action is a key word in understanding the romanticism that Babbitt did find acceptable and, by his own prescription of a balanced temperament, healthy and necessary. So hostile were many of his references to the romantic spirit that one might justifiably infer that Babbitt did not always heed his own exhortation to avoid extremes. The romanticism he did approve was exemplary of the "masculine" qualities he lauded in other contexts. Against the imputed femininity of French romantics, he argued that the Elizabethans were proper romantics. They were not "mere sensitive plants, recoiling from the rough and tumble of the world"; "they were interested in actual adventure, caring little for the mysterious dalliance of soul and sense in the tower of ivory."[42] Elizabethan romanticism embodied a representative, human inclination for wonder and adventure. This characterization, which Babbitt may have borrowed from Dr. Johnson's *Preface to Shakespeare*, had an actual as well as fictive basis: the Elizabethans not only wrote tales of adventure, but they lived them. Similarly, American society had once enjoyed in fiction such as Cooper's Leatherstocking sagas an embellished commentary upon its own adventurous expansion into wilderness. Romanticism as recreational art carried some purpose if only in reflecting purpose in life itself.

That delight in and need for adventure amid the rough-and-tumble world would seem to have found expression most exuberantly in so patently expansive a romantic as Walt Whitman. But even from the vantage of recreational romanticism, Babbitt could see no merit in Whitman, for he, like Rousseau, wrote from the perspective of an overcivilized society, that is, one in which romanticism manifested itself only in retreat from actual conditions of life. (Babbitt had forgotten *Democratic Vistas*.) Babbitt implied that, although some romanticism was common to all epochs, its primitive and unreflective character could be allowed only in a naive age: "Such a difference, for example, we feel between the author of a genuine old Irish Saga and some modern Celtic revivalist" because the latter sought the artificial restoration of the child-like, undeliberated spirit that the former expressed free of self-consciousness.[43]

Babbitt's distinction between the naive, the civilized, and the self-consciously overcivilized societies is crucial not only to his notion of the breakdown of aesthetic standards. Its implications extend into his views on the imperialism of degenerate democracy and the humanitarian distortion of Christianity into a false spirituality. Nowhere did Babbitt make so clear as in his dismissal of the aesthetic of the false naive the ethical danger in abandoning a convention of artistic standards. Aesthetic trends were an intimate gauge of a civilized culture's stability and of the ethical balance of its members. Babbitt held so firmly to this belief in the ethical nature of art, to the degree of order and proportion in form and expression, that, living in an age that he viewed as one of "prodigious peripheral richness joined to a great central void," he was unremittingly suspicious of contemporaneous arts.[44]

So implacably dour and negative was Babbitt's view of modern arts that Heine's criticism of Lessing applies equally well to him: he was as strong in negation as he was weak in affirmation.[45] Heine ascribed Lessing's deficiency to a lack of philosophical system or *Grundprinzip*. Babbitt had, at least inferentially, a humanist ethic, but he was unwilling to argue for a complementary aesthetic that was anything more than a series of arbitrary distinctions. His own fondness for *le genre tranché*, or the functional separateness of literary and artistic modes, placed upon him an unfulfilled obligation to update, revise, and reaffirm such distinctions if only in a corrective rather than prescriptive way.

The strange lack of contemporaneousness in Babbitt's aesthetic arguments, a lack most noticeable in *The New Laokoon*, stemmed partly from his disdain of the most modern literary genre, the novel. "The triumph of the novel," he generalized, "has been, if not the triumph of formlessness over form, at least the triumph of diffuseness over concentration."[46] He rejected not only the genre itself but the attitudes that he conjectured to be integral to the reading of fiction. While he could accept recreative poetry because "the need of escape is deep-seated and universal" and "one need not quarrel with imagination of this quality when it shows itself frankly for what it is," he saw the writing and reading of novels as symptomatic of decadence.[47] Fiction tended to become an antidote to the rigors of Whitman's overcivilized industrial society. It offered vicarious indulgence of emotion as a narcotic to the mundane uglinesses of life.

Babbitt's remarks on Dreiser's *An American Tragedy* reveal a deeper objection. His conclusion that "it is hardly worth while to struggle through eight hundred and more very pedestrian pages to be left at the end with a feeling of sheer oppression" summed up his sense of the wastefulness of fiction in conveying often dubious points of ethics.[48] A novel like Dreiser's was wholly opposite to the Aristotelian catharsis that Babbitt felt all great literature provided, that release from "human agitation" to "a deeper sense of calm" and universality by comparison with which one's particular life would seem feverish and vain.[49] The novel tended largely to reflect life's agitations so as to make people seem not better but worse than they were, that is, incapable of elevation to a sense of a higher will. Naturalistic or realistic novelists such as Norris and Sinclair, carrying on Rousseau's charge that evils are rooted in institutions rather than in people, not only depicted life more sordidly than it was, but reduced people to puppets of environmental circumstances.[50]

The 1928 essay, "The Critic and American Life," gives the most concrete notion of Babbitt's tastes and distastes in contemporary literature. His target was the wholesale antitraditionalism of the most influential critic of the decade, H. L. Mencken, and the sort of literature that Mencken promoted. Included in his assault upon Mencken's view of criticism as "the satisfaction of a temperamental urge" to self-expression was a restatement of Babbitt's vague plea for a "correct scale of values," a "poise" that would give literature dignity and worth beyond the passing fashions that influenced its creation. Instead of applying critical norms to postwar literature, Mencken's "intellectual vaudeville" absorbed much of the romantic disillusion of the time into the province of criticism itself.[51]

Babbitt subscribed to the common assumption that literary trends in Europe tended to be reborn a generation later in America. The Gallic decadence of the fin-de-siècle was regenerated among American "exiles" in Paris in the 1920s. Three years before Edmund Wilson's study of symbolism in *Axel's Castle* (1931), Babbitt wrote: "Anyone who resided in Paris in the nineties and later in America, will, as I can testify from personal experience, have the sense of having lived through the same literary fads twice."[52] Zola, for instance, prefigured Dreiser in a naturalistic depiction of societal evils, a perspective that obscured "the principle of control on which the inner life finally depends."[53] An imbalancing stress upon particulars, as in the characterization of social problems, betrayed a lack of insight among novelists into the abiding, universal elements of human nature. The trouble with fictional dramatizations of "the evanescent surface of life" was that they passed to posterity not as literature but as "sociological documents."[54]

Babbitt's harsh verdicts on modern fiction were a function of his stringently held classical bias. Unwilling to confer even documentary status on *An American Tragedy*, he concluded that it was not tragedy at all since it was void of "the final relief and enlargement of spirit that true tragedy succeeds somehow in giving, and that without resort to explicit moralizing."[55] Even more severely, he faulted Dos Passos's *Manhattan Transfer* as beyond the ancient criteria of credibility or probability, "unless one is prepared to admit that contemporary Manhattan is inhabited chiefly by epileptic Bohemians." Like Dreiser, Dos Passos exaggerated "the clutter and incoherency of the mundane spectacle instead of eliciting its deeper meaning."[56] But where in those postwar years, an era that Babbitt looked upon as a chaos, was there any "deeper meaning" to be found? His literal application of Aristotle's terms served him as a kind of bludgeon against literary trends that confounded any rules. His only defense was that he was a true modern in wanting literature to be more than a reflection of an age or its fetishes.

It was a basic tenet of Babbitt's humanism that a critical mind should not only address the age but rise above it to an intuited sense of order and proportion based upon a broad knowledge of literary history. In contrast to such an informed critical spirit, a modernist of Mencken's stamp, boosted by fleeting fashion, was certain to become its victim and lose authority when that fashion changed. Babbitt's rigid preference for a wisdom of the ages over that of Mencken's hour intensified his denial of any substantive literary worth in the twentieth century. His reversion to the masterworks of tradition—to Sophocles, Dante, and Milton—was his somewhat invidious way of keeping modern letters in the dimmest light. He had once attested that

> some of the ancients and a few of the greatest of the moderns, may be regarded as the fixed stars of literature. We may safely take our bearings with reference to them and be guided by them in deciding what is essence and what is accident in human nature. They are a sort of concrete *idea hominis*. There is something definitive in their rendering of life—something that is purged of all localism and deserves to be received as typical.[57]

Babbitt conceived of this exalted, almost metaphysical view of letters as a basis for ethical standards in an era he contemned as defiantly accidental. Arguing for ethically sound aesthetic criteria was his singular way of being a humanistic modern, as it had been Lessing's way nearly two hundred years before. Mention of Lessing serves to turn us to nonliterary aspects of Babbitt's thesis in *The New Laokoon*.

Babbitt intended this book to be more a polemic than a treatise, but he extended his argument beyond literary genres into musical ones partly on the ground that modern literature and music had close philosophical associations and partly in deference to the classical notion that music was a factor in one's moral education. He may also have accepted, perhaps too seriously, the Germanic view that music is the most transcendental of arts and thus the most certain haven for the romantic sensibility.

Babbitt was quite ignorant of music and musical theory. What little education he had came largely from the wife of a colleague, Edward Sheldon, who spent some afternoons with him at her parlor piano in the 1890s. He may have felt that music, like the reading of novels and other "cultural" activities, was the pastime of women and dilettantes and so have reacted with some aversion to it. The only composer to whom he ever responded positively was Mozart, who appeared to be the paradigmatic master of a balance between form and expression and next to whom romantic composers invariably appeared errant. Babbitt attempted to arraign the romanticists of music on the same charges he had brought against romantic poets and naturalistic novelists, finding in them "the same growing emphasis on the individual, . . . the same tendency to confuse the original with the bizarre, the paradoxical, the eccentric."[58]

Drawing largely from British musicologist Edward Dannreuther's *The Romantic Period* (1905) in the *Oxford History of Music*, Babbitt centered his attack upon the foremost romanticists of the nineteenth century, Hector Berlioz and Richard Wagner. Berlioz's flamboyant excesses of temperament, so evident in his *Memoirs*, were, Babbitt presumed, certain to appear in his music as well. After reading an analysis of Berlioz's *Requiem*, Babbitt, not having heard a note of it, concluded that it was in parts "mainly noise and sensationalism" and on the whole "not an illumination from above but an insurrection from below."[59] This example reinforced, or so Babbitt believed, the case against a pseudo-spirituality latent in romantic aesthetics, an exaggeration of expression at the expense of form that could evince no real ethical intent.

Babbitt was on more solid ground reviewing the theories of Wagner. Thanks to Bernard Shaw in England and James Gibbons Huneker in America, Wagner had become a stock figure of controversy among literary critics. Babbitt's view of him was based largely upon his writings in the psychology of aesthetics. Wagner's theoretical fusing of literary, musical, and visual genres to reveal, in his words, "the Unconscious, the Instinctive, the Purely-human" sufficiently exhibited to Babbitt what he considered a cardinal romantic anti-intellectualism.[60] "Nothing could be conceived more Rousseauistic than Wagner's theory of opera; . . . men are to meet, not in a common discipline but a common sympathy; . . . love is to triumph over restraint."[61] His criticism of Wagner's union of music and verse was naive, of course, because that union was the essence of opera itself and antedated Wagner by two centuries of development. It would have been as just to attack a composer such as Christoph Gluck, a contemporary of Lessing and no less a seminal figure than Wagner in operatic literature. For once, Babbitt was awkwardly ignorant of the historic breadth of a generic development.

Moreover, Wagner's theories on fusing the arts into a *Gesamtkunstwerk* remained for the greater part abstract and were never practically integrated into the performance of his operas. Babbitt was misled here by the assumption he had always applied to letters, that the derivation of a creator's philosophy determined the worth of his creation. But Wagner, like Rousseau, exerted an incalculable influence and had to be held to account: he had exercised an especial fascination upon two generations of French writers, from Baudelaire to Mallarmé.

What Babbitt failed to note was that this fascination, which included French poets, painters, and musicians, was but an addendum to the attraction that an earlier generation, led by Madame de Staël, had felt for an apparent Arcadian purity in feudal Germany—a purity that a decadent, pseudoclassical France could not hope to emulate. In other words, aesthetics was a cosmopolitan force that bridged national differences. In Wagner's era the enemy of the arts was no longer pseudoclassicism but the philistine bourgeoisie that reduced the arts to entertainment for the affluent. In Germany, burgeoning industrial power was furthering the growth of a class that had emerged in France mainly through revolution and war. Had Babbitt treated such non-aesthetic factors within the framework of his thesis, he could have seen perhaps that the profuse advocacy for mixing genres was a transnational counteroffensive against the bourgeois depreciation of the arts.

But Babbitt was no historian. He was so much the moralist that he was inclined to forget his own concession that "art rests primarily not on ethical but aesthetic perceptions."[62] Review of a basic theme of Babbitt's humanism in the context of *The New Laokoon* will provide a bridge to discussion of some final points about his aesthetic views. He reiterated from his first book that the essence of a humanistic method was mediation between temperamental extremes, that in art, as in education, self-discipline was essential not merely to effective but right thinking. One proves oneself to be above natural law by exercising restraint according to a human law or "inner check," a phrase Babbitt borrowed from Emerson and Colebrooke, who had derived it from Eastern mysticism. Exercise of that check, claimed Babbitt, accorded with "the highest law of which man has finite knowledge, the law of measure," "the law of concentration."[63]

Although the physics, not to say metaphysics, of this law's operation remained vague to Babbitt, he was once more attempting through such a formulation to give humanism a spiritual base: whereas "measure" inevitably referred to Aristotle's metron, "concentration" connoted the Buddhistic practice of meditation. Such abstractions may have seemed remote from the problem of aesthetic anarchy that Babbitt tried to analyze in *The New Laokoon*, but in his essay, "Schiller as Aesthetic Theorist," he made clear that it was the separation of the arts from an ethic of restraint that lay beneath the whole matter: "Art that is not in the service of the supersensuous is likely to become, not an end in itself, but a mere servant of the senses."[64]

That Babbitt was convinced the arts had been reduced to that servitude in the twentieth century is clear from his remarks on one of the few aesthetic theorists of his age to whom he directed critical attention, Benedetto Croce. In Babbitt's characterization, Croce denied the intellect any role in art because he dissolved aesthetics itself, along with religion and philosophy, into a historical continuum of ever-evolving process. Denying a oneness according to generic standards in favor of a processive multiplicity that dispensed with all standards, Croce championed a spontaneity of instinct that could not be integrated with that of insight: "With his expansive view of beauty he looks upon the whole attempt to set up literary and artistic genres as an unwarranted meddling of the intellect. . . . All the talk that has gone on in the past about the proper boundaries of the arts is, as he would have us believe, a mere logomachy."[65] But the talk was, indeed, past as Babbitt seemed to admit in concluding that the influence of Croce, Henri Bergson, and other philosophers of the flux was attributable principally to "the fact that they have the whole age as their accomplice."[66] Babbitt's attention to aesthetic criteria of the past and his almost exclusive moralistic stance caused him to neglect an essential aspect of modern aesthetics most notably propounded by Henry James. This was the function of the critic himself in creating art by the imposition of his own sensibility and taste held free from moralistic formulas or prejudices. Babbitt was simply too skeptical about any individuality at the center of an artistic or critical process. His suspicion of originality and spontaneity as terms of a romantic legerdemain was too strong for him to relax on behalf of contemporary critical theory. He was unable to comprehend Croce's aesthetics as a kind of caveat, which attempted to show that the seeming tyranny of expression (the polar extreme to the pseudoclassical tyranny of form) was an urge felt in art as in politics and religion; it expressed a human need to affirm the will if only as a part of incalculable historical processes in which no value was certain.[67]

After publication of *Rousseau and Romanticism* in 1919, Babbitt had a brief but pointed exchange with one of its unsympathetic reviewers, Arthur Lovejoy of Johns Hopkins. It included an articulate characterization of Babbitt (offered by Lovejoy as a parody of Babbitt's own technique), which came to be stereotypic among his critics: Babbitt's objection to the extremes of romanticism was itself so extreme, willful, and inclusive as to betray him as a romantic. Babbitt's rejoinder indicated that in the face of criticism he tended to hold the more tightly to terms that he could never fully define.

Lovejoy's sharpest criticisms concerned Babbitt's discussion of Friedrich Schiller, who was the model of an artist deeply imbued with philosophical suppositions which, in Schiller's case, came largely from Immanuel Kant. In Schiller, Babbitt was able to analyze ethical intent as a background to aesthetic execution. He noted Schiller's endorsement of Kant's view that art is disinterested unity between imagination and understanding and has no objective concept within the working of these faculties. From Schiller's aesthetic theories, he concluded that Schiller had appropriated art's "purposiveness without purpose" (*Zweckmässigkeit ohne Zweck*) to promote his own longing for an Arcadia indistinguishable from the idylls of Rousseau, save that it was futuristic rather than elegiac.

Armed with copious citations, Lovejoy argued that Schiller was actually a dualist who continually reformulated the delicate balance between the imagination and the sense of lawful limits to its expression. Arcadia was an aesthetic conception or ideal to which moral progress was to be directed though without hope of finite attainment. Lovejoy granted that "'expansive' Schiller's ideal undeniably is, in the sense that it aims at a larger and more general realization of the potencies of human nature than has yet been reached."[68]

Here was the rub. Babbitt conceded to Lovejoy that Schiller's aesthetic technique was dualistic, but he maintained that the direction in which that technique was directed was vagrant. He shared Schiller's attention to Greece as a model for the modern problem of aesthetic forms, but he emphasized that Schiller's celebration of Hellenic naiveté was itself naive. The primitivistic view of the Greeks as healthy children of nature was a sentimental belying of the mastery inherent in Greek literature and art. Babbitt himself had distinguished the Homeric age from the Periclean in terms of the latter's increasing self-consciousness, expressed through the questioning of conventions that initiates their subversion. Schiller's own position was one of acute self-consciousness that he rationalized into a longing for the ideal. Art was at once an empirical, problematic working for balance and an expression of its own need for a nonrational harmony, for which the Greeks served as enchanting models. But to be enchanted by the Greeks, Babbitt insisted, was to forget the example of their discipline, a discipline that was not a will-o'-the-wisp like Schiller's unreflective harmony but a practicable, indeed essential part of aesthetic expression.

Babbitt's persistent tagging of Schiller's idealism as expansive and idyllic rather than ethically concentrated overshadowed perhaps the most critical point of similarity he shared not only with Schiller but with Goethe. This was the problem of restoring integrity and wholeness to the arts in a utilitarian age that debased aesthetic creativity. Babbitt reasoned that art that took an idyllic or escapist turn played into the hands of the utilitarians; it became increasingly recreative, a mere holiday for the senses of weary materialists:

> The momentous matter is not that a man's imagination or emotions go out towards this or that particular haven or refuge in the future or in the past [but] that his primary demand upon life is for some haven or refuge; that he longs to be away from the here and now and their positive demands upon his character and will.[69]

Babbitt's rugged allegiance to his notion of will, which veiled a Hellenic idealism akin to Winckelmann's and Schiller's, kept him belligerently attentive to the "here and now," but the very use of his terms in arguing for that will removed him to a vacuum. He failed to perceive that the fluid nature of semantics weakened the meaning of his appeals to "circumscribing law," "the principle of restraint," and "higher intuitions."[70] And yet he remembered how pathetically his genteel precursors, Norton prominent among them, had become isolated in their reliance upon the aesthetic expression of an idealism that could only be described as "higher." Late in his life, Babbitt told More, "It is my conviction that if the critic is to exercise a useful function he cannot afford to get too much out of touch with the contemporary situation."[71] But few men were ever so remote by disposition as Babbitt was from his time.

4. Les Épreuves Françaises
Babbitt's French Masters

> Il faut des mouvements de bassesse, non de nature, mais de
> pénitence, non pour y demeurer, mais pour aller à la gran-
> deur. Il faut des mouvements de grandeur, non de mérite,
> mais de grâce, et après avoir passé par la bassesse.
>
> Blaise Pascal, *Pensées*

> Chère amie, ne savez-vous pas que la vertu est un état de
> guerre, et que, pour y vivre, on a toujours quelque combat à
> rendre contre soi?
>
> Jean-Jacques Rousseau, *Julie ou La Nouvelle Héloïse*

Irving Babbitt first visited France in July 1887, at the beginning of
a year's tour of Europe with a high school friend. He stayed only
five days in Paris and then walked to Madrid. Four years later he
was back in Paris to study Sanskrit and Pali. A third visit extended
over the summer months of 1896 when he browsed through book-
stalls along the Boulevard St. Michel, purchasing some three hundred books in preparation for his course work as a French instructor
at Harvard.

"The function of books is to teach us to despise them," remarked
Babbitt in those early days.[1] Apart from a deeper philosophical application, this maxim was perhaps simply one more slighting commentary on the literary world, that is, Paris as he found it in the
1890s. It was the Paris of an ultra-aestheticism, of Mallarmé and Verlaine, of Lautrec, Debussy, and Rémy de Gourmont.

Having recovered from defeat in the 1870–71 war with Germany
and the nightmarish exorcism of the Commune, France had become
industrialized and prosperous at a high political price. Paris in the
1890s was an arena of sustained excitement and turbulence. The
prolonged crisis of the Dreyfus affair, while polarizing French society
over the question of a Jewish army captain's innocence or treason,
exposed the dangerously fragmentary state of the Third Republic.
Royalists, Jesuits, militarists, anti-Semites, socialists, anarchists, and
libertarian artists formed tenuous, improbable alliances. Successive

government crises continually opened the way for possible dictatorship from any faction.

When Babbitt returned to Paris in 1908, two years after Dreyfus had been pardoned and promoted, he found the uproar had not abated but had assumed ideological forms. As he wrote to More:

> In all purely intellectual ways I always find this contact with Paris and with France immensely stimulating. My opportunities are unusually good because a number of the friends of my student days are now professors at the Sorbonne and the Collège de France, and through them I see a great many of the so-called *intellectuels*. This whole group strikes me as extremely confident, not to say cocky at the present. The reactionary elements ever since the later stages of the Dreyfus affair have been in a state of demoralization. The Revolution has passed from the acute to the chronic state and nearly everybody I meet has something of the toploftiness that one often finds in people whose ideas encounter no effective opposition. Everybody is proud of *les expériences sociales* that France is making for the benefit of the world. These *expériences* so far as I can see may be reduced to one, the attempt of a great nation to dispense utterly with everything that has been traditionally recognized as religion and to offer social sympathy as a substitute.[2]

He proceeded to note that the only alternative the French offered to this Rousseauism was a reactionary traditionalism, but he had already refused that stance by insisting that he and his humanism were positive, critical, and modern.

The French, so agile in wit and thorough in tradition, seemed ever to be at odds with themselves, as their often frenetic politics outwardly demonstrated. At critical times they appeared almost ridiculously disposed to sacrifice long-held standards and decorum for the cleverness of new dogmas; France had more than once proven to be a laboratory for the creation and dissemination of deadly sophisms.

Babbitt's study and instruction of French letters was less a literary than a psychological or clinical experience, one through which he became a pathologist of French historical culture. Of course he had nothing of a scientist's dispassionate objectivity. His study was a crusade to indict the sins of the intellect as committed against itself when it abandoned the vital props of willed discipline and the ancient legacy of humanistic dualism.

"You mustn't turn to French if you wish to visit either Paradiso or l'Inferno," he once said in a lecture.[3] Did he find in French letters a sort of purgatorial compromise between the two, some evidence of both torment and hope, of the human power of expiation and its ineluctable inadequacy?

In the multivariety of the French literary experience, from Du Bellay to Bergson, Babbitt searched in vain, perhaps predisposed to find only vanity, for what Montaigne had called the "common model" to which "the finest lives" conformed themselves.[4] Since Richelieu's time that model had been the French language, itself a surrogate for the proprieties of the ancient, especially the Roman, world for which France, more than any other nation, maintained a special affinity. When Babbitt told Sumichrast, the head of Harvard's French Department, that French was "a cheap and nasty substitute for Latin," who could say that he was not echoing misgivings that the more self-conscious members of the Académie française may have had in their unique enterprise? Babbitt's charge came early in his teaching, and though, as he seldom changed his mind about fundamentals, he may not have regretted his restive remark, he had cause to become more charitable to his French masters. He turned their defects to his advantage.

Not one of them wholly passed his muster. Each seemed predestined to reveal some aspect of what he termed the "intellectual lightness" of the French.[5] He did not refer, to be sure, to any superficiality or shallowness in their mentality; their problem was the very opposite, that they gave too exclusive attention to keenness of mind, to logical acuity and wit at the expense of the individual will. Babbitt was merely sounding a vague echo of Goethe's remark that the French were constricted in form and motivation: "The French have intelligence and l'esprit but lack grounding and piety."[6] Their fascination with German letters in Napoleon's time was simply to make it one more battleground for their intellectual partisanships. It was their lack of humanistic "grounding" and of pious deference to Montaigne's "common model" that drove them into fits of dogma and counterdogma.

One such bout of false absolutisms Babbitt cited from contemporary Paris where Jules Lemaître lectured on the horrifying influence of Rousseau. While old-guard elements of respectability applauded his judgment, thousands of Jean-Jacques's devotees sponsored harangues outside the Sorbonne. Babbitt concluded:

We may smile at these characteristically French proceedings, but at bottom the French are right in perceiving how much in modern life is involved in one's attitude toward Rousseau; they are

right in centering their attack and defense on the great father
of radicalism, instead of fixing attention on some contemporary
radical, who is usually only his remote and degenerate posterity.[7]

But Babbitt's smile was more incredulous than amused, and he felt
some chagrin, too. For the point closer to his intent, though unstated,
was that the French combat, however right in its focus, was wrong in
its weaponry. It would have to be fought again and again, as it had
been since the epoch of Rousseau and Voltaire, because the decisive
powers of will remained unreckoned.

The French indeed labored under an excess of their own criticism.
The nineteenth century, Babbitt found, amply supported his generalization that "critics have at times been so numerous in France that
they have had to fall to criticizing one another."[8] This excess meant
that everything was called into question so that no standard could
arise to mediate between principles and impressions. The French
tended to polemicize their intellects.

Did Babbitt realize, in acclaiming Pascal's designation of excellence
as harmonization of opposite virtues, that Pascal had prescribed what
was perhaps impossible to the highly political French intellect? After
all, who had become the foremost master and victim of this politics but Rousseau? And it is Rousseau who reveals how deeply Babbitt himself was a party to this self-victimizing to which Frenchmen
seemed almost universally subject. As the Genevan magus had convinced himself and much of the world that Paris was the antithesis
to and the betrayal of man's natural society, so Babbitt was sure
that Rousseau was the antithesis, the direct spiritual threat not only
to Parisian but to all civilization. He could no more exclude Jean-
Jacques from his argument than Jean-Jacques could exclude the
idyll. Both imprisoned themselves to a past of their own fashioning:
the pseudoclassical decadence of Paris became Rousseau's emblem of
human nature's fall and Rousseau himself became Babbitt's.

The father of *Émile* and the *Contrat social*, of Julie and Saint-Preux,
remained the unannounced presence in Babbitt's assessment of every
major figure in French letters. Those who came after the fall bore
the obvious signs, sometimes the stigmata, of this consequence. And
those before Rousseau? Although generally indulgent to their faults,
Babbitt felt some compulsion to locate in them covert manifestations
of tendencies leading to Rousseau's romanticism, that is, to a coun-
terreaction. In assailing Rousseau, Babbitt almost invariably included
criticism of the decadent pseudoclassicists who made his ascendancy
inevitable, even desirable, as a corrective to an excess of formalistic

veneer and lifeless artifice. Babbitt hinted at this excess in glancing at the seventeenth-century poet, Malherbe. Exercising an intensely scrupulous diction and an almost fanatical technical control, Malherbe, said Babbitt, "turned to best account the resources of the French temperament and was a living embodiment of a need of his time." But in making lyric poetry into an exact science, Malherbe had also "paved the way for literary absolutism," for "the literary despot who brooks no contradiction" and is "impervious and dogmatic" in the "proud sense of his own infallibility."[9]

No less hazardous than this formulaic strait-jacketing was the temperamental aspect that usually attended such exclusiveness. In no one, perhaps, was rancor more unremitting and consuming than in the Renaissance Latinist Julius Caesar Scaliger who, as though inspired by his imperious namesake, polemicized his way to a pedantic authoritarian command over his age. Remote in time, Scaliger was nonetheless a vivid spectacle for Babbitt, an exemplar of dangers one might run with oneself in seeking to revert to tradition merely for its own sake. Babbitt sensed empathically from "that highly astringent genius" and "colossal pedant" that a militant recourse to tradition was too arbitrary and would compel its own undoing.[10] In the wilderness of American letters, out of which Lowell and Norton had hacked some byways, Babbitt felt all the greater need for self-admonition, through the citation of Scaliger, to resist incendiary tendencies against his own time. He had to check his own astringency, but in lecturing he was seldom disposed to do so. It was fitting that Van Wyck Brooks, describing a lecture in which Babbitt "roared down his opponents . . . tossing and goring" writers he despised, included Babbitt's reference to the histrionically austere Scaliger.[11]

But Scaliger profited from a historic convenience that Babbitt could well envy. The unbridled individualism that the decline of medieval scholasticism had initiated required ultimate constraints. They came in the Council of Trent and the reign of Henri IV, during whose rule Malherbe and his academic purists purged away the stylistic excesses and indulgences of the poets who formed Les Pléiades. The transition signified not only the exchange of some standards of purism for others but the emergence of criticism over poetic creativity. Malherbe, Babbitt concluded, was a "critic rather than a true poet."[12] From that time, the hegemony of the Académie française was preordained. Babbitt longed in vain for the artifice, the superstructure of such an institutionalization of criticism for American letters, and quoted Lowell on the need for an American criticism to *precede* an American literature. At the same time he had to concur with

Arnold that academic conventions of the French sort were beyond the capacity of the English and certainly the American temperament. To have luxuriated in such a tradition on home grounds might have spared Babbitt his cautionary view of Scaliger, but he was not inclined to belabor the hypothetical and fanciful. Without detracting from the gravity of Lowell's plea, because the impossibility of its fulfillment made his own moorings as a critic uncertain, Babbitt used it wistfully. It was both epigraph and apologia for his attention to a literary tradition distant from and in some respects alien to American persuasions.

Attention never became unqualified adulation. From the naturalistic skepticism of Sainte-Beuve, he adopted a critical technique by which the estimation of the subject's merits and virtues proved an antecedent for the exposure of some fatal fault. Nietzsche, despising what he called Sainte-Beuve's feminine sensibility for vengeance, said that no one knew better how to mix poison with praise, and concluded that this French critic had a plebeian resentment of the power of greatness in men.[13] Babbitt had other reasons for deploring Sainte-Beuve but maintained through his mimetic practice the soundness of this undercutting technique. Whereas Nietzsche wrote as though Sainte-Beuve defaced statues, Babbitt found that he pricked the overinflated balloons of hubris.

The consummate expression of the cultural hubris of the French classical ideal was the golden age of Louis XIV. It had an order and majesty precedented only in the Roman world, but in that its regularity was conventional, it could not dazzle Babbitt from afar into pleading for a restoration. To explain the peculiarly Gallic passion for logical, almost sterile verisimilitude and dependence upon sclerotic rule-making, he referred to Rousseau: "The Frenchman does not wish to be seduced."[14]

But Rousseau erred on two points. His own appeal to unbounded imaginative fervor, which he had pitted against the classicists' properties of measure and logic, was to seduce generations of Frenchmen. Further, it did so because the classical norms had themselves proven too great a seduction; they had been carried to an excessive formalism. Babbitt was enough of a Frenchman, if only as a Francophile, that he, too, had no desire to be captivated, but he was also a staunch, individualistic Yankee (as his accent always betrayed) of a time when one's sense of American distinctiveness was no longer duly defensive and self-conscious. The too-near achievement of perfected social discipline in the France of Louis Quatorze had something about it finally repelling to him. Surely it was not the order, clearness, logic, and precision of language and conduct, which he identified as humanistic values, but an impersonality, a lack of feeling typified in the manicured parks of Versailles. The otherwise auspicious epoch of the Sun King was strangely lacking in regard for organic forces, among them the ones that make an individual's integrity inviolable. Even Boileau, the giant of critics in that august time, despite "an almost infallible literary intuition," had a formulaic narrowness that was without a "sense of evolution and flux."[15]

Boileau appeared frequently in Babbitt's notes on French classicism. Babbitt tended to displace from their epoch those men whom he believed had embodied its qualities, values, and assumptions. Disengaged, they were not incorporeal but somehow the more vivid to his imagination. Boileau is a case in point. Babbitt used him neither to justify nor to censure the classicism to which he belonged, but to underscore the central importance that a personalized philosophy held for humanism. Babbitt believed and hoped that such a man as Boileau could survive out of his age: a classicist could endure, even thrive in an anticlassical time. This point hints at Babbitt's need of appropriated humanist models that would form luminary ranks against the gloom of his own hour. He was the paradigm of Mencius's gentleman-scholar who, missing the best men of his age, made company with antiquity.

In *the New Laokoon*, where Lessing generally loomed as the *scriba ex machina*, Boileau was described as "the leader of a reaction against formalism . . . simply a wit and man of the world, not especially logical or imaginative or profound," withal sensible enough to scorn the neoclassicism of literature by recipe.[16] Two years later, in *The Masters of Modern French Criticism*, Boileau reemerged bearing the charges of "narrowness of range" and "formalism" that Babbitt had previously dismissed as rubrics of "a romantic bugaboo."[17] Yet he made Boileau's attractive qualities seem by compensation almost the greater: it was Boileau's tact and intuition that inspired Babbitt's wish for "a modern Boileau" not only as a critic capable of making "keen and crisp discriminations" but of furnishing "constructive satire." In a rare allusion, he indulged the prospect: "Nothing could be more inspiring than some twentieth-century equivalent for those first satires of Boileau when the bad authors went down before his epigrams like the suitors before the shafts of Odysseus."[18] In both senses of the word, there was a precious quality about this view, but Babbitt left the negative denotation of affectation and overrefinement to Boileau's historical character. When Babbitt transmogrified him into a modern satirist, Boileau became precious solely in the sense that he would be of inestimable worth, to Babbitt, in purging contemporary letters of mediocrity and banality.

Babbitt's penchant for dualizing a personality into historically defective yet contemporaneously wholesome aspects was more forceful in the instance of Pascal. The morose, ascetic Pascal, who believed in predestination and innate depravity, was deplorable and Babbitt would gladly have discarded him from his estimate. It was as "one of the last great representatives of medieval idealism" that Pascal launched an attack upon imagination and, "flouting ordinary good sense," divorced reason and intuition.[19] Pascal was further guilty of a "stark supernaturalism" that confounded the humanistic efforts of unaided virtue to rise above nature.[20] (We will shortly note Babbitt's curious shift of emphasis on this point.) Such an obscurantism—a term that Babbitt made a predicate of Christianity more than of Pascal—invited a counter-extremism that was to be epitomized later by Rousseau, with whom Babbitt stood in unacknowledged sympathy when it came to yawning abysses, infant damnation, hellfire, and the like.[21] Finally, as more than a corollary, there was Pascal's view of life itself as a sickness, a view which, though Babbitt could find ample substantiation in the nineteenth century, he could not accept. Neither was there a sanctuary such as Pascal's Port-Royale into which he might retreat to entertain such a dismal, passive notion.

What, then, would Babbitt salvage from Pascal to make him an enlistee of humanism? He found that if a medieval dogmatism against imagination was sophistical, a kindred dogmatism aimed at scientific investigation and calculation might be altogether wise, at least in the age of Darwin and Spencer. Pascal's slurs against the rationalist Descartes had to be rephrased for the evolutionists and others who had a too confident grasp upon natural or cosmic phenomena. In the context of Darwinism's apparently brutish aspects, by which man had demythologized himself from Eden, Babbitt had an especial concern for what he called Pascal's "sense of a principle of superiority in man to the monstrous, blind forces of nature."[22]

These words were somewhat hedged. The "sense of principle" was at several vague removes from the divinity that Pascal recognized and by which he was able to conceive of the utter wretchedness of humankind when unaided and unredeemed by it. Likewise, human nature's grandeur was entirely a function of being God's answerable creature. Babbitt used Pascal as a foil to the desperate skepticism that tended to recur in French letters, from La Rochefoucauld to Chamfort to Sainte-Beuve, and contrariwise against the prolix optimism of Goethe and Emerson. Treating a man who had made this balancing of extremes an exquisite art, Babbitt was unavoidably forced to some delicate balancing of his own. Thus, the alter ego of a gloomy fanatic (and geometrician) was almost the true modern, gifted with what Pascal himself termed *l'esprit de finesse*.

The "almost" is crucial. Had Babbitt's transformation been total, had Pascal been resurrected merely as a neophyte of humanism, Babbitt's method would not have differed greatly from Sainte-Beuve's. Twice he cited this critic on Pascal: first, in what he called Sainte-Beuve's "very superficial" and invidious comparison of Pascal's "spiritual elevation" with its absence in the pagan Goethe; second, in a passage where Sainte-Beuve switched sides to join Goethe in contempt for converts, centering the point on Pascal.[23] But Babbitt omitted to mention Sainte-Beuve's deeper insight into Pascal which occurs in the pregnantly titled *Portraits contemporains*, though he was almost certainly familiar with it. Touching upon Pascal's faith and his skepticism, Sainte-Beuve judged the latter triumphant to posterity: "it is a skepticism we fully comprehend and which we feel ever more and better," whereas for Catholicism, "we are increasingly in the course of forgetting it or at least of transforming it vaguely, no longer giving it any fully effective meaning."[24]

The skepticism that was fully commensurate to Sainte-Beuve's bleakness could not be so to Babbitt's humanism, if only because it would debilitate further "the effective sense." But Babbitt's effort to retain a humanistic "sense" of faith came on the very terms that Sainte-Beuve had indicated, "of vague transformation." In the minor key that sounded his wistful call to the saving remnant, Babbitt concluded his essay on Pascal:

> There may be some . . . who, in Pascal's words, feel the need of discovering some firm island of faith in the midst of the "horrible flux of all things." Any *wholesome* revival of Pascal must depend on his power to appeal to persons of this kind, . . . the Pascal who summed up his experience of religion in the words, "Joy, certainty, peace."[25]

But for Pascal the joyous and peaceful bearings of the isle of faith were inseparable from the terror of being without it, or perhaps more precisely, they could be experienced only as a consequence of the terror and misery of being in the flux. In Pascal's own words, "There must be great stirrings not by merit but by grace and after having endured lowliness."[26]

Babbitt eventually realized that the humanist decorum that sufficed as his own joy, certainty, and peace was, from Pascal's ascetic

view, too worldly a part of the "horrible flux" to be more than a
floating island, a facade: "Pascal sees in decorum a disguise of one's
ordinary self rather than a real curb upon it, and feels that the gap is
not sufficiently wide between even the best type of the man of the
world and the mere worldling."[27] One recourse against a fanatically
stringent either/or was historical relativism, itself an abyss into which
Babbitt usually refused to stare. But Pascal's comparison of the person of faith with someone who has a watch among others who have
none was too much for him. Babbitt noted privately: "Unfortunately,
different watches have different time and [there is] no central time."
Then, in a striking change of images, he added: "Have made painful
discovery that looking glass faces render back the mental lineaments
of the man who consults them."[28]

It was an admission the subtlety of which he could not afford to
probe too deeply if he were not to compromise his own looking-glass
image. Babbitt had perhaps sensed that only through the drastic
weaponry of relativism could he allay the unease that Pascal caused
him. Elsewhere, he appealed to "strict psychology" to confound Pascal's arbitrary and absolute discriminations between imagination and
reality, reason and faith.[29] But this argument, too, confounded Babbitt's own hard and fast distinctions which themselves bifurcated reason and imagination, illusion and reality into lower and higher levels.[30] And, using such terms as argumentative conveniences rather
than as conceptual blocks, he could not share Pascal's claim to l'esprit
de géométrie, nor to a more than figurative sense of divinity. To counter Pascal's geometry, Babbitt had to weigh and vindicate his own
humanistic finesse, but he wanted to put the verdict aslant and to
have another deliver it: "We are forced at last, like Voltaire, 'to take
the side of human nature against this sublime misanthropist.'"[31]

Against Pascal, this invocation of the most powerful satirist in modern literature had to be guarded. Babbitt did not care to exchange
for the rigorous dogmas of Pascal the meliorist humanitarianism that
lay beneath Voltaire's barbed wit. Boileau, it will be remembered, was
the archetype for the satirist that Babbitt wanted in his own time
because, in spite of bearing the vices of classical formalism, Boileau
bore as well its resplendent virtues. Voltaire, a classicist often
paired off against the chief romanticist in modern history, would
have proven a convenient, obvious, seemingly inevitable ally (far
more than the remote Boileau) in Babbitt's attacks upon Rousseau.
His grounds for rejecting Voltaire were based, as was many times the
case, upon the touchstones of key terms in the humanist lexicon. "So
far from being capable of high seriousness, he is scarcely capable of

ordinary seriousness. And so the nobility, elegance, imitation, and decorum that he is constantly preaching have about them a taint of formalism."[32] It is odd that Babbitt had found the same "taint" in Boileau yet fashioned him a modern. Apparently, Boileau was at least capable of what Arnold and Babbitt called "high seriousness." Moreover, unlike Voltaire, he had made positive appeals to literary fashion rather than "spreading abroad a spirit of mockery and irreverence that tended to make every traditional belief impossible."[33]

Summarily, Babbitt's implied objection to Voltaire was that he was too much of his age, that his satiric brilliance in annihilating foes and his reformist liberalism aimed at societal abuses were alike rooted in the Augustan gospel of utilitarian reason that Babbitt considered shallow and facile. Voltaire was too zealous an opponent, not merely of religious superstition but of Christianity, and thereby made himself alien to a humanism that included Dante and Pascal in its periphery. Besides, he had misused his predominant influence in failing to rout Rousseauism. And his acerbic unorthodoxy went far to spark a new orthodoxy, a new piety, a new seriousness that pretended to be high, from the *vicaire savoyard* to Chateaubriand and the lesser hosts of romantic religiosity. So far as the residual effects of that romanticism extended into the faith of Ruskin, Pater, Bergson, and Nietzsche (who idolized Voltaire), with no visible cyclical regression to a new classicism that might redeem him, Voltaire's historic position was that of a decadent, and so an easy butt for Babbitt's recrimination.

Babbitt's French company did a double service: as well as providing case studies for his humanistic standard, they were fallible minds ever prone to some kind of self-perversion, some damaging extreme. Marking these, Babbitt served notice on himself as though in a severe assessment of another's defect he might profit to correct his own. Such plumbings of deficiency and error also made him feel a kind of intuitive commiseration for his subjects, especially those in the generations after Rousseau. *The Masters of Modern French Criticism* ironically reflected this commiseration, for there was not one true master nor thoroughgoing humanist to be found within its pages, and yet each to his particular degree elicited a telling intellectual sympathy from Babbitt.

Perhaps to no one, not even to Sainte-Beuve, did Babbitt's sympathy extend further than to Joseph Joubert. Nearly fifty years before *The Masters*, Matthew Arnold had celebrated this maximist out of obscurity and pronounced him a second-order genius, an "outskirmisher" who, though never securing public recognition, would win safe passage for men of greater literary genius to pursue. Like Arnold, Babbitt, and other humanists, Joubert felt himself at a wayward remove from some better, surer world of antiquity: "It seems to me much more difficult to be a modern than to be an ancient."[34] Joubert's maxims often mirrored Babbitt's own biases, yet Babbitt did not perceive how well, too, they revealed a lack of the contemporaneous in his own thought.

Joubert won high marks from him. He had survived the turbulence of Revolutionary society with acute contempt for its maniacal utopism, and he kept intact his sense of order, albeit one too personalized. But, self-sequestered in reactionary disregard of contemporaneous clamors, Joubert mistook the ghost of tradition for its spirit. Babbitt found him futilely attempting "to impose the past too despotically upon the present . . . to see only the benefits of order just as Emerson sees only the benefits of emancipation." To rigidify society into "a sort of hieratic immobility" was the ambition of a humanist who allowed social upheaval to shape, partly to warp, the individual temperament.[35] Joubert signified to Babbitt the hazard of withdrawal, "the shrinking of the valetudinarian from the rough and tumble of life," and his own sense of this hazard was the stronger in his dread of an isolation indistinguishable in its effects from Joubert's voluntary withdrawal.[36] However, within his eremite's cell, Joubert set down standards of taste and intellectual decorum too approximate to Babbitt's own for him to withhold a general enthusiasm. From Joubert he drew the consoling notion that humanists "are recognizable through the diverse accidents of time and space by their agreement on essentials."[37]

A maximist rather than a critic, Joubert concerned himself less with being a man of letters than with telling others how to become so. He assumed, in the manner that seems increasingly quaint in Arnold and Babbitt, the need for an encompassing moralism. Some of his *aperçus* strikingly anticipate Babbitt's.[38] Further, befitting what Babbitt conceived to be the true humanist, Joubert discriminated provinces of the mind and accordingly restricted them to particular functions. Babbitt was pleased to find anticipation of his own prejudices in these arbitrations. For example, Joubert accused Bacon of taking ideas for facts and so violating the proper use of imagination. Likewise, he scored Voltaire for depriving mankind of the "severity of reason" and concluded that "in no age is a Voltaire good for anything."[39]

Abuses of reason or imagination Joubert and Babbitt alike found unpardonable, but their grounds for objection differed. Joubert's ontology rested on a Platonic mysticism, an intuition of the One above the Many; that is, he had a sense of a fixed and permanent reality above that of change and instability. Greatly as Babbitt admired, perhaps even craved, this higher intuitive sense, he never claimed to possess it, and he suspected the legitimacy of many others' claims. He estimated that the sense of the One and the Many shifted back and forth through consciousness rather than remaining a static metaphysical reference point. Wholly foreign to him would have been Joubert's eulogistic remarks on Plato, that the ancient had put a light in men's eyes by which all things became illuminated: "He teaches us nothing but makes us fit to know everything."[40] Babbitt might well have detected too much presumption in such praise, because he found Platonism involved "such subtle and baffling perversions" (by comparison with a pedestrian but trustworthy Aristotelianism) that one's light might easily prove a will-o'-the-wisp.[41] He had in mind the romantic parody, as he called it, of religious intuition as revealed in Rousseau's admission that, though not religious, he was at least intoxicated with religion. Babbitt's critical departure from Joubert came with the latter's allowance that "a Rousseau corrected would today be most useful, even necessary."[42] That Babbitt could never imagine and would never concede.

Skirting that perilous thought, Babbitt used another from Joubert that seemed to contradict it: nothing but religion could cure one of Jean-Jacques. Babbitt's citation is strange because, in making it, he believed that Joubert realized as he did that "in the final analysis the irreligion of Voltaire is a less insidious danger than the pseudo-religion of Rousseau."[43] But Voltaire had already been sentenced as a good-for-nothing, and what about a "corrected" Rousseau? And if Rousseauism were a disease that only religion could cure, of what avail was humanism? Faced with the same kind of void that he encountered from Pascal's fanaticism, Babbitt rescued himself in the same tactical way from Joubert's liberality. Experiencing strong intuitive sympathy with his subject, he stressed the humanistic aspects and ignored or downplayed potentially or actually irreconcilable ones. That endeavor was, to be sure, facilitated by Babbitt's central literary concern, the examination of a historical continuum of criticism. But as moralistic rectitudes were part of that occupation, quasi-religious issues were certain to obtrude.

Whether because or in spite of his scrupulous estimation of Joubert, Babbitt's notes on him are far less penetrating, that is, self-revealing, than those he made on Sainte-Beuve. There are apparent reasons for this fact that precede an understanding of more intricate ones. Sainte-Beuve's stature as a critic was far greater than Joubert's, greater for that matter than anyone's in modern letters—his only possible contemporary rival was Arnold—and his analytic grasp as reflected in the capacious span of his topics (virtually the whole of French literary history to his own time) was awesome. Of the eleven critics discussed in *The Masters*, Sainte-Beuve rightly occupies more than a fourth of Babbitt's effort. But historical stature was no sure gauge of a writer's importance to Babbitt, as his slighting of Voltaire indicates. And the nearer that writer to Babbitt's own time, the more likely it was that he would appear minor or derivative, for Babbitt was convinced that the vulgarizing literature of the tabloid and the mass-produced dime novel represented some downward cultural curve.

An epoch such as the nineteenth century, mediocre in its poets, might flourish in its prose artists, novelists, and critics, as did the England of Victoria and the France of Louis Napoleon. In the midst of a humdrum bourgeois age, Sainte-Beuve conferred anew upon the art of criticism the high status it enjoyed in the opulent ages of Henri IV and Louis XIV. Sainte-Beuve could do so because he wrote "when it was still possible to receive a living initiation into tradition, that is to say, to see the past as it saw itself, which means in practice to live in a world of absolute values." But simultaneously, there was the possibility that one might "detach one's self from the past and see it relatively and phenomenally," and in the crisis between the absolute and the relative, Sainte-Beuve, rather than filling the space between opposite virtues, wavered so as not to lean too heavily on any doctrinaire props.[44] Although Sainte-Beuve was a kind of paragon to Babbitt, unqualified adulation was foreign to Babbitt's disposition and would have been grotesque and ironic if expressed toward a critic who prided himself on being no one's dupe.

Babbitt's estimation and emulation of this master critic are exceedingly delicate matters for delineation. They do not defy analysis but, as it were, almost compel an excess of conjectural inference. "It is difficult to make too many distinctions in writing of Sainte-Beuve," Babbitt wrote, and the point must be extended to include his own efforts to judge him fairly.[45] Each of the courses that Babbitt taught at Harvard bore debts to Sainte-Beuve, and in the half-courses, "Pascal and Port Royale" and "Chateaubriand and His Influence," he might well have been designated the principal critical voice beyond Babbitt's own. The issue, however, is not one of mere academic scrutiny, continually refined and restated. It involves an intimacy that, although lasting most of Babbitt's lifetime, he could not fully resolve into an affinity, an empathic rapport.

The model critic, Sainte-Beuve was also a self-victimized intellect, an accomplice to the dreary and sinister drifts of his spiritless age, and it was perhaps in this dual role of exhortation and admonition that his portrait loomed, alone, in Babbitt's study at Widener Library. Sainte-Beuve had yielded to the dark penchant of pessimism and despair that dogged some of the greatest minds of his age. For the expansive impulse that he had defined as the hallmark of romanticism was not simply a euphoric projection of the idyllic temper, but a kind of will to nothingness, a dissipation of values and self. Once he had outgrown the anachronistic attractions of Jansenist Catholicism, Sainte-Beuve rationalized the claims of flux by embracing a scientific skepticism. At the same time, he shared with the maximists of neoclassicism, particularly La Rochefoucauld, a disgust with mankind sufficient to keep him free from binding allegiance to any of the partisan illusions of his age.

Sainte-Beuve was a humanist almost in spite of himself and by default of other paths: "His perfect tact and measure and good sense can always be counted on to put him on his guard against everything that is extreme and one-sided, whether it claims to be ideal or naturalistic."[46] But the extremes occurred in his own sensibility. Babbitt distinguished in him, besides the humanist and the humanitarian believer in scientific progress, the "cold disillusioned observer of human nature with marvelous psychological finesse and naturalistic tendencies, and . . . without [an] ideal that would correct his observation of facts."[47] It was perhaps this disillusion without ideals that enabled Sainte-Beuve to depict his subjects so as to reveal "each in his inner psychological truth."[48]

In this probing, Sainte-Beuve exposed the susceptibilities of human character as expressed through what was classically known as the master or ruling passion. Babbitt wanted to discredit this notion as inhumanistic, if not inhumane, in its express denial of the power of will over impulse, but it was precisely that denial that served as the *clef-de-voûte* of Sainte-Beuve's "marvelous psychological finesse." In an epoch of wrong-headed prophets—Comte, Proudhon, Taine, to name only some French ones—and hollow shibboleths, it was well and good for a critic such as Sainte-Beuve, who had subscribed to and outlived the uses of so many of them, to practice the art of deflation. The legitimate negative function of the critic, said Babbitt, was "to keep mankind as far as possible and in spite of its natural proclivity, from being devoured by charlatans."[49] On the other hand, Sainte-Beuve's deflation, his "getting behind the scenes and examining the cloth on the wrong side," disclosed an absence of faith in what even Pascal granted to be a grandeur in human nature.[50]

By demolishing as many idols as he found, Sainte-Beuve anticipated Nietzsche's advice to beware of statues that might fall and crush one. But some belief in the human ability to attain the statuesque was fundamental to the humanism of individual progress, the only progress that Babbitt ever recognized, and so he felt obliged to interpret Sainte-Beuve's demolitions as evidence of a defect in humanistic balance. Yet, having documented amid Sainte-Beuve's several fallacies and misdirections his acuity and perspicacity, Babbitt was reluctant to leave him wholly responsible for a lack of center. In what appears a most uncharacteristic concession to behaviorism, he resolved: "That so shrewd an observer as Sainte-Beuve could find no firm anchorage for the spirit in the movements peculiar to this century may in the long run turn out to be not to his discredit but to the discredit of the century."[51]

Did Babbitt's assumption of Sainte-Beuve's predestination to failure conceal a self-protective rationalization? He adhered to Sainte-Beuve's practice of extolling his subject only to undercut him by revelation of a grave fault, but he departed from this technique in tracing that fault not to some defect of personality or master passion but to the age. It was a condemnation no less inclusive than had he employed the generalizing overviews of a Herder or Taine, who dissolved distinctions of personality into the compass of racial and national traits. Babbitt eschewed these mechanistic biases because he found that they not only confounded individual will but were usually, as in Taine, the complement of an idyllic view of life and nature. Within the determinist hid the dreamer. Sainte-Beuve shone the more in having rejected all mechanistic doctrines, albeit he found nothing to serve positively as a counter to them. In arguing that Sainte-Beuve's psychological perceptions were antithetical to Taine's reduction of all behavior to scientific law, Babbitt relaxed for a rare moment his own geometric notion of the planes of being. Sainte-Beuve's mercurial intellect reminded him that in addition to the religious, humanistic, and naturalistic planes, "there are, of course, intermediary stages, the rungs of the ladder, as it were, by which man may mount or descend from one level to another of his being."[52]

In the century of Darwin and Marx, those rungs had become so dangerously slippery that one could only pretend to remain secure upon any one of them. Sainte-Beuve's successive disillusionments seemed to hint that slipping was a horizontal rather than a vertical process. With the postmortem of religious faith, any doctrinal elevation of mankind was bound to be a pretense or an adulteration, if not both.

Humanism was not excepted. It was even likely to include antihumanistic elements. Babbitt took the critic and politician, Edmond Scherer, as an instance. A stern moralist, antidemocrat, and defender of austere literary standards, Scherer was also an enthusiast of Hegel and a relativist who forced himself into a false elegiac posture toward religious orthodoxy and any sense of absolute values because he was convinced that the pluralistic drift of his time was scientifically justifiable. Recording Scherer's as the Rousseauistic conflict of head versus heart, Babbitt employed a favorite ironic device, condemning the subject from his own mouth: "Nowadays, nothing is any longer for us either truth or error," Scherer wrote in 1861. "We no longer know religion, but religions; not morality, but manners; not principles, but facts."[53] As Babbitt depicted him, Scherer failed to comprehend his inner conflict, for the only effect of it was a sangfroid toward the valueless delusions of the hour. The harsh lesson of Sainte-Beuve was repeated: a mind of scruples, insight, and moral sense was set against itself. Intellect became as deadly an agent of self-perversion and temperamental aberration as faith had been in "darker" ages. Sainte-Beuve, Scherer, and their time exercised a reinless *libido sciendi*, a drive to expel any illusion because they could not distinguish it from delusion.

Just as Babbitt refused to accept the intellectual gambit of these French humanists in relegating traditional standards to the somber chill of nostalgia, so he rejected the lure of an intellectual satisfaction with his age that would, he was certain, vitiate the mediating power of will and leave nothing in the end but enervating despair. Much of his enthusiasm for the otherwise reactionary Joubert was based upon Joubert's insight into man's need to maintain illusions as a medium, necessarily an imperfect one, between the phenomenal and noumenal worlds. People, Babbitt believed, were fated to see through a glass at best darkly, but it was essential that they make the effort to see at all. A resigned downward glance upon the Darwinian world of whirl and process would cost them their sense of its "mysterious interconnection with the whole."[54]

The apparent and fatal error among French intellectuals was that they suffered a confusion of spiritual or noumenal claims through their rationalized endorsement of the naturalistic world. Babbitt argued that without the median of will to rise above the flux and to affirm standards set over circumstance and relativity, they were lost to the fortunes of their own sensibilities. Either, like Sainte-Beuve, they displayed an impressionistic critical spirit or, like Brunetière, a rigorous but pseudological one.

Next to Sainte-Beuve, Ferdinand Brunetière was perhaps the exemplar most illuminating and most painful in Babbitt's review, and he was the only one vivified by personal acquaintance. Babbitt had met him in Paris in the 1890s and was one of his hosts at Harvard when Brunetière lectured there in 1897. The first version of Babbitt's essay on him appeared in the *Atlantic Monthly* that year; soon after, he translated Brunetière's "The French Mastery of Style" from its manuscript for the same journal. As he indicated to the *Atlantic*'s editor, the article on Brunetière's "dogmatic" criticism as opposed to the "impressionistic" criticism of Lemaître would serve to convey the lively and high-level qualities of French polemics, the very qualities that he longed to witness in American criticism.[55]

The second version of the essay, included in *The Masters*, abounded in thinly veiled encomiums that Babbitt knew might well be applied to himself. Brunetière, who had died in 1906,

> persisted in the somewhat antiquated notion that books exist primarily to express ideas, whereas most people nowadays turn to books for entertainment or at best for elegant aesthetic sensation. He made himself the champion of the classical tradition and proclaimed the supremacy of reason at an epoch when art was given over to every form of morbid subjectivity. He was stern and ascetic in a period of easy-going self-indulgence. He produced work marked by eminently masculine qualities at a time when literature had fallen to a great extent under the influence of women.[56]

Clearly, these remarks were Babbitt's tokens of prejudice against his age, which, after all, was also Brunetière's. Having characterized him thus, how could Babbitt not have felt a warm empathy? Yet, the unmistakably present commiseration was tempered by his dismay over Brunetière's inability to establish a positive basis for his humanism against the impressionism he had rightly read as the main current of thought in fin-de-siècle literature. Brunetière failed partly by his sophistical attempt to wed a scholastic view of literary genres to Darwinian evolution. Worse, he sought to compensate his sense of the inefficacy of individual will by endorsing the reactionary elements of church and state. He was, for all purposes, within the church of Rousseau's civic religion. In that way, he became an example of a critical mind such as Babbitt dreaded probably as much as that of the self-divided man of letters, a reactionary whose fight against his age was somehow only one more symptom of its ills.

Recalling Joubert once more, Babbitt found that Brunetière "lacked the intuitions by which alone one can escape from the spirit of the age into the spirit of the ages."[57] Babbitt, however, insisted that the humanistic modern had not only to survive the age and its pitfalls but to rise above it so as to shape it to a controllable future. Brunetière's renunciation of individual will for militant social orthodoxies was more than a personal quirk; it was the emblem of the crisis that afflicted all the critics in Babbitt's study.

The unwritten but often hinted keyword was passivity, which Babbitt conceived as a putatively feminine yielding to extrinsic forces in a process of progressive intellectual debauch. The French mind, for which the art of speech has scarcely ever been distinguishable from the art of argumentation, seemed prone to give itself too much to intellectual fashions. Of course, schools continued to form one against another; there would always obtain some variant of the antipathy between Voltaire and Rousseau. Flaubert's Homais and Bournisien showed that these intellectual bouts could be carried down to the level of the bourgeoisie. But minds of great critical stature betrayed themselves, consciously or not, into becoming crucibles for the various idioms of their time.

It was probably inevitable that flux itself should eventually receive philosophic sanctions, which it did in the works of Henri Bergson. His transnational popularity over the first decades of the twentieth century reinforced as a pestilent gall Babbitt's ill-humor toward his whirling age. Bergson, as Babbitt saw him, was but one more sophist who conjured up Rousseau in confounding all attempts of the will and intellect to impose order upon life. Babbitt may have taken the cue for his antagonism from an enthusiastic reading of Bergson by William James. Not only did James celebrate the novelty of Bergson's dynamism, but he stated that it proved to him that "philosophy had been on a false scent ever since the days of Socrates and Plato."[58] Babbitt construed this to mean that Bergson, like James, intended to obscure the claims of the One in favor of the Many and to relegate intuition to what Bergson termed "immediate givens."

Anticipating Bergson's visit to America in 1913 (he had lectured at Oxford in 1911), Babbitt, with an alarm to which only a Rousseauist could stir him, wrote to More at the *Nation*:

The signs are multiplying that the world is going to go crazy over Bergson. The last number of the *Revue des deux Mondes* proclaims solemnly that he is at least as great as Kant and probably as great as Socrates. I hope that when he comes over to give his lectures at Columbia, the *Nation* will take up a position on the firing line.[59]

He delivered his own fusillade in that journal late in 1912. It may have amused him that on the Gallic side of the ocean Bergson had been likened to Socrates in stature, while on the other, James, now dead, had taken him to be the confounder of Socratic and much subsequent philosophy. But if Bergson were comparable to anyone, Babbitt suggested, it would be to Protagoras.[60] More important to the moment, however, was that Bergson was the true congener of Rousseau. (It was a likening that would have pleased Bergson.[61]) In *Rousseau and Romanticism*, Babbitt repeatedly referred to "the whole movement from Rousseau to Bergson" as one "filled with the glorification of instinct."[62] The basis for this conjunction was compacted into the *Nation* article.

In Babbitt's view, Bergson had legitimately refuted the efforts of scientism to impose formulas upon human behavior, but he had done so in the perverse fashion of Rousseau, not to try to restrict science humanistically to its proper areas of phenomenal inquiry but to exalt spontaneity and to give a pseudomystical aura to temperamental urges. Sensing in Bergson's notion of time an *invitation au voyage* to Rousseau's realm of idyllic revery, Babbitt returned to the motif that predominated in *The Masters*, the debilitation of the will through passivity:

> It is hard to see how even its admirers can claim virility for a philosophy that would have us turn away from both thought and action and seek our vision in an aimless aestheticism. It is at just the opposite pole from the philosophy of Aristotle, with its emphasis upon acting with a purpose . . . linked intuitively by a series of intermediary purposes with the supreme and perfect End itself.[63]

From reading Bergson's *L'Évolution créatrice*, he derived the imagery of romantic vertigo, claiming that Bergson nullified "higher intuitions" by prescribing a "facing downward into the vast swirling depths of the evolutionary process."[64] It was because such giddiness had become too much *le mal de siècle*, too akin to the anarchy that Babbitt believed ascendant in the arts, in politics, and in society, that he employed *le frein vital*, or vital check, against Bergson's *élan vital*, or vital impulse. In addition to this metaphysical catchword, he attempted a *contre-coup* toward Bergson's aesthetics. The Frenchman's plea that one must see life artistically did not include an account of how most people were to attain the artist's special vision, especially the ethical vision, the sense of the good that necessarily preceded the pleasurable.[65] Further, in proclaiming life a perpetual and incalcu-

lable process of change, Bergson implicitly endorsed a kind of pedestrian aestheticism by which anyone might become a mere passive
recipient or collector of novelties, like Pater's aesthete for whom
the maintenance of momentary impulses, the burning with a "hard,
gem-like flame," was "success in life."[66]

While Bergson lectured at Columbia, Babbitt admonished his own
students that a more valid aesthetic was one bridging what Pater presumed to be "that thick wall of personality through which no real
voice has ever pierced."[67] "To attain to true discipline, to work toward
a true human centre is an imaginative act," Babbitt insisted, meaning
that there could be no admissible hiatus between ethical and aesthetic
endeavor. A mere return to formalism, as Bergson's French opponents seemed to want, was no longer possible; there had to be what
Babbitt called "an imaginative reaction": "Simple good sense will not
suffice. Imagination should rest on good sense about the way religion
rests on morality but vastly transcends it, and this combination we
have in great poets."[68]

In effect, Bergson's international influence dramatically justified
to Babbitt his claim that romanticism was a living, pressing danger to
civilized values, and it made his own punitive posture seem more
than ingrown academic rancor. He was not shadowboxing with the
ghost of Rousseau but indicting the latest Protean form of Rousseau's
idealism, revealing that, like Bergsonian duration, romanticism had
continuous indeterminate properties.

In 1912, Babbitt had no evidence of a defensive front against
Bergson. The most articulate opponent of scientific romanticism
would be George Santayana, in whose *Winds of Doctrine* (1913) several
of Babbitt's charges would be duplicated.[69] For the while, Babbitt was
content to insert some points from his *Nation* article as prefatory
remarks to *The Masters of Modern French Criticism*, so as to show that
Bergson's philosophy was the consummation of the central intellectual failure of the critics under study. Having found that they lacked
the crucial intuitive power of reconciling the One and the Many, was
Babbitt not obliged to indicate some *via media*?

In the concluding essay of *The Masters*, in style and thought one of
his best efforts, he attempted to fill the gap of his patently negative
criticism: "What we are seeking is a critic who rests his discipline and
selection upon the past without being a mere traditionalist; whose
holding of tradition involves a constant process of clear and hard
thinking, a constant adjustment, in other words, of the experience of
the past to the changing needs of the present."[70] It is strange that
Babbitt, whose critical endeavor centered principally on French let-

ters, found the man closest to his archetype of the modern humanist
not in France but in Germany. The peculiarity is compounded when
we consider that he regarded Germany as a hotbed of some of the
worst excesses of romanticism.[71] The enlightened Germany of Lessing and Kant had descended into the false lights of *die Geniezeit*,
when anyone of a mediocre pen could pose as a genius. This was the
certain pattern of Rousseau's self-exalting otherness. Among the
worst offenders was Babbitt's paragon.

It was Goethe, of course. He had attained a wholeness of personality, a genius for proportion and balance in spite of, no, because of
his quondam susceptibilities both to Rousseau's romanticism (a debt
he acknowledged in *Dichtung und Wahrheit*) and to Bacon's naturalism. And, in addition to the multiple hazards of being German, he
had lived out what the Chinese call the curse of exciting times. Like
his Faust, Goethe survived everything; unlike Faust's, his own redemption was self-wrought and contained a humanistic insistence
upon earthbound virtues, not least of which was the capacity to stand
apart from and against one's age. That, undaunted, he had once
towered (more than physically) over the greatest imperialist in modern history was itself an emblematic feat.

Although Goethe despised converts, Babbitt treated him as one. If
"the whole of life may be summed up in the words diversion and
conversion," Goethe was the olympian antithesis to the indolence and
indulgence epitomized in Rousseau, and the fact of his putative transition from the romantic to the humanistic way was "almost as in-
structive as the final result."[72] Much of Babbitt's esteem for Goethe,
as on a lesser plane for George Sand, was based on an imputed conversion, that is, on the assumption that Goethe had learned the error
of his romanticism.

Conversion as a rejection of the romantic and an espousal of the
classical temper posed a somewhat sinister question that Babbitt either did not consider or could not answer: Was not Goethe's endorsement of what he famously called the health of classicism necessarily a
result of his having experienced and survived the disease of romanticism? Was not a seeming chaos preconditional to the establishment of
order? Conversion, like redemption, could make sense only if there
were a predicated diversion (sin) to rectify. We can infer that Babbitt
believed that cultural and individual degenerations were so pervasive
by the turn of the century that he felt it unwise and unnecessary to
participate even experimentally in them. "Everyone must risk lop-
sidedness in an endeavor to redress the balance we have lost," he

explained to a student who tried to modify his extreme character-ization of issues.[73] In his *Laokoon* he had warned that an age of temperamental excesses, meaning his own, had as its stigma "one of those violent oscillations from one set of half-truths to another."[74] Risking lop-sidedness on his own, he found a model in Goethe, who "lived in an age of formalism and tended, as all well-balanced men will do, toward the side of that which was being neglected. If he were living now he would undoubtedly lean to the other side."[75]

So, then, Goethe's youthful romanticism was neither a contracted disease nor an apostasy from sense, but a tactical criticism of pseudo-classicism; his growth to a neoclassicism (itself romantic, according to Santayana) was as much a complement as a purgative to the romanti-cism he had helped to foster in *Die Leiden des jungen Werthers*, *Wilhelm Meister*, and the early dramas.

Still, even Goethe was not without defects. As he remarked in an uncharacteristically modest disclaimer, he was but the sum of many men, so that if all his debts to them were paid, little of him would remain. This was an eclecticism that Babbitt hailed as vital to the modern humanist, but it was bound to have blemishes. Referring to the humanitarian ethos concluding *Faust*, Part 2, Babbitt observed that "the wisest of moderns is not free from the suspicion of having encouraged an undue expansiveness," that is, of disguising a roman-tic egotism under "social sympathy."[76] Condemning Faust's utilitar-ianism in the final act as "an egregious piece of sham wisdom,"[77] Babbitt failed to perceive that Goethe himself was depicting Faust to the last hour as an errant, reckless, deluded mind. But one of Goethe's essential points, one lost to Babbitt, was that such mental aberration was concomitant with the struggle by which alone one makes oneself capable of redemption.[78] So, in his serene and aged austerity, Goethe extended an olive branch to the wayward parts of his nature that Babbitt believed he had simply overcome. Byron had ample reason for calling Goethe an old fox.

Never so aware as his contemporary, John Jay Chapman, of how cleverly Goethe rationalized his works as a process of self-enlighten-ment, Babbitt could not reconcile the humanitarian Goethe of *Faust* with the pontifical Goethe who talked with Eckermann. Far from the "sham wisdom" of the romantic lapses was an almost mystical eleva-tion in which Goethe seemed to speak for Babbitt: "We are not made free by wishing not to acknowledge anything above us but that we revere something which *is* above us. In so far as we revere it, we elevate ourselves up to it, we carry in ourselves this something higher and become worthy to be of its nature."[79] Apart from its agnosticism, Goethe's elevation rested upon antidemocratic and antirevolutionary biases to which Babbitt could give full assent. Also, dismissing metaphysics and religious faith as vain, Goethe's egotism was the more clearly a self-absorbing exercise of will, and on that ground, Babbitt likened him to Buddha and Samuel Johnson, almost the very best of humanist company. True, an imp of the perverse named Emerson prodded him to concur that Goethe lacked reverence for "the highest unity," but Babbitt lacked it too, and no amount of deference to the grimly celestial humanism of a Dante or a Pascal could compensate.[80] Free of the terrorism and morbidity of these earnest Christians, Goethe was more fully the self-survivor, the self-savior in whom Babbitt was able to see some reflection of his own temperamental struggles and overcomings.

Sainte-Beuve once acclaimed Goethe as the union of all traditions. From this lofty generalization Babbitt derived the note of Goethe's singularity as that union within an epoch of fragmentary and spiritless values. A generation after Darwin and Marx, whose influences had devalued man as surely as Copernicus had devalued God, Babbitt stubbornly reaffirmed self-mastering individuality through the character of Goethe. Finally, there was a cosmopolitanism in this German, a taste in contemporary and classical literature joined to his own Herculean breadth of expression. In his esteem of the ancients, he rose above the historicism that from Herder and Hegel implicitly or explicitly downgraded antiquity. Goethe had even remarked that had he known the ancient literatures in his youth, he would never have lifted his pen. Apart from such modesty and obscurantism, his suggestion that one finds in antiquity "the model of man in his true beauty" to which the modern age might raise itself complemented Babbitt's assertion that humanism was processive but required fixed standards, which the Greeks especially were so prodigious in offering.[81]

So much—perhaps too much—of Babbitt's French experience was an interplay of essence and accident, a kind of irresolvable limbo or purgatory of the intellect, with accident too often in the ascendant. The French tended, in their adept but parochial wars of words, to embrace one extreme against another; and those seeking to renounce all extremes, minds like Montaigne and Sainte-Beuve, could not rise above a middling plane.

In his high station as the Titan of modern letters, Goethe served Babbitt as no Frenchman could, as a personal reinforcement to his abstract faith in a disciplined individuality, in man as his own work of art. But this "creative illusion," this convenient, almost pagan fiction, did not satisfy Babbitt's deeper need to reconcile humanism to the religious "plane" that he had from the first recognized as the highest element in human nature. The attempt to achieve this reconciliation was to dominate the next decades of his life.

5. The Craving for Immediacy
The Search for a Humanist Culture

Nothing is so horrible, says Goethe, as ignorance in action,
and nothing is so depressing, one might add, as right knowledge that remains inactive.

> Irving Babbitt, Miscellaneous notes

On the whole one feels as if one were straining one's lungs
to be heard by a small audience sitting at the back of a great
and half-lighted hall. It is not very encouraging. There has
been some recognition in this country; and the coupling of
our names as engaged in the same campaign is a good
sign—but the audience is very small and the hall very large!

> Paul Elmer More to Irving Babbitt, August 11, 1913

In the last year of his life, the irascible octogenarian Charles Eliot
Norton mellowed momentarily. To his friend Horace Howard
Furness, the variorum editor of Shakespeare, Norton recorded
his enthusiasm over a book from a former student:

> Its author, one of our younger professors, has more of that old-
> fashioned literary culture which you and I value, than most of
> the younger Germanized scholars of today. His essays show both
> wide reading and independent thought . . . and his conclusions
> are in the main such as you and I should approve. . . . It is a
> great misfortune for us nationally that the tradition of culture is
> so weak and so limited. . . . But I hail such a book as Mr. Bab-
> bitt's as an indication of a possible turn in the tide.[1]

Norton, who had never fully succeeded in freeing himself of a youthful libertarian's optimism, even in reproving Emerson's irrepressible
shows of it, seemed to have transformed his cultural expectations
from national to individual terms. Shortly after the Civil War, he had
proclaimed American society a "paradise of mediocrities" in which
"shallowness of thought and life" flourished, but he believed that
that condition was temporary and that the "genuine and inevitable

result" of unimpeded democracy would ensure a superior culture.[2] A generation later, he was no longer confident of such a result: corruption in public office; the unabated ugliness of industrial power; a reckless war against Spain (his opposition to which earned him brief calumny); and still "no body of educated men competent to pass correct judgment in matters of learning."[3] Against such sources of disillusionment a book whose author was "interested in the perfecting of the individual rather than in schemes for the elevation of mankind" made ironic sense to Norton.[4]

When he published *Literature and the American College* in 1908, Irving Babbitt was forty-two, hardly one of Harvard's "younger professors" and certainly old enough to realize that Norton's genteel assumptions about an inevitable upward course of democracy had been mistaken and need not be renewed. But Babbitt shared Norton's concern for the life of letters in America; he simply did not construe "literary culture" as in any way "old-fashioned." Neither, to Babbitt, was there anything old-fashioned in James Russell Lowell's call for an American critical tradition as a foundation for a native "literary culture." But before there could be any tradition worthy of the name, there had to be standards. Reading over the initial chapter of his first book, Babbitt owned, "I am sorry to have to begin with a rather arid and abstract discussion of first principles, but we are living in such an impressionistic muddle nowadays that it is about the only way to avoid misunderstanding."[5] Babbitt found that these "first principles" were not only essential to his argument but basic to that tentative enterprise, the making of a desirable culture.

When he subsumed his principles and definitions under "humanism," he meant an aristocratic doctrine and discipline. As he characterized it, humanism was not a dogma but a process whereby some people would overcome as much as possible, but never totally, their innate proneness to temperamental or intellectual extremes. Almost as though he were describing a law of dynamics, Babbitt stated that "any point of view works out into an ironical contradiction of its own principle, unless it is humanized through being tempered by its opposite."[6] This tempering was not a neutralization of thought and energy but a never fully achievable balance between them. Babbitt's mediatory humanism operated within the phantom-like dualistic construct that philosophy and science had successfully eroded through the nineteenth century. In a pluralistic world, Babbitt wanted a restoration of a dualism that would not be merely a resuscitation of theological corpses. A radical but essential note in his thought was that "strictly speaking, one does not need to revert to anything,"[7] yet he had, like the humanists of old, a "will to tradition."[8]

Eschewing broad social issues and causes such as had occupied Norton, Babbitt in his early works concentrated his exhortations to balance wholly upon the individual. People would do better to reform themselves before they undertook to reform society. To remove humanism above the "impressionistic muddle," Babbitt prescribed that, free of overt institutional controls and sanctions of the past, one "must at least do inner obeisance to something higher than his ordinary self, whether he calls this something God, or, like the man of the Far East, calls it his higher Self, or simply the Law." Humanism, then, was a surrogate for "religious obligation" and "religious restraint."[9] Its medium was not the marketplace of social serviceability but an educational system that would provide "training for wisdom and training for character."[10] Babbitt's forum was Norton's, the college lecture room as a kind of secular church.

If there was a humanist gospel, it was to be derived mainly from ancient Greece, the *fons et origo* of everything that Babbitt, like most humanists before him, recognized as civilized. In his essays on education he had perceived the decline of collegiate studies in Greek and Latin as the subliminal cultural crisis of his era. To be sure, Greece served as much for admonition as for emulation; at its apex, it produced Socrates but also the sophists, and they had tipped the balance from "character" to serviceability, from "wisdom" to efficiency. So antiquity had a lesson for modern cultures that prided themselves upon power without direction and energy without control. Apart from historical lessons, there was an imperishable classical literature that maintained a consistent and high appeal "to those faculties which afford us an avenue of escape from ourselves, and enable us to become participants in the universal life."[11] Babbitt's humanism was a testimony that that "universal life" existed and served critically above the flux of the hour. The classical and neoclassical literatures that he had read and loved from his undergraduate years enforced upon him the defense of values that he conceived to be universal and therefore diametrically opposed to the values of particularity that predominated his own time. Thus, antiquity became an immediate cultural force.

Accordingly, the injunction of the humanist was that people lead a supratemporal life against their own natural inclinations to follow the claims of contingency and circumstance. Babbitt never underestimated the difficult, impracticable nature of the task. The nineteenth century had ripened the historical consciousness that awoke in the English and French Enlightenments at such a high price:

> The historic sense only became possible when men had ceased to take the past as an authority, when they no longer looked upon themselves and it as common partakers in an absolute ideal; when in short they had arrived at the degree of detachment that made it possible for them to see in the past, not a standard, but the mere relative product of the circumstances of time and space.[12]

He attributed to this relativity on the positive side of the ledger "an immense decline in fanaticism" on the negative, "a great falling off in vital conviction."[13] He attempted to reconcile historical method with humanistic standards by conceiving that method as a legitimate means solely for determining the evolution and transmission of ideas. Although, as we have seen, he had little esteem for most modern literature, Babbitt dismissed the traditional contest between ancient and modern literary values as false and futile. He suggested that ideally a tactical ballast should operate between them so that literature itself might continue to convey "avenues of escape" from the indeterminate and relative to the abidingly human.

Babbitt noted that during the Italian Renaissance, humanism was a movement against the confines of medieval scholasticism, but it became too prone to a loss of discipline. He favored the later Renaissance humanism of Castiglione, Sidney, and Malherbe that reversed the trend toward expansiveness in favor of selectivity. Yet the later humanists had been subject to a crabbed narrowness and dogmatism in their views and thus stifled thought and expression. It seemed to Babbitt that no period in history and no culture had long been able to maintain the humanistic balance of discipline and what he called "sympathy." Apart from hallowed antiquity, seventeenth-century France had come closest to a culture based upon humanistic standards, but it had left no continuum, no viable tradition with which the modern mind could ally itself, so that "the individual, left to his own resources, must seek a substitute for it in humane reflection."[14]

It is on this point that the character of Babbitt's concept of humanistic culture displays some affinity with that of Matthew Arnold. Arnold's thesis, in *Culture and Anarchy*—that culture was not a fixed end but a person's internal pursuit of perfection, apart from or even against the material and mechanical forces in an affluent industrial society—was undoubtedly a model, perhaps *the* model for Babbitt's own plea. Arnold warned of popular tendencies among societies and individuals to embrace novelties or to pursue action for its own sake without reference to what he, following Milton, called right reason. Babbitt subsumed Arnold's term in his own *frein vital*, or vital check —the law of restraint. Arnold had written:

> Now, it is clear that the very absence of any powerful authority among us, and the prevalent doctrine of the duty and happiness of doing as one likes, and asserting our personal liberty, must tend to prevent the erection of any very strict standard of excellence, the belief in any very paramount authority of right reason, the recognition of our best self as anything very recondite and hard to come at.[15]

Thus he anticipated in the drift of mid-Victorian England Babbitt's indictment of an aimless American society two generations later. Both called for harmonization of ideas: Arnold, for a balance between the spontaneous Hellenic consciousness and the strict Hebraic conscience that he found peculiar to English character; Babbitt, the more partisan, for a redress that would afford humanistic standards equal status with humanitarian ones. Following Arnold in the use of these abstract intellectual polarities, Babbitt exaggerated in the manner of his English mentor the power of ideas upon conduct. But whereas Arnold hankered in his subdued, wistful way after the moribund norms of "spiritual perfection" and "the will of God,"[16] Babbitt addressed himself only passingly to "the sense of communion with absolute being."[17] His notion of culture was agnostic. He could never have followed with Arnold Cardinal Newman's contention that "philosophy, however enlightened, however profound, gives no command over the passions, no influential motives, no vivifying principles" in that it could not make a Christian but only a gentleman.[18] Hence, the humanist virtues—moderation, decency, common sense—were emphatically secular ones. For an epoch of specialized knowledge and conflicting dogmas, Babbitt found the exemplar of these virtues neither in the saint nor the scientest, but in La Rochefoucauld's courtly gentleman who prided himself on nothing. This courtly ideal was meant to be more than a corrective to the modern pressures of specialization. An age of collective material expansion that diminished one's individual worth required some spiritual denominator that would bind people together. Babbitt's notion of decorum as "the grand masterpiece to observe because it is only thus [one] can show that he has a genuine centre set above his own ego" was a cultural formula, a prescription for the deference of the individual to the ethical conventions agreed upon by the community.[19] Perhaps more fitting than La Rochefoucauld's ideal was Montaigne's, which Babbitt recorded privately: "The most beautiful lives are, to my mind, those that submit themselves to a common standard, without wonder or extravagance."[20]

Babbitt's early essays suggest, in their forceful, vigorous, sometimes caustic tone, that he believed the college to be the bastion for the preservation of humanist values as it had been for their propagation in Europe centuries before. He joined to a Gallic affirmation of *le sens commun* an Aristotelian attention to education as the inculcation of proper habits. As there was an etymological link between habit and ethics, so there was a necessary conjunction between education and convention. Basically identical with "decorum,"

> convention is only the organized common sense of one's time. Civilization rests, more than upon any one thing, upon the orderly transmission of right habits. A society that does not come to some kind of working agreement as to what habits are civilized and then insists on these habits being perpetuated through education in its children is at once cowardly and degenerate.[21]

But now the enemy was within the gates and furthering some habits the civilizing value of which Babbitt severely questioned. He analyzed the pervading aims of collegiate education as twofold: first, it was humanitarian in lowering academic standards to accommodate a democratic average; second, it was scientific in promoting the phenomenal values of calculation and mechanization.

Babbitt made no concession to the fact that industrial processes and the rise of urban populations from the time of the Civil War had to a great extent predestined these developments in education, making the agglomerates of universities from parochial colleges. (The process at Harvard itself was lengthily described by Charles William Eliot in his 1869 presidential address.) He insisted upon a longer than circumstantial view. The ethics of service and power alike represented a close identification of humankind with nature that would prove as deleterious to the human spirit as had the medieval identification of humankind with the claims of divinity.

In his early works, Babbitt characterized the utilitarian aberrations: "the proper study of mankind is not man, but chemistry; or perhaps, our modern attitude might be more correctly defined as an attempt to study man by the methods of physics and chemistry. We have invented laboratory sociology and live in a nightmare of statistics. Language interests us only in so far as it is a collection of facts."[22]

No less a threat than scientism, however, was the humanitarian notion that made the individual impulses of the student the guide in determining the worth of studies. The combined effect would be "that 'encyclopaedic smattering and miscellaneous experiment' which according to Plato are especially harmful in the training of the young."[23] If the ascendancy of scientific studies in college curricula could be traced to the prestigious rise of scientific theory and invention through the nineteenth century, the humanitarian influence was explicitly traceable to the growth of the elective system at Harvard and soon elsewhere in the generation following the Civil War.

President Eliot furthered the elective system greatly after 1896 by increasing the number of electives and reducing prescribed studies to the freshman level by 1874. By 1883, shortly before Babbitt entered Harvard, classical language requisites had gone; only French and German were required, in addition to sophomore and junior themes and two courses in physical sciences. According to the Faculty Report of 1899–1900, more than half of the undergraduates elected mostly elementary courses; about a quarter took half of their courses in one department. By that time students frequently crowded four-year programs of study into three.[24] These were some of the grounds for Babbitt's charge of "encyclopaedic smattering and miscellaneous experiment."

The great experimenter behind these changes Babbitt likened to Francis Bacon in his unqualified faith in quantitative progress and to Rousseau in his naive celebration of adolescent potential. At the expense of established disciplinary norms, Eliot fused the worst aspects of humanitarian idealism: "having bestowed upon the student the full liberty of Rousseau, it is evident that President Eliot would have him use this liberty in a Baconian spirit; he is not to profit by his emancipation to enjoy a 'delicious indolence,' but he is to work with great energy with reference to his personal interests and aptitudes."[25]

Babbitt's assessment of Eliot did not change from the time of his first book to his essay on Eliot written in 1929, three years after Eliot's death. It is a view that reflects the peculiar consistency of Babbitt's thoughts and attitudes; his premises and arguments remained unchanged even in basic vocabulary over forty years. Trends in education over a generation merely reinforced his conviction that his initial criticisms were sound.

Babbitt was not a proponent of the "genteel tradition," but he shared the assumption of its spokesmen that a democracy was best served through its ablest minds occupying positions of authority and influence. He defined the cultural nature of the college negatively as the elimination of special favor or privilege on any extrinsic basis for any student. In a somewhat Jeffersonian manner, he called for an "aristocracy of character and intelligence" to replace the artificial aristocracies of wealth and ancestry—a point that might have appalled genteel patriarchs—but his explicit prompter in this plea was Tocqueville, who argued that the true test of a democracy would be its ability to produce superior people.[26]

Besides the balancing of instruction between modern fields, literary and scientific, and those resting upon tradition, a curricular reference to antiquity would perpetuate what Babbitt called "the total experience of the race as to the things that have been found to be permanently important to its essential nature."[27] His whole concern for attention to standards was based upon a kind of historical empiricism, a belief that through innumerable generations came certain centralizing hallmarks of human experience. He never presumed that such cultural standards, historically derived, were progressive in any Hegelian fashion. Almost paradoxically, these standards were static in that, to the humanist, they were irrefutable—the laws of measure, balance, and restraint were constant to a person's nature and conduct—but they were dynamic in that each generation had to apply them in its own contextual terms. In the re-creation and maintenance of these standards for a culture, colleges played a role so crucial that Babbitt was wont to mystify its execution; it was "to coordinate the scattered elements of knowledge and relate them not only to the intellect but to the will and character; that subtle alchemy by which mere learning is transmuted into culture."[28] But now in the "progressive" epoch of Deweyan education, rather than advancing the assimilation of knowledge together with "permanent human values," the colleges were perpetrating mere proficiency in the investigation and accumulation of facts. The consequence was not only a disregard of the past as the foundation of and for a cultural continuum, but a pedantic attention to learning as a means of self-promotion. A culture worthy of the name would have to be more than the sum of fragmentary persons absorbed in their particular research.

Babbitt did not deny that the quantitative, dynamic criteria of science afforded valuable indexes to a culture's progress in a material sense. But the more crucial progress was one that retained a sobriety of right values and depended upon the individual's balance of knowledge with insight, "the harmonious rounding out of all the faculties," rather than upon a talent for specialization. Scientism as postulated in education rested upon the fallacy that the wholeness of a society as a condition for its "progress" depended upon a one-sidedness in its members.

Positivism's mechanical objectification of people and society into phenomenal laws, and romanticism's exaltation of subjective temperament were the Scylla and Charybdis between which the humanist as the educator for culture would have to steer a narrow course. Although both movements had influential formulators in France since the Enlightenment, Babbitt regarded Germany as their more ominous harbinger in his own time. He offered no historical grounds for his suspicion, such as Germany's rapid rise to industrial power and its bureaucratized nationalism as outward aids to a positivistic ideology. Instead, he dwelt upon a quasi-racial view of German character. The German penchant for productive efficiency came in part from a lack of the classical restraints and decorum that the French had been able to achieve in forming their culture upon La Rochefoucauld's *honnête homme* and *le sens commun*. Hand in hand with a prosaic mechanical life of efficiency went the idyllic intoxication of the romantic sensibility which depended upon that mechanization to justify its escapism. And the Germans, from Schiller to the Schlegels, from Schopenhauer to Nietzsche, had proven masterly practitioners of escapism.

Germany's cultural scientism, the complement and rationale for modern romanticism, reduced education to a system of searching into origins and causes (*Quellenforschungen*) and a rigorous application of method (*strengwissenschaftliche Methode*) that treated knowledge as, in Babbitt's words "something that is dumped down on one mind and then 'distributed' in the same mechanical fashion to other minds."[29] Here was the paradigm of education as industry. The hazard, Babbitt suggested, was that Americans, like Germans, were prone to confuse knowledge with efficiency and so violate the humanist laws of sense and discriminative judgment. The superficiality of the American temperament was that it used the past largely for folk ideology and otherwise had an obsessive futuristic prejudice. The academic fetish for novelty and innovation as in the elective system and fledgling doctoral programs would, to be sure, continually elicit shows of brilliance among the educated, but virtuosos were not necessarily learned people. Neither would they qualify as makers of culture.

Chief of the sophisms about standardless virtuosity was Eliot's rationale of electives, that students knew better than faculty the best course of study. Against this total reverse of the meaning of pedagogy, Babbitt scoffed, "The wisdom of all the ages is to be as naught compared with the inclination of a sophomore."[30] But on the graduate level he defended the student against "the German incubus" and "the fetish of productive scholarship," in reasoning that young minds needed to expend their fullest energy in broad assimilative learning rather than in prematurely restrictive efforts of research.[31]

Babbitt's antidotes to the aberrations of collegiate curricula were only partially and tentatively proposed. English humanism (he never referred to an American humanism), embodied in men like Arnold, Samuel Butcher, and Gilbert Murray, proved itself a model for emulation, if not imitation. Yet that England's hallowed humanist culture was endangered seemed evident from the closeted epicureanism of a classicist like Walter Pater and, even more scandalously, in the cult of aestheticism he fostered. But the eminence of men like Arnold and Murray allowed Babbitt to plead that advocacy of a humanistic culture, realized through education, was not tantamount to obscurantism: "In general the humanist will not repudiate either sentimental or scientific naturalism; for this would be to attempt an impossible reaction. His aim is not to deny his age, but to complete it."[32] This completion or balance was as essential as the correction of one-sidedness in the individual. Baconian utility and Rousseauist sympathy unimbued with humanist discipline meant chaos for education and society and the confounding of any hope for humane culture.

Searching for corrective models, Babbitt concentrated upon a hypothetical honors system for the humanities patterned loosely after English and French archetypes. He looked enviously to Oxford and the Sorbonne where honors were bestowed only after years of rigorous study that coordinated ancient and modern fields. He was encouraged by the Harvard program of interdepartmental honors, which the Lowell Committee had instigated in 1903, but he found that its critical fault was its Germanic attention to specialized research. Whatever reforms might be initiated to humanize degree requirements, they would have to depend on recognition of the permanent worth of literary and philosophical masterworks, that is, "books which so agree in essentials that they seem, as Emerson puts it, to be the work of one all-seeing, all-hearing gentleman."[33] This agreement on essentials was, of course, the literary component that made for a cultural decorum. For centuries, the Chinese had maintained that sort of decorum in the Confucian analects.

Increasingly, however, Babbitt had reason to believe that his appeals for a humanistic reform of education were echoing in a cultural void, like those of a seemingly reactionary Jansenism in French Christianity that, for students of his course on Pascal and Port Royal, he characterized as a "desperate rear guard action" against the secularizing influence of the Jesuits.[34] Not only had Eliot's delight in the "department store conception of education" won manifest triumphs in American schools, but Dewey's instrumentalism and John Watson's behaviorism were proving potent, decisive influences in educational psychology.[35] Nor did it seem that World War I made as evident to others as to Babbitt the worst possible perversions to which an unrestrained ethic of serviceable power might extend. But he persisted in sounding an indomitable note of expectation that humanism would rally enough adherents to confront, if not reverse, the trends of the age. As in 1907 he had cheered Norton in noting "signs" auspicious for a return to what they both understood as culture, so on the eve of the Great Depression he submitted that "there is probably even now a minority of shrewd observers who are ready to get together to resist successfully the stupid drift toward standardization."[36]

Babbitt never posed to himself the question of how this minority would exert a humanistic sway beyond their own isolated institutional perimeters—how, that is, humanism would become a societal as well as individual force. Here his failure to follow the broad and flexible model of Arnold's social criticism becomes apparent. Rather too formulaically, Babbitt adhered to his favorite humanist: "Society is chiefly important in the eyes of Aristotle for the aid it may give the individual in realizing his higher self," and that outer aid was necessarily subordinate to the far more fundamental inner helps of the individual's will in working to that higher self.[37] Culture had to be realized first, if at all, as an individual effort known as leisure.

Leisure, according to Babbitt, was not properly the loafing of the materialist but a setting for meditation. Like decorum, it was the mode by which the individual through reflection cast off his sense of particular self. A scholar, etymologically considered, was a practitioner of leisure. But under the aegis of materialistic efficiency academic life had produced "that strangest of all anomalies, the hustling scholar," overburdened with teaching, publishing, and administrative duties. In this hustling, Babbitt found, Eliot's gospel of work reached its dismal acme.[38]

Against the rush of a society dedicated to mechanical prowess, Babbitt conceived the college to be ideally a kind of vital check, an institutionally vested curb, a cultural counterforce energized through the right practice of leisure. Unless Eliot's joy in work were tempered by a joy in leisure, his industrial democracy would beget a tendency "to live in a perpetual devil's sabbath of whirling machinery, and call it progress."[39] Unlike Henry Adams, Babbitt was not disposed to mystify mechanical processes as somehow beyond human control. He recognized that mechanization wisely employed would afford leisure to a greater number of people than had ever been possible. But it would prove a bane to civilized persons and to culture if mechanical activity became a rationale merely for more such activity. Lost would be the humane sense of effort, of an Aristotelian *telos* or purposeful end, of which true leisure was a fundamental part.

Because humanist leisure was a singular, contemplative activity, Babbitt could not give it a broad social meaning. He would not have equated it with William James's "gospel of relaxation" even though it was intended, as was James's "gospel," to serve as a release from the mundane anxieties of the industrial present.[40] Rather, leisure was the requisite basis of a private well-being, a *eudaimonia*. In it a man could exercise what Aristotle defined as speculation or thought for its own sake ($\vartheta\varepsilon\omega\varrho\eta\tau\iota\varkappa\eta$ $\dot{\varepsilon}\nu\dot{\varepsilon}\varrho\gamma\varepsilon\iota\alpha$), as both means and end. In this Hellenic fashion, Babbitt divinized the will's contemplative intellect as the highest and happiest activity. It was this ancient view of leisure as the ground for the only substantial happiness, this heightened mental action (not a true mystical conversion) that allowed Babbitt to propound a principle complementary to the vital check—a vital release —which, like the check, presupposed a limited number of participants. The enduringly great thoughts, the art and poetry that in no explicit way figured in Aristotle's notion of contemplation, were both patently Nortonian elements of culture and Babbitt's points of reference to the leisure which that culture required. They were literally the educative or guiding means by which humanistically trained students, fit though few, could become the arbiters of culture. An education that should "liberate the whole man" to leisure would thus become a cultural event.[41]

Had Babbitt espoused a dogmatic involution, he would have made his humanism into what James called a hegelism, a complacent intellectual exclusiveness blind to the variety of experience. Babbitt abhorred metaphysical constructs so far as they pretended to explain reality, but he felt that the pendulum of thought and inquiry had swung to an opposite excess in the nineteenth century, that "experience" had won sovereignty over reflection of any kind. The sciences, exalting experience as the ground of experimentation, had made reason and speculation seem idly abstract and barren. Society itself was becoming an experiment through the laboratorial ethic epitomized in men like Charles Sanders Peirce and John Dewey. If a community, a culture, were to be an exercise in experimental controls or a rendering of human experience into scientific formulas, then, Babbitt concluded: "It follows that immense areas of what the past had taken to be genuine experience, either religious or humanistic, experience that has been transmitted to us in consecrated masterpieces, must, inasmuch as it is not subject to test in a laboratory, be dismissed as mere moonshine."[42]

Babbitt's censure reflected his overreactive subscription to the antinomy of religion (and humanism) versus science (an antinomy that neither Peirce nor Dewey recognized as valid), but he rightly perceived that the experimentalists reduced the claims of religion by making scientific norms paramount. The future of a religion, Peirce warned, depended upon its being "animated by the scientific spirit."[43] For his part, Dewey averred that cooperative observation, experiment, and "controlled reflection" were the "one sure road to truth."[44] This experimentalism neglected the aspect of culture upon which Babbitt most firmly insisted: a selective regard for the past, not on the basis of generational deference, but because the past furnished a succession of experiments of permanent human value, embodied in the works of those who had risen above their time in a sense that experimental philosophy could neither accommodate nor comprehend. Babbitt thought that a society became a humanistic culture only to the extent that it balanced its immediate concerns with reference to "certain constant factors in human experience" historically revealed.[45] Such a culture would work to harmonize the practicable, experimental activities of mind—what the Greeks termed *phronesis*, or purposeful activity—with the transcendent ones of contemplation.

The singularity of Babbitt's view of the past as a component of modern culture is that it is not "historical" in any progressive sense. He believed that Aristotle and Confucius were not only more edifying but more immediate to one's interest than, say, the daily newspaper or the paperback novel. In a deleterious way, so was Rousseau. "To debate Rousseau is really to debate the main issues of our contemporary life"[46] meant that Rousseau was a cultural microcosm, the datum of proof that society's ills as well as its aids find their impetus in the individual's imaginative and ethical qualities.

Babbitt rejected as a false application of natural law to human behavior any deterministic or cyclical view of history: "I do not believe in any such fatality, and am in general skeptical of every possible philosophy of history—of the Spenglerian variety most of all."[47] Determinism, even under the most benign presuppositions such as those of Comte or Hegel, jeopardized any faith in the efficacy of individual choice and action. Yet he could not deny that his exhortations to culture were too austere, exclusive, and academic to accommodate people en masse; like Arnold, he wrote against the very fact of their collectivity. Rather than yield to the collectivistic trends of the late nineteenth century when, as Nietzsche said, spirit passed from man to mob, Babbitt resorted to Arnold's notion of the saving remnant. The term connotes an elitist's reactive concession to the power of numbers but also suggests a species of collectivism in itself, albeit a restrictive one.

Babbitt had models for a self-congratulating, involuted society in the "genteel" generation immediately preceding his own, in Brahmins like Lowell, Stedman, and Norton. But more important than their genteel affiliation per se was the cosmopolitan character of their learning and taste. He himself had only the shell of an American tradition had he been disposed to retreat into it, but the sense of an *esprit européen*, an *esprit mondial* came in his training at Harvard and in several trips to France, the most cosmopolitan of nations. There, in salons that included partisans of Charles Maurras and Léon Daudet, and in lectures at the Sorbonne, he became acquainted with the critical lights of Paris—Lasserre, Brunetière, Seillière—contacts that gave immediacy to his call for "a mobilization of the sages."[48] Although he did not agree with the reactionary conservatism of men like Julien Benda or Pierre Lasserre, whose solution for the anxieties of the present was "what seems to me a mechanical return to the past," he recognized that they worked within a viable community of ideas; they had a responsive press and a reading public, the kind of press and public for which Lowell and Norton had hoped and vainly sought on native soil.[49] Babbitt was convinced that the fourth estate in America had so declined as to become an index of national degeneracy rather than of national culture as Godkin and Norton had once intended: "A glance at a current display of our newspapers and popular magazines suggests that, though we are not fools, we are reading just the things that fools would read."[50] A "mobilization" of America's "sages" was not likely to occur through journalistic media.

Babbitt did not attempt to solicit a slavish imitation of European literary or cultural trends, because he knew that too often Americans borrowed the worst from them. American literati in "exile" in France after World War I seemed to be acting out a generational tutelage that prompted Babbitt to inquire whether America's literary culture was "always to be the dumping ground of Europe."[51] By arguing for a body of scholars capable of criticizing and educating American writers, Babbitt resisted this almost ineluctable tendency among

American academics to express fealty—resentfully or obsequiously—
to Europe. But his sense of how this saving remnant would become
culturally effectual remained rhetorical. After the World War, Babbitt's argument for the creation of a humanist culture became increasingly international in its compass.

Just as American cultural standards had long been under a tutelage to Europe, in the wake of the war, the Old World was increasingly subject to the tastes and fashions of American acquisitiveness.
"Average men of different nationalities tend to borrow faults rather
than virtues" from one another, Babbitt concluded upon seeing a
poster outside the Moulin Rouge in five languages.[52] Even as far as
the Orient the claims of an untrammeled Western materialism had
extended. Babbitt learned directly from his oriental students at Harvard, several of whom corresponded with him after their returning
home, that Japan especially was applying too well the lessons of occidental materialism: "The lust of domination, which is almost the ultimate fact of human nature, has been so armed in the Occident with
the machinery of scientific efficiency that the Orient seems to have
no alternative save to become efficient in the same way or to be reduced to economic and political vassalage."[53] Shortly after the World
War, he pointed to the rise of sensationalistic anti-Western journalism
in Japan as a portentous symptom of how well the Orient was learning occidental ways.

This alarm over the ominous westernization of the East is related
directly to Babbitt's hope for a humanistic culture. As he had maintained that human nature is doomed to occasional excesses of one-
sidedness, so too, he felt, were national cultures. From his earliest
writing he had urged a curricular perpetuation of classical literatures
as balancing complements to modern literature; on similar grounds,
he urged attention to religious and humanistic traditions of the Orient for the appropriation of civilized norms absent in the West. In
that sense, Babbitt's humanism was a kind of imaginative harmonization of cultures. Plato's concept of the reconciliation of the One and
the Many as the most crucial problem of philosophy Babbitt applied
critically to diverse cultures. The ever restless multiplicity of Western
thought, abetted by utilitarian sciences, had its counterpart in the
unifying quietism of Confucian China and Buddhistic India. Separately, East and West labored under the aberrant tendencies of half-
truths: the West was prone to a materialistic anarchy that broke down
restraints of authority and tradition; the East was subject to the fossil-
ized obscurantism of a millennial tradition. The ideal of a "oneness
that is always changing," of "activity in repose" became Babbitt's ab-

stract predicate for a cultural interaction between the Asian and European intellectual communities.[54] The oriental concentration upon an inner absolute he conceived to be an especially needful corrective to the "vain surface agitation" of America: "Nothing at bottom could run more counter to the gregarious and humanitarian instincts of the present age," he wrote in 1899, "than insistence on renunciation and meditation, on the essential loneliness of the human spirit."[55]

Such supranational elements figured throughout Babbitt's writing. In his first essays he employed Buddhism as an adjunct or cross-reference to Western humanism. As he became aware that humanitarian trends in Western cultures had immediate implications, even direct influences beyond the West (Dewey's influence in Russia and China was an instance), he urged an integration of Eastern and Western humanism and religion. By the early 1920s he defined his "method" as one placing Confucius behind Aristotle and Buddha behind Christ.[56] The ascendant importance of Buddha in Babbitt's later works, beginning in *Rousseau and Romanticism* and culminating in his translation of the *Dhammapada*, signified his resolution of the problem of finding a religious reference to which as humanist he might adhere and his designation of a *point de repère* in the midst of a growing international crisis.

Babbitt's initial prescription of a meeting between Eastern and Western intellectual traditions seemed to suggest a dialectic: the Heraclitean flux of the Occident, manifest in its material wealth, industrial power, and scientific knowledge, would, once tempered by the oriental absorption in transcendental peace, conceive a middle way, a humanistic mean of sobriety and temperance. The elements of culture, like the principles of aesthetics, required the balance of opposites rather than the clash manifested in mercantile and military rivalries. Yet at no point did he presume humanism as a plea for measure would provide a historically valid synthesis either within or among societies. He eschewed any abstract deterministic imposition upon people and culture; the power of the will, however enfeebled by materialism, remained his paramount assumption; collectivization of the will to whatever end necessarily canceled its meaning and effectiveness. He rejected pessimism in any form but could not deny that modern collectivistic democracies endangered what he considered civilized, a culture of standards and decorum consciously created and maintained by individuals. That such a culture was a fact he knew from the polite cultivation that oriental students invariably showed. A culture was not merely given or received but willed, and as its livelihood was a delicate task, only the sobriety and intuition of disciplined wills could perpetuate it. It might survive within a national society but not upon the terms that Eliot had supposed, not through democratic agencies and powers, but in spite of them.

The attacks upon radical democracy that Babbitt developed in a series of lectures at Kenyon College, Stanford University, and the Sorbonne between 1920 and 1924 came simultaneously with a widening breach between his humanism and Paul Elmer More's quasi-religious orthodoxy. At about the same time, Babbitt's former protégé, Stuart Sherman, became disaffected with both men as inflexible, unyielding antidemocrats. Despite Babbitt's affirmation that "the unit to which all things must finally be referred is not the State or humanity or any other abstraction, but the man of character," he was forced to realize that a humanistic remnant, composed of such men of character, was an abstraction too precarious in any concrete manifestation.[57] Charles William Eliot, after all, was the Puritan who had subjected educational standards to the antitheses of his heritage, to scientific and sentimental humanitarianism. Similarly, Sherman rejected the exclusiveness of a saving remnant in favor of a "divine average" against which humanism stood, according to Babbitt, in an "opposition that is one of first principles and not therefore subject to mediation or compromise."[58]

The absence of an estate of critical tradition in America had made this democratization of the intellect irreversible.[59] The same leveling trend seemed to be operating in Europe, even in France, where the Académie française had for three centuries served as an institutional check that prescribed and proscribed the conduct of its men of letters. This trend seemed to accelerate in the postwar years. Babbitt upheld the thesis of French essayist Julien Benda in his *Trahison des clercs* (1927) that, in former ages, philosophers, writers, and artists had held themselves and their standards above the immediate dictates of their societies; they were "dedicated to the service of something in man that transcends his material interests."[60] But in modern times these men had become secularized and, instead of resisting the suasions and drives of the hour, flattered them. Violating their common service to a decorum, they became the European equivalent of the hustling scholars.

Nowhere, perhaps, were the effects of this unseemly yielding more evident than in what the radical American journalist Randolph Bourne called the "herd intellect" of American intellectuals in support of American participation in the World War.[61] Bourne localized the source of the betrayal to war rather than to imperialism and thus had no effective counterstance to the delusions of Deweyan liberalism other than to urge that "irreconcilables" and "dissenters" allow their minds to "roam widely and ceaselessly" so as to avoid "premature crystallization."[62] To this surrender to the flux of impressionism, Benda, who saw the betrayal of the intellectuals as a cultural crisis, failed to provide a remedy and drifted toward what Babbitt characterized as Swiftian misanthropy and fatalism.

Babbitt's analysis was free of Bourne's disillusion and Benda's pessimism. He contended that the political and social ills of nations had a common source in the breakdown of traditional constraints upon institutions and individuals since the eighteenth century. More crucially, those ills came with the waning of cultural standards that tradition had sustained. Revolutionary romanticism was the source to which Babbitt could always refer his humanist sense of déjà vu and from which he could derive a formulaic understanding of historical catastrophe. If he would not allow himself to view history as a process of fixed laws, he did accommodate a no less convenient view of it as a display of recurrent patterns of individual and collective behavior. The present became a telltale addendum to the past, charging Babbitt's lively apprehension of imminent dangers by warning signals that had leitmotivs generations or centuries old.[63]

Not the least foreboding of symptoms was what he came to regard as a transcultural phenomenon: "A boundless intoxication with novelty is indeed the outstanding trait of the modern era that sets it off from all the ages of the past."[64] America, he feared, was particularly subject to this virulence. Yet he decried as specious the European's stereotypal condescension toward America, the proclivity for diagnosing European ills by presuming their sources transatlantic, even though the vehemence of foreign critics had a match in his own attacks upon the quality of American life. Just as he never tried to improve the clipped Yankee accent with which he spoke French and German, so he retained a native pride that told him America's best critics should be her own. Besides, the extroversion of professionals into mechanical hustlers was an intercultural epidemic, infecting Europe and Asia no less evilly than the United States. He could even believe for a brief while that the very absence of a sound tradition in America (an absence he usually deplored), to which there might be reactionary recourse, enabled it to further, better than Europe, "a genuine cosmopolitanism."[65] But his faith in that possibility died with America's entrance into the World War.

As for this cosmopolitanism, it was of course humanism writ large. Babbitt wrote of it almost synonymously with internationalism but invited confusion in doing so: he had only contempt for the humani-

tarian internationalism of the League of Nations and its pacifist af-
filiates, and he supported no governmentally based internationalist
policies. The World War seemed to have documented conclusively
the incapacities of nations to overcome their competing nationalisms.
In the wake of the war he denounced as "the most dangerous of all
sham religions of the modern age—the religion of country."[66] The
remedy was not the pacifist's pretense that minimized differences
among nations. Neither was it a sentimental escapist appropriation of
other cultures than one's own as palliatives for internal crises as had
been the way of German exoticists headed by Schlegel and Schopenhauer, who made the East a narcotic dreamland. No, it would have to
be based upon a recognition among educated persons of all nations
of a need for "the defense of the disciplines that tend to draw men to
a common center *even across national frontiers*."[67]

Although he never ceased to reaffirm Norton's and his own plea
for an indigenous culture of educators and critics, Babbitt in the last
decade of his life transmuted his tenuous hopes for a saving remnant
in America to an equally tenuous cosmopolitan sphere. In private
notes he defined a cosmopolitanism in which "elites of each nation
can communicate with elites of others, escape from one's national
limitations by assimilation of cultures, . . . graftings of one form of
national culture upon another."[68] From these elites the "higher democracy" of sound political leadership would presumably emanate.
How far such intercultural "graftings" and "assimilations" might be
realized Babbitt did not attempt to suggest; he gave the notion no
development in published works. He did argue that the religions and
ideologies of nations might serve as barriers to communication, and
through that point argued for the "humanistic side" of Eastern and
Western faiths as a basis for "closer agreement" among elites.[69]

Babbitt's cosmopolitanism included his familiar appeal to a "higher
will", which, as it did not claim an absolute nor an ideal rooted
in dogma, might prove a denominator for an intercultural decorum,
a convention. To affirm the higher than natural law meant to elevate oneself above the province of nationality, which, indeed, was
far more one's circumstantial condition than the result of conscious
choice or will. In political terms, exercise of the humanist virtues—
moderation, "common sense," decency—among cultural leaderships
was so reasonable an aim that appeals to it would have seemed commonplace had not Babbitt obtruded his almost metaphysical notion
of the will by which to signify that humanist elitists had a common
ground deeper than mere politics and politenesses.

He had felt the force of that higher will in the benign, sequestered atmosphere around the home circle of Norton. He perpetuated this almost spiritual sense among a small group of responsive students. This ambiance of gentlemanly restraint was especially marked between him and his oriental students. Babbitt extrapolated the genial, almost courtly rapport of his microcosmic community to a transnational realm. The amenities of the salon society that he enjoyed in visits to Paris furthered even more his wistful presupposition that a higher will was not the figment of an isolated humanist but a socially attainable integer. But these acquaintances and coteries did not substantiate his ideal of a humanistic communion; they afforded at best only approximations to an unwritten protocol.

Babbitt characterized the humanistic will as "this superrational and transcendent element" that would perhaps prove "to be alone capable of supplying a sufficient counterpoise to the various 'lusts' . . . that result from the free unfolding of man's natural will."[70] Paul Elmer More challenged this vague formulation for the employment of a transcendentalism that was without reference to a supernatural, divine agency. Expunging any religious connotation, Babbitt replied that he accepted the higher will "simply as a primordial fact, something of which one is immediately aware."[71] This intuitive affirmation hints at Descartes, but Babbitt rejected the Cartesian conception of will as too mechanical, too insistent upon reason as the sole guide of conduct. Rationalism was a gambit that ultimately impoverished the will. Lacking Descartes's adhesion to a perfect and immutable divine will and resting his claim for a higher will upon an "awareness" that "exists in different degrees in different individuals so that one encounters in purely psychological form the equivalent of the mystery of grace," Babbitt contrived a mechanism as arbitrary as that of Descartes.[72] But he believed its vagueness was vindicated by its embrace of a cosmopolitan humanity.

So Babbitt made high claims for his intuited will as a cultural factor. History had shown, he argued, that one's unity with oneself and with others "must be based primarily . . . upon an exercise of the higher will"; without it, the intellect would resort to the conceit of metaphysical or mechanical determinisms.[73] Kant, for example, had mechanized traditional dualism into rigid abstractions "without reference to the happiness of the individual or the special circumstances to which he needs to adjust himself" and so "his philosophy does not satisfy the craving for immediacy."[74] That immediacy and a unity among those within it had been grounded since Kant's time upon scientific rather than metaphysical claims. Thus, in 1868, Charles Peirce called upon philosophy

to imitate the successful sciences in its methods, so far as to pro-
ceed only from tangible premises which can be subjected to careful scrutiny, and to trust rather to the multitude and variety of its
arguments than to the conclusiveness of any one. . . . We have no
power of Introspection, but all knowledge of the internal world
is derived by hypothetical reasoning from our knowledge of external facts. We have no power of Intuition, but every cognition
is determined logically by previous cognitions.[75]

Although Babbitt, no less than Peirce or any other social philosopher,
was concerned to realize a community of values, he denied that they
could rest upon a logically experimental basis. His will to tradition
referred values almost exclusively to a kind of transcultural aggregate or what has been termed a historical empiricism.

Like Matthew Arnold, suspended between a dead world and one as
yet powerless to be born, Babbitt felt obligated to improvise a rationale for humanism that would satisfy the claims of immediacy. He
could do so, however, only by hedging his terms, by admitting that
the "truths" of the humanistic "inner life" were "not clear in the logical or any other sense" but were "a matter of elusive intuition."[76]
Babbitt wanted to reconcile the transcendence of a cosmopolitan oneness and the immanence of a nationalistic plurality through a mediatory humanist decorum, but he could pretend to achieve this reconciliation only by ignoring the disappearance of the former into the
mists of philosophical and theological history, and the reduction of
the latter into the laboratories of war. Only thus could he rationalize
for his time that the higher will "though it concerns primarily the
inner life of the individual, will be found to involve finally all the
main issues of civilization."[77]

To make humanism compatible with immediacy, Babbitt referred
to Confucius, the abiding genius of Chinese culture and "a master of
them that will," and he looked ever more scrupulously to Buddhism,
an atheistic, dualistic faith, "the most critical," "the least mythological
of religions."[78] He discerned in Buddhism a "remarkable tendency to
take the cash and let the credit go," the cash being the "immediate
peace" that Western philosophers had neglected and that Western
science would never fully be able to provide.[79]

Immediacy tended to render arbitrary philosophical systems inop-
erable, but it accommodated, even demanded, eclecticism. Babbitt
felt this demand was satisfied in the "purely psychological," "intensely
analytical temper" of Buddhism.[80] It was an ethic that employed scientific or, more properly, Socratic means for humanistic, quasi-tran-

scendental ends. Because Buddha was a teacher who instructed in purification of the inner self, he was timeless and cosmopolitan. But Babbitt failed to recognize that as Buddha was only a teacher and not a savior, he could not give the cosmopolitan element a popular depth or even a cultural base.

In his last years, in the midst of translating the *Dhammapada*, Babbitt transformed to his own satisfaction a humanistic mediation into the remoter, more private realm of meditation. He did not renounce or abandon his claims for the values of humanism in making a culture, but they became less pressing. Possibly only in a late hour did he realize that if he were to find a humanistic equivalent to grace that it would, like grace, have inherently exclusive properties that could in no way be given amplification into the broader reaches of culture.

In the attempts to formulate a cultural dimension for humanism, he depended upon an adjudicative posture, a mediating force of will that could only be individual and that was in a social frame fictive or at best tenuous, especially in American society, where the "inner life" itself seemed but the shadow of stale religious proprieties. Babbitt's eclectic transcultural norms rendered humanism even more abstruse than it had appeared in the confines of a native American culture. Going far beyond the parochial standards of an American humanism, Babbitt's hope of combining the geniuses of culture reflected an overestimation of the force of personalities, albeit historically powerful ones, as continually effective cultural delineators. The East was more than the sum of Buddha and Confucius, Mencius and Lao-tzu, as the West was more than that of Aristotle and Kant, Bacon and Darwin, Rousseau and Robespierre.

6. Limiting Democracy
Humanism in a Political Context

Si vero populus plurimum potest omniaque eius arbitrio
reguntur, dicitur illa libertas, est vero licentia.

> Cicero, *De Re Publica*

Mettre la loi au-dessus de l'homme est un problème en
politique que je compare à celui de la quadrature du cercle
en geométrie. Résolvez bien ce problème; et le gouverne-
ment fondé sur cette solution sera bon et sans abus. Mais
jusque-là soyez sûrs qu' où vous croirez faire regner les lois,
ce seront les hommes qui regneront.

> Rousseau, *Considération sur le Gouvernement de Pologne*

The consolidation of capital in the American economy following
the Civil War initiated a prolonged social crisis. Financial pan-
ics and nationwide depressions from 1869 to 1898 buffeted
an economy that survived not in spite of inherent instabilities but
because those instabilities allowed growth and, under a few shrewd
hands, direction.

The most dramatic response to corporate expansion came from
the laboring classes that made it possible. The Chicago Haymarket
Riots of 1886, followed by a general strike of white and black labor in
New Orleans; the 1892 strike against Carnegie's Homestead and one
in 1894 against the Pullman Company—such incidents were but the
most sensational proof that workers, too, were moving toward a kind
of corporate power. In their reactive strength, many immigrant laborers from Europe espoused a political radicalism that repeatedly
figured in conservative minds as a vague portent of another civil war,
this time on class lines. In the 1880s and 1890s, the centralization of
federal power to regulate the chaotic economy came as part of a
general tendency to massive organization.

In collegiate education, too, there was a move toward collective
order. President Eliot's ethic of training for service and power was a
formula for direct accommodation of newly rising social and industrial conglomerates. Nowhere was the academic thrust better characterized than in an 1886 oration at Harvard Law School. The speaker

was Oliver Wendell Holmes, Jr., and his theme was "The Use of Law Schools":

> I know of no teachers so powerful and persuasive as the little army of specialists. . . . they furnish in the intellectual world a perfect type of the union of democracy with discipline. . . . Perhaps in America . . . we need specialists even more than we do civilized men. Civilized men who are nothing else are a little apt to think that they cannot breathe the American atmosphere.[1]

The breathing became easier so far as each group interest, bloc, or economic faction influenced and shaped the political process. At no time was the accommodating breadth of the party system more apparent than in the electoral campaign of 1912 when conservative, liberal and progressive, and socialist philosophies competed. A volatile, experimental progressivism, shaped in the rhetoric of Theodore Roosevelt and Woodrow Wilson, emerged to form a consensus.

But the recurrence of familiar plagues—depressions in 1913 and 1919 and the upsurge of a militant unionism among laborers (some overtly revolutionary)—reasserted a challenge to traditional democratic assumptions. Although America's commercial expansion abroad and participation in the Great War had given the public a nationalistic optimism and ideological fervor, in 1919 the nation's attention turned broodingly inward upon domestic turmoils following Germany's defeat.

This overview, brief and necessarily incomplete, of the American society and its economy between two great wars may serve to frame the essential political issues for Babbitt's humanism, the preservation of constitutional constraints upon an expansive democracy, and the survival of the aristocratic principle of leadership. Babbitt's view rested upon a dualistic conception of the state that was derived ultimately from Plato's *Republic*: the state is man writ large and so may be said to have a higher and a lower self. The American Constitution, embodied institutionally, had long served as an indispensable check upon the undifferentiated popular will, but could it survive the transformations that rapid industrialization and an upsurgent populism had produced in little more than a generation? Retrospectively, the question now seems idle, but in the epoch of the Great War it was a protracted and nagging concern to many men other than Irving Babbitt.

It was at that time that Babbitt was composing his essays on democracy. In spite of its seers, Eliot and Holmes, Harvard retained men of retrograde sentiments going back to or beyond the genteel era.

Theodore Roosevelt could rightly complain to his friend Barrett Wendell, professor of English, that Harvard was incurably provincial. Wendell, a sympathetic biographer of Cotton Mather, had done his share to keep it so, being proud, as he said, never to have uttered a liberal sentiment in his life. Like Henry Adams, one-time professor of history, Wendell worried over the seemingly inborn inconsequence of the Boston Brahmins, many of whom still had chairs at Harvard in the progressive age.

Babbitt, outside of the patrician class and unable to savor its moody provincialism, undertook to bolster the political efficacy of the veto power that was dear to its conservatism. He would refurbish the long-hallowed tradition of judicial restraint and insist that democracy worked only within strictly constitutional limits. But rather than accept this view as conservative or reactionary, he insisted that it was the only true liberalism.

"If philosophy means anything different from a practical sagacity in viewing the facts of human nature, we should hesitate to call ourselves philosophers." Babbitt wrote.[2] He was unable to employ this sagacity to promote a humanist culture. There seemed to be no discernible social base for the claims of what was an essentially private experience; the *via media* of humanistic measure and selectivity tended irresistibly toward a withdrawal into a *vita contemplativa*. Yet, as a stalwart advocate of Aristotle, Babbitt took in earnest the view that humankind belonged in the polis. Committed to the modern experiment, the humanist was necessarily a political being.

Babbitt's politics, far more than his views on education, aesthetics, or culture, though related to them all, reflected his sense of a sustained crisis through the early twentieth century. He observed the drift of nations to imperialism and war, intermittent with economic collapse and social revolution: "So far as I have any vision of the future at all, it is one of frightful social convulsions brought about by the present materialism and childish illusions as to the real facts of human nature. *Bella, horrida bella!* Only, I have a special dislike for these lurid speculations as to the future of society."[3]

His polis, the genteel Cambridge, was, if we credit the biased testimony of Santayana, drearily respectable. Harvard, wrote Henry James in 1904, was monastic: "A new and higher price, in American conditions, is attaching to the cloister, literally—the place inaccessible (to put it most pertinently) to the shout of the newspaper, the place to perambulate, the place to think, apart from the crowd."[4] But Babbitt sensed crisis well within and far beyond the eremitic confines of the Yard. Higher education, as he had analyzed it, had become a workshop of apprentices enlisted on behalf of some of the most dangerous illusions of the age.

His writings and lectures were attempts to indicate historical and contemporaneous sophisms and to draw lines of battle against them. Early aware that success in the first task did not ensure it in the second, Babbitt was haunted by the fate of the Pratyeka-buddhas, men who were somehow doomed to attain insight in an age when it could not be imparted to others. "A critic of today would have to play the part of the pratyeka-buddha," he concluded.[5] Dread of ineffectuality; resentment of the encompassing influence of materialistic science at the expense of the reflective life; most portentously, revulsion before democracy's leveling powers—these Babbitt shares with other aristocrats manqués such as Nietzsche, who was driven to question whether the elevation of human nature was any longer possible and whether its promoters, the philosophers, were not to be condemned to "play badly."[6]

Babbitt's central political criticism was directed to the bad performance of American democracy and whether its drift from the foundations of constitutional limitations would end in irreversible erosion under the force of a radical or direct, unlimited democracy. In constitutional constraints, he said, "we probably have the best thing in the world," but democracy free of constraints "as all thinkers of any penetration from Plato and Aristotle down have perceived leads to the loss of liberty and finally to the rise of some form of despotism."[7] He had no faith in the workability of many hallowed nostrums of American ideological tradition that assumed a collective wisdom. Conjuring up the Socratic analogy of people needing a gadfly to keep them from sleep, he told his students: "Mankind as a whole never wakes up and stops dreaming but it at least turns occasionally in its sleep. The illusions of the past age become absolute for the present, but with a minority good sense never goes out of fashion."[8]

His support of constitutional democracy was founded on a belief that it provided institutional checks upon the occasional popular enthrallment with flattering illusions and that by these checks the minority of "good sense" would find spokesmen. He was a tacit partisan of the Tory camp that believed the people sometimes needed to be rescued from themselves. Meanwhile, the spectral eminence of men like William Jennings Bryan, the Democratic presidential nominee in 1896, 1900, and 1908, and the socialist Eugene Debs, who ran in 1912, convinced him that the sensible minority or saving remnant might not be sufficiently powerful or authoritative to resist the radical democracy that such men threatened to impose.

There are three main approaches to the democratic crisis as Babbitt analyzed it: first, a psychological assessment of democracy as a precondition for the operation of romantic illusions; second, a review of America's historical implementation of democracy in its limited and direct forms; third, attacks upon contemporary manifestations of direct democracy. Babbitt himself did not make such distinctions. He wrote, as he lectured, discursively, revealing his sense of intimate interplay between past and present, the one fortifying or condemning the other, and both reinforcing some abstract dictum to emphasize an abiding truth about human nature. As a scion of his age, he did not make clear distinctions between philosophy and psychology. As a dualist, he set himself the task of affirming the human law above the natural, but his writings indicate subtle, inextricable comminglings of the two in operation.

Babbitt thought that people wished to be deceived by flattery about their innate virtues so that they might avoid submission to the necessarily rigorous discipline of the human law, the law of self-control, the curb of reason and will upon impulse. Probably no one in history fulfilled this wish for deception better than Rousseau:

> Perhaps no one has ever surpassed Rousseau . . . in the art of . . . giving to moral indolence a semblance of profound philosophy.[9] We can scarcely form any adequate conception today of the daemonic charm that Rousseau's admonishing call to nature and originality, to renewal and rejuvenation, exercised upon his immediate contemporaries.[10]

But Babbitt's conviction that the romantic temperament inhered in everyone, so that the appeal of Rousseau as its most effective proponent was an abiding danger, belied the latter claim. Rousseau had contemporaries in every age; all people were, in fact, romanticists insofar as they were subject to the natural law of impulse.

The basic distinction making Rousseau the romanticist par excellence was his eloquent denial of any other but the natural law. Among an extensive store of references, none recurred more frequently in Babbitt's writing than Rousseau's "confession" that his head and heart did not seem to belong to the same individual. Rousseau's political implication was that people and society could live on terms of the one only at the expense of the other. Scarcely less often, Babbitt cited Rousseau's "the man who thinks is a depraved animal" as indicative of Jean-Jacques's preference in this dualism. It was Babbitt's intent as a polemicist to revert repeatedly to these incendiary pronouncements as though they had telltale conclusiveness. To be sure, that is exactly how he regarded them. They were not wrenched from a context but singularly sufficed in themselves as a context, that is, for Babbitt's own dualistic construct. They were the essence of the man, a pithy summation of the main direction of his arguments. Following Taine, whom he once scored for a "dry and mechanical intellectual habit," Babbitt assessed Rousseau's works as a logical whole, a unified impulsive impressionism.[11]

The centrality of Rousseau Babbitt based not merely on a sense of his historical influence nor on the lasting appeal in much that he wrote. Either might have been easily documented. Rather, it was that Rousseau employed, like Babbitt, the dualistic mode and exploited dramatically the implied tensions between head and heart, civilization and nature, the solitary idyll and the decadent salon. He did not originate these dualities but, in Madame de Staël's words, set them afire. Babbitt was convinced that Rousseau's fires were as unabated in the twentieth century as they had been at the close of the eighteenth. To make the world safe for Wilsonian democracy, for example, would entail the same illusions and ultimate barbarisms as to make it safe for Jacobinical republicanism.

The ironic common ground that Babbitt shared with his adversary was an outraged sense of standing alone against an age of corrupted standards and false ideals. The ones that Babbitt fought were, in altered form, the ones that Rousseau had enthroned. Their most succinct formulation came in Rousseau's discourse on inequality. There he argued for a return, not to nature, but to what he conceived to be "the natural man." Rousseau felt that civilization (à la parisienne) had imposed false norms, obligations, proprieties, and ambitions upon people by creating artificial relations among them: divisions of labor, rights of property, privileges of class. Law itself was an artifice. The proper basis for human association was equality; the cohesive emotion to maintain it was pity.[12] A natural goodness among human beings would perpetuate individual liberty without compromise or competition.

Rousseau vaguely presupposed a perfectibility in human nature from which to condemn social inequality. That is, society tended to create standards that obliged the individual to live only by approval from peers and so hampered innate development. Thus a primitive society would achieve "a fitting medium between the indolence of the primitive state and the petulant activity of our conceit."[13] Babbitt contended that Rousseau had in effect created a new religion, "a new set of myths that have, in their control of the human imagination, succeeded in no small measure to the old theology." Pity and sympathy as means of recovery from man's fall from nature were "a sort of parody of Christian charity."[14]

Rousseau took this "parody" further. Against the individualistic primitivism of the *Discours*, his *Contrat social* posited an opposite extreme in the conception of a general will (*volonté générale*) to which every member of society would be subordinated. This ultimate source of sanction was not a collectivized expression of divine right but in itself the only right. Rousseau's popular will was thus a subrational parody of divine will. In making a religion of state in which all as citizens had their civic faith, he adumbrated not only a modern secular patriotism but totalitarianism as well. Any denial of personal liberties, such as were to flourish in the crude, pitiful society of the *Discours*, could be made in the name of the people.[15]

To Babbitt, the two seemingly irreconcilable postulates of Rousseau's politics were logically connected expressions of direct democracy: the anarchy of the one was a precondition for the dictatorship of the other. Historically, it appeared, social chaos always portended tyranny, but the worst tyranny would be imposed not on the basis of mere naked power as in the eras of sovereign kingship but under the sophistical guise of popular will. It was no paradox to Babbitt that Rousseau, who admitted he could find no median between all and nothing, was himself unable to accommodate society. His paranoiac retreat to the Île de Saint-Pierre signaled the humanitarian's inability to live out his own illusions.[16]

But the sentimentalist's flattery of the populace into the belief in its unlimited virtue (*pitié*) and unlimited power (*volonté*) invariably set the stage for his successors, the utilitarian manipulators and the Machiavellians. Behind the ethic of pity and sympathy that Rousseau and Shaftesbury espoused came the cynical ethic of selfishness and exploitation propounded by Hobbes and Mandeville. So far as they deduced a general good from the mutual cancellations of vices among individuals, they anticipated both Rousseau's view of civilization as the corruptor of humanity and his espousal of a benign collectivism.

Babbitt found "the tendency to make of society the universal scapegoat . . . only one aspect of the assumption that because man is partly subject to the natural law he is entirely subject to it."[17] He addressed himself not to aspects but to the stylistic effect of the whole. He did not attempt to refute Rousseau point by point, nor did his citation of isolated statements even begin to serve such an end. Sophisticated and adroit, Rousseau was capable of alternating an intensely emotive apologia (as in his *Confessions* and *Rousseau, Juge de Jean-Jacques*) with an abstract, unemotional dialectic (the *Contrat so-*

cial). He could appeal to head and heart, but consistently his intent resided in what he called his "moral instinct" or what Babbitt called his "idyllic imagination," which never ceased to create artificial paradises.[18] By abstracting Rousseau's imagination to a prototype and by underpinning this abstraction with imputedly exemplary quotations, Babbitt shaped Rousseau into what Karl Jaspers has called "the paradigmatic individual," one who exerts a universal appeal upon the basis of a wholly transforming insight.[19] Unlike Jaspers's examples, however—Buddha, Confucius, Socrates—Rousseau appealed to no higher authority than the claims of his own temperament, to his "moral instinct" as he termed it in high-minded moments.[20] So far as he quickened his readers' sense of utopian illusion, of a false transcendence of their dualistic nature in the name of communal sympathy or common will, Rousseau became the spokesman of radical democracy.

The effect of primitivistic pleading for the natural goodness of humankind against the unnatural artifices of convention was to incite class warfare, to set the presumed virtues of the less privileged against the presumed vices of the more. Babbitt was quick to note the psychic inversions that Rousseau's political romanticism manifested: that the abolition of all self- or socially imposed constraints in the name of fraternal love culminated in class strife or, beyond that, in international war. Rousseau's contract proscribed intolerance but condemned to death or exile all citizens who did not act according to the civic creed. Not coincidentally, Robespierre's Age of Reason dissolved into the Reign of Terror. The fondness of sentimental and utilitarian humanitarians for "all kinds of easy short cuts to heaven which do away with the need of discipline and concentration" guaranteed some kind of hellishness on earth.[21] Sure that one could not overestimate Rousseau's "subtle psychic indolence" and that his exhortations to attend to one's "nature" would never fail to persuade one's will to self-deception, Babbitt reminded his students: "Those of you romantic in sympathy and disquieted by . . . attacks on romanticism . . . may be consoled by the reflection how deep-rooted romanticism is in human nature." Here was the psychological basis for Babbitt's attack upon direct democracy; no other form of government was so certain to perpetuate the somnolent illusions of the general will: "Man is not a thinker but a dreamer and when he does think he is likely to put his thoughts in the service of his imaginative illusions. . . . The future of romanticism seems to me assured by the fact that very many people can always be counted upon to remain children all their lives."[22]

He implied that there would always be more than these "very

many" to endanger society, and the danger was greatest in a democracy, which would supply implementations and rationales for the activation of popular impulses. Hence, his *Democracy and Leadership*, written as "a defense of the veto power," was "devoted to the most unpopular of tasks."[23] This veto power was, of course, the political expression of a humanistic check upon temperament. It was a part of a person's ineradicable moral sense. Unable to verify its force or even its existence beyond his own experience, Babbitt affirmed the check as an exercise of will, "one of the immediate data of consciousness" that served as an imperative upon conduct.[24] He was not content simply to refer to the "familiar oracle of his daimon" even though, like the Socratic oracle, his inner check was always a hindrance, never an incitement to action, and beyond rational analysis.[25] Socrates' oracle was idiosyncratic (at least, he never claimed it was otherwise), but Babbitt insisted his own was an integer of human experience. Indisposed to paradox, he yet maintained that one paradox fundamental to life was that one's willed negation of impulsive thought and conduct might be the source of true affirmation, that is, of one's distinctive power of control over oneself.[26] Presuming himself a realist, Babbitt acknowledged that few people ever exercised that will and that most thereby forfeited rights to self-government. No democrat, he meant an aristocracy when espousing "limited democracy" or at least "the recognition in some form of the aristocratic principle."[27] This form was perhaps best indicated in one of his favorite Buddhist proverbs: a person who conquers the self is greater than one who conquers millions of others. But where was a political context for this self-conqueror? Babbitt's attempt to answer this question came through appeals to the authority of the Confucian Analects and the works of Edmund Burke.

In Babbitt's conception, Confucian ethics were the oriental complement of the Aristotelian, but with the critical difference that in the former there was a stress upon humility as a check upon self-reliance and, in the aggregate, upon popular will. Like Aristotle, Confucius placed mediatory virtues in a social setting; his teachings concerned not merely the individual of breeding but such a person's power to influence and regulate the masses. Babbitt's claim that "not justice in the abstract but the just man" or "man of character" was the only security for society was inspired by the Confucian keynote of exemplification.[28] As a check upon the democrat's belief in the divinity of numbers, Babbitt posed a basically Confucian model in finding "here and there a person who is worthy of respect and occasionally one who is worthy of reverence."[29]

For Babbitt, Confucius himself was an exemplar in fulfilling the potential of a nonreligious cultural mediator, having aspired "at most to be the channel through which the moral experience of his race . . . should be conveyed to the present and future; in his own words, he was not a creator but a transmitter." The Confucian influence in China and beyond, embodying the power of an individual's humanism over nearly twenty-five centuries, seemed "to offer more warrant than anything in our Occidental experience for the belief that man may after all be a reasonable animal."[30] Babbitt found that belief so shaken in the midst of the World War that the West appeared to him to have no immediate remedy for its deterioration. Against a spiritual crisis greater than any Wilson could resolve at Versailles, Babbitt found himself "trying to recover my respect for human nature at present by immersing myself in the sages of the Far East—for the moment Confucius and Mencius. No one ever had a firmer faith in the final triumph of moral causes than these old boys."[31] By contrast to the hierarchic demands of Confucius, the American program to make the world safe for modern democracy represented not the triumph of a moral cause but its debauchment.

In spite of the appeal of the oriental tradition, Babbitt recognized that much of the outer conventional strength of Confucian ethics betrayed a debilitating tendency to decline from spirit into mere letter, much in the way that Catholicism in the nineteenth century had degenerated into reactionary claims to papal infallibility. So far as the present could be "held in a perpetual spiritual mortmain by the past," it would be rendered passive and immobile.[32] There was a similar passivity in the model Confucian ruler who was said to rule wisely in practicing nothing but self-contemplation. Babbitt was willing to concede that tradition, even one of Confucian humanism, might too readily paralyze behavior and nullify the importance of individual will.

He stopped short of an Emersonian antinomianism. Seeking to find a proper balance to oriental passivity, Babbitt found considerable merit in the Platonic republic where only wise men could become kings and in which society was strictly stratified according to the mental capacity of its members. But Plato's antidemocratic bias was too rigid, too theocratically constrictive to satisfy Babbitt's jealous and wholly American regard for the ultimate autonomy of the individual. He found Aristotle likewise deficient in appreciation of individual freedom even though Aristotle's attention to constitutional order and adherence to law evinced as an implicit criticism of direct democracy "a startling relevance to existing conditions."[33]

For a sound individualism and a critical sense of immediacy, Babbitt turned to the redoubtable foe of Rousseau, Edmund Burke. It was Burke who had argued most sensibly for an imaginative balance between the claims of tradition and those of the passing hour, between the abiding oneness of the state's ethical ideals and the multiplicity of immediate problems. Burke reasoned that a society's genuine leaders appreciated and interrelated both. He argued, and Babbitt concurred, that "the wisdom of life consists in an imaginative assumption of the experience of the past in such a fashion as to bring it to bear as a living force upon the present."[34] Further, Burke upheld one of Babbitt's tactical notions, that of concord between religion and humanism. In Burke's words, civilization depended upon "the spirit of religion and the spirit of a gentleman."[35] Partly for the sake of political convenience, Babbitt, like his British model, did not ask under what conditions these two spirits might be fundamentally in opposition, as they had been in the early Italian Renaissance.

Burke was not an apologist for the nobility per se. As a Whig, he forwarded the bourgeois idea of a "natural aristocracy," of leadership deserved not by privilege but by "shows of wisdom and virtue."[36] Unlike the Confucian Orient, the West underwent constant changes in status and power; for change to be wisely guided, there had to be maintenance of order and constitutional, traditionally based processes. Without them, any change might prove too sudden and chaotic. It was all in the difference between 1688 and 1789 or, no less accurately, between 1776 and 1789. The English and American revolutions were based upon gradually realized constitutional rights, whereas the French revealed a people's capacity for precipitous and extravagant political claims, not only as citizens but as scions, or, in Babbitt's view, children of Rousseau.

Ultimately, Babbitt found he had to fault the soundness of Burke's political theory, but he did so on unfair grounds. Burke had underestimated the subversive force of humanitarianism in England; he was almost too medieval in his view of an organically stable, divinely directed society to comprehend the impact not only of sentimentalists like Shaftesbury or Rousseau but the more fateful utilitarianism that burgeoned in nineteenth-century industrialization. Babbitt judged Burke's "psychology" obscurantist because it was not that of "the great urban masses."[37] It was as though Babbitt wanted to discredit Burke's theistically directed society because it had not withstood the man-directed utilitarian society of the Victorian age, an age that presupposed human perfectibility while relegating deity to the role of shadowy spectator. But to discount Burke's god-in-nature, Babbitt had to weaken his own support for Burke's "spirit of religion and the spirit of a gentleman" so as to make religion a mere institutional bulwark for the courtly humanist to revert to in the face of the modern humanitarian menace. There was, besides, no inherent conflict between Burke's society and, say, Bentham's, particularly insofar as utilitarianism would reinforce its opposite, the human sense of ulterior purpose.[38] Babbitt's real protest seemed to be based upon an awareness that, lacking a countervailing power such as Burke's theism, his own anthropocentric humanism could not resist the sway of an atheistic gospel of progress in which life would become "an infinite and indefinite expansion of wonder and curiosity."[39]

Babbitt ascribed Burke's doctrinal strengths and weaknesses partly to his British character. Burke was representative in his dislike of abstract formulas and phrases, in his defense of party, and in his denunciation of any breach with the past—the latter being a major factor in his violent hatred of French revolutionaries. The hazard to such conservatism had proven to lie in what Burke called "the unalterable perseverance in the wisdom of prejudice" that he thought so valuable to the British but that Babbitt feared would tend toward a "Chinese immobility."[40] As much as he envied Burke's rock-bedded conservative prejudice for tradition, Babbitt had to believe that he could do without it. Indeed, he disavowed any adherence to an American past simply because he found it not sufficiently sound. Unlike the stereotypic conservative who fears the future for the sake of a cherished, often mythical past, he was alarmed *because* of the past, because the constitutional restraints of the American government had, he felt, too effective a foe in the ideologies of a wayward popular will.

Babbitt documented his skepticism about American democracy in a highly selective view of the national history. During a New Hampshire summer of 1919, he took notes for a book he intended to call "Democracy and Imperialism."[41] At that time, he wrote More, "I have been reflecting a good deal on the psychology of Thomas Jefferson. It seems to me to have a good deal in common with that of Woodrow Wilson."[42] There was no little contempt behind the neutral tone of the comparison. It was the greater in that 1919 was a year of prolonged nationwide labor agitation and sensational advertisements of syndicalist radicalism. Keeping his usual attention to the ideational or psychological basis of conduct, Babbitt quickly traced the immediate turbulence to Jefferson.

With the father of the Declaration of Independence centrally in mind, Babbitt noted that "declamation about liberty," which was becoming the hallmark of modern politics, would have to be succeeded by a "Socratic period of strenuous definition about liberty or we shall lose our liberties."[43] He reasoned that much of the historical protest in the name of liberty had been based upon an abuse of "the pursuit of happiness": "We have interpreted this to mean the pursuit of pleasure—and indeed we have the authority of the author of the phrase itself," for Jefferson once confessed himself an Epicurean.[44] But Jefferson had failed to take account of the pursuit of power that could fall under the same rubric.

Babbitt's criticisms of Jefferson partly rested, as did those of Henry Adams and Theodore Roosevelt, upon his character. Roosevelt and Adams scorned the president's apparent femininity and vacillation in policy insofar as these traits eroded governmental authority. Adams especially delighted in the paradox by which "the Moses of Democracy" gained monarchic powers and as "the apostle of peace" embarked the nation upon a disastrous war.[45] Applying his Rousseauist touchstone, Babbitt rejected any such paradox and contended that Jefferson's sentimental humanitarianism produced a monarchic imperialist as surely as Rousseau had produced Robespierre and Napoleon. In Jefferson, Babbitt found the embodiment of his old maxim that "any point of view works out into an ironical contradiction of its own principle, unless it is humanized through being tempered by its opposite."[46]

His reading notes on Jefferson enforced this conception of an American Rousseauist. From an unsympathetic biography, Babbitt recorded testimony of Jefferson's youthful "mood of dreamy virtue"; his "visionary tendency"; his "always moving and feeling with the huge multitude"; and his gazing "with instinctive confidence over the sea of ignorant but countless faces upturned towards himself."[47] Having these characterizations at hand, Babbitt felt no need for a rounded estimate. Moreover, he could impute to Jefferson a Jacobinical streak; Jefferson had called for a revolution every twenty years and had said that tyrant's blood was necessary to water the tree of liberty. Such a tree, like the Norwegian firs in A Tale of Two Cities would likely make a guillotine. The real tyranny of the twentieth century, Babbitt was convinced, would come from a source that Jefferson had never considered—the general will.

Lacking a historian's interest in Jefferson's policies and the breadth of his political philosophy, Babbitt, just as he ignored Rousseau's recommendation of an elective aristocracy under the social contract, gave no heed to Jefferson's espousal of an educated elite (Burke's "natural aristocracy" was the term he used) to serve as an enlightened governmental bureaucracy. Instead, he concentrated on Jeffersonian liberty as a fundamental contradiction to the unionist liberty whose champions he found in Washington, Marshall, and Lincoln. Basically, it was a contest between the democrat's insistence upon individual rights and the unionist's adherence to constitutionally guided order. This dualistic construct of the national history was, to be sure, a transparent restatement of Babbitt's scheme of contention between the "higher or permanent" and the "ordinary" selves. He alleged that the truly "irrepressible conflict" in America's history lay in the ambiguity of its "experiment with democracy," and, as it was irrepressible, it would have to be "fought to a conclusion."[48]

In his omission of Hamilton, the most consistent of Jefferson's opponents, it was clear that the terms of the conflict that Babbitt foresaw were remote from the progressivism of his age. Against the Jeffersonian progressives—Bryan, Wilson, Josephus Daniels, and the Southern Bourbons—Hamilton stood as the darling of the "nationalists"—Lodge, Croly, Beveridge, and Roosevelt. Babbitt gave no allegiance to the latter camp because he distrusted the motives behind their reliance upon increased centralization of government. In his own time he saw realized the antinomy that Burke had noted: a government could be made to work easily when conceived as an authority or ultimate source of power; conversely, liberty could be effected simply by abolition of all controls. But a free government could come only when there was a delicate balance of the two polarities, and it required for its perpetuation "a sagacious, powerful and combining mind."[49] Roosevelt, Babbitt was certain, had no such mind because his essential concern was accretion of governmental, especially executive, license. That men like Croly and Roosevelt could rationalize Hamiltonian means by pretending to Jeffersonian ends was a sophistry that did not occur to Babbitt, yet it indicated the bond he detected between "idealistic" and "realistic" humanitarians. The latter were more likely to succeed in any contest with their apparent opponents, because they could resort unabashedly to naked shows of force: "A formidable mass of evidence has been accumulating (the Great War was for many a convincing demonstration) that, in the natural man as he exists in the real world and not in some romantic dreamland, the will to power is more than a match for the will to service."[50]

Caught in any political contest between these wills, the decorum of the humanistic "higher will" would prove ineffectual unless it were institutionally buttressed. Babbitt had witnessed from his youth the passing of the Whiggish concept that limited executive power to administration. Even the presidency of Grover Cleveland, whom he admired as a sober constitutionalist (and a stubborn foe of labor strikes), had been tinged by imperialist jingo—a practice that was amplified greatly under Roosevelt and Wilson. Both the Machiavellian and sentimental idealist had proven unscrupulous in expanding executive privilege. Wilson's claim, in the 1912 presidential campaign, that the president was the true representative of the people as the nationally elected officeholder, increased Babbitt's apprehension as to the outcome of the irrepressible conflict. The presidency was too likely to become the expedient tool of direct democracy. The moral indolence of the public would tend to develop in it "fanatical devotion" to "some leader who offers them nostrums and curealls" together with "corollary denunciations of a gang of traitors."[51] Most executives, especially in recent times, seemed unable to resist this invitation to demagoguery.

The exception making the rule, according to Babbitt, was Lincoln. But having dismissed any similarities between the democracy of Jefferson and that of the mythic emancipator as "peripheral overlappings," he could find as the highest point for commending Lincoln only his "element of judicial control" and "a profound conception of the role of the courts in maintaining free institutions. The man who has studied the real Lincoln does not find it easy to imagine him advocating the recall of judicial decisions."[52]

In the Supreme Court's enforcement of the Constitution Babbitt found the surest agency for a limited democracy. The Court, as well as but far more than the Senate, represented "the higher or permanent self of the state."[53] It was the Confucian arbiter that preserved order and tradition, and the Burkean guarantor against absolutism from either the populace or its minions in executive and legislative branches.

Babbitt was by no means alone in extolling the checks of the court upon "the immediate will of the people."[54] His colleague at Harvard in the Department of Political Science, and subsequently the president, A. Lawrence Lowell, reflected the same quite literal conservatism in writing, in 1890, that the Court's business was "to defeat the immediate will of the people."[55] A fine abstraction, however, was a tenuous reality. The Court's legitimacy as a vital check for constitutional democracy was valid only as long as the parties it constrained acknowledged its authority. Just as Lowell was confident that ultimately "the sober good sense of the people themselves" was the only control over the caprices of their collective will, so Babbitt, in the months of postwar labor agitation expressed hope that "the latent good sense of the people will rally at the last extremity."[56] But he saw no end to the working of virulent partisanships within and among nations that would render void any pious assumptions of an aggregated good sense.

Babbitt saw the class antagonisms of the postwar years as part of a fundamental conflict that emerged in the age of Victorian industrialism between the "stodgy bourgeois" and the "wild-eyed romanticist"; the handmaid of mercantile routine was an idyllic hysteria implacably set against it.[57] He was disinclined to defend the crassness of the Gradgrinds of commerce, but he gave short shrift to socialists, pre-Raphaelites, and other radicals who advocated alternatives to it. Unable to propose an activism to resolve or mitigate social conflict, he could only insist, rather lamely, that such conflict was invariably the effect and cause of the romantic presumption that good and evil were a dualism of society rather than of individual conscience and conduct.

This fallacy had begun, as had so much else that appeared askew in Babbitt's world, with Rousseau. Having given the most eloquent appeal to the natural man, Rousseau, who had condemned the French aristocracy for their arrogation of property rights that reduced the populace to dependent laborers, had his natural progeny in American radicals who damned capitalist magnates on similar grounds. Babbitt found this Rousseauism epitomized in a Boston orator's reference to John D. Rockefeller and Henry Huttleston Rogers as "ghouls and vampires in human form."[58] Had not Rousseau likened the aristocrats to wolves that ate human flesh?[59] There could be no wonder, then, that Rousseau's discourse on inequality "should still be a direct source of inspiration to the bomb-throwing anarchist."[60]

Although it was Rousseau who found people in chains, it was Marx who exhorted them to throw off those chains. Marx figured so little in Babbitt's argument that it is clear he underestimated a decisive intellectual force in modern political thought. There is no evidence that he ever read Marx or his explicators, but he felt he had exposed the central flaw in Marxism: the materialistic value of labor, a fallacy "already known in ancient China and refuted by Mencius."[61] "It is both proper and inevitable that the man who works with his mind should hold sway over the man who works with his hands."[62] Any quantitative view of labor obliterated a Socratic distinction that anteceded differences of class or economic power.

Horrified contempt kept Babbitt from any support for labor unions. He was certain that their leaders harbored Jacobinical intents. During the depression that followed World War I, he observed: "Labor wishes to escape work and to be free from control while exercising despotic sway over others. This is the tyrant's dream."[63] He was particularly critical of Woodrow Wilson's deference to labor unions, the power of which revealed "a form of the instinct of domination so full of menace to free institutions that, rather than submit to it, a genuine statesman would have died in his tracks."[64] Strangely, Babbitt generally ignored the more leftist and violent labor bodies such as the International Workers of the World and focused his scorn upon gradualist unions like the American Federation of Labor. Making no differentiation between the ideologies or legalistic purposes of the several labor movements, he seemed to select his targets according to their public influence. Thus, in "the rant of Gompers and his kind" he detected the threat of "the domination of the laboring class" and tagged Gompers its own certain dictator.[65] He wrote to More in alarm over "the insolence of organized labor" but was unsure as to how it might best be checked:

> Unless it receives a pretty prompt setback, the outlook is not bright for our form of government. . . . There is of course not much hope in the politicians at Washington unless they feel the pressure of a powerful public opinion. At the present rate, the last hope for the rights of private property may be the Supreme Court, though it may not prove easy to protect its less radical members from dynamite bombs.[66]

Babbitt could neither understand nor sympathize with labor because he accorded it only one grievance, which was that the managerial and capitalist classes "have concentrated so exclusively in their mental working on the material order."[67] It was a peculiar, if not arcane, grievance to grant the unionists, and one obviously contrived out of Babbitt's own grievance toward the utilitarian's ethic of material efficiency.

Despite his fearful strictures against organized labor, Babbitt was no apologist for the managers and dynasts. His first book, composed during the initial federal prosecution of trusts, reflected the public consciousness. He was especially critical of the philanthropic activities of corporate magnates whose will to service veiled their abusive will to power. Proficient exercise of either would be dire—"a few more Harrimans and we are undone," he wrote in 1907—unless there could be a humanistic inducement to the magnates "to liberalize their own souls, in other words to get themselves rightly educated."[68] Without explaining how the liberalization of a Morgan or a Rockefeller was to come about, Babbitt seemed to presume the benign efficacy of a just paternalism. At no time did he censure the great corporations as he had the unions for showing "an instinct of domination," even though his own insight that an excess of power and doctrine breeds and partly justifies its opposite should have led him to an even-handed condemnation of abuses.

According to Babbitt, not the least point of Aristotle's pertinence to twentieth-century politics was his positing a large middle class as the basis for social stability (*Politics* 1296a). Factions were born from social and economic extremes. When Babbitt expressed faith in "the latent good sense of the people," he surely meant this mediatory class. But he was contemptuous of the professional reformers, educators, and journalists especially who came largely from that class and made humanitarian appeals to its readers and legislators. He singled out for special scorn the muckrakers who promoted notions of conspiratorial powers in industry and commerce. The essential danger in this "progressive" bias was not political or economic but psychological and ethical; it externalized issues and encouraged scapegoating: "With the help of the muckraker we are developing an almost preternatural nimbleness in dodging responsibility and shifting the burden on some individual or some other class of the community."[69] That a public broader than the laboring class could be swayed by a demagogy parading as humanitarian idealism made the need for sober leadership the more crucial.

Babbitt's hierarchic models, the Hellenic polis and the Confucian system, rested upon a concentration of virtues in leadership as the basic criterion of social health. His "limited democracy" was a transposition of this kind of hierarchy to a society of strong egalitarian proclivities. Although apprehensive, particularly during and after the World War, over working-class insurgencies, Babbitt placed all his hope for justice and temperance among those on whom society depended for direction. The Confucian assumption that justice from above would keep the populace submissive and that an upright officialdom was the true regulator of social harmony figured in his argument that the proper corrective for the evils of capitalist enterprise was to be discovered "in the moderation and magnanimity of the strong and successful, and not in any sickly sentimentalizing over the lot of the underdog." Hence, the turbulence of the postwar years was partly attributable to "an extreme psychic unrestraint" in leadership.[70] Woodrow Wilson was undoubtedly the foremost instance in his mind.

If only by implication, Babbitt had to concede the historically based

Marxist premise that a quantitative valuation of work might be as integral to a reactionary society as to the revolutionary counterforces that it engendered. The conservative's defense of property for its own sake rather than as "an almost indispensable support of personal liberty, a genuinely spiritual thing" formed an impasse with the progressive's scheme for redistribution of wealth, an impasse that Babbitt saw as endemic to the party system of a representative democracy and that might at any time intensify into class warfare.[71] Even more likely was the prospect that the society would yield to a utilitarian collectivism, that an unethical insurgency would interfuse a corrupt materialistic hierarchy. (Babbitt would not have been surprised at the rise of fascism in Germany under this very formula in the 1930s.) In anxiety over that possibility, he exclaimed in a moment of untypical melodrama: "We seem, indeed, to be witnessing in a different form the emergency faced by the early Christians. The time may come again, if indeed it has not come already, when men will be justified in asserting true freedom, even, it may be, at the cost of their lives, against the encroachments of the materialistic state."[72]

It remains unclear whom he expected to perpetrate these encroachments. Would it be the benighted plutocracy or the Jacobin labor unions or the humanitarian "uplifters" in public offices? The vagueness of his omen seemed to include them all and fittingly so, for their society offered no apparent accommodation of the leadership that Babbitt promoted in his appeals to the "just man."

Like the Confucian exemplar who practiced rulership by meditative self-restraint, Babbitt's "just man" remained a stylized figure, an "imaginative symbol."[73] His attribution of a will-to-justice to this figure hardly went far to diminish an austere privacy, a Solon-like impartiality and detachment from political partisanship. Too, Babbitt forfeited the Aristotelian presuppositions of a class of *aristoi* that ideally would be ever present in serviceable advantage to the state. This forfeit was an obligatory concession to the decline of the "genteel" political influence. (By familial right, Henry Adams had long expected that he would one day assume the presidency.) But, in stricter conformance to his idea that balance of character was at best an approximation, not an achievable goal, Babbitt also had in mind the fastidious ideal of Confucius's "manhood-at-its-best" that no political leader, however much a sage, would ever embody adequately. Through such furtive hedging from explicit partisanship, Babbitt disengaged himself from either a theoretical or programmatic reform politics. Besides, since the day of genteel reformers like Norton, Boker, Curtis, and Charles Francis Adams, the very notion of reform had become the legerdemain of sentimentalists and utili-tarians.[74]

Two prominent reform movements that Babbitt enjoyed ridiculing were prohibition and women's suffrage. His opposition to the Vol-stead Act and the Eighteenth Amendment made clear that he was neither a strict constitutionalist nor a "Puritan." Prohibition was to him a capital instance of the humanitarian's concern to meddle with other people's conduct, not to mention their taste. (It was his one point of agreement with H. L. Mencken.) His objection to the rights of women was more psychological than political. He believed that women as crusaders tended to further the most sordid kind of social conflict, that between the sexes. Himself a distant father and hus-band, Babbitt estimated that the covert danger in feminism was that it would undermine the basic unit of social order and civilization, the family:

> Certain feminine reviewers in particular remind me of a suffrag-ette at whose side I happen to be seated at a dinner party and who said when I had explained to her my point of view about women that she would "like to stick me full of pins." The time will come at the present rate when work that runs counter to the "uplift" will have no chance of getting a hearing at all. I already feel that I am printing for private circulation.[75]

Babbitt was willing to leave society to its own and fortune's ca-prices. Having demoted the authority of a popular will to nullity, he was forced to place a high stake on its leadership:

> The notion in particular that a substitute for leadership may be found in numerical majorities that are supposed to reflect the "general will" is only a pernicious conceit. In the long run de-mocracy will be judged, no less than other forms of government, by the quality of its leaders, a quality that will depend in turn on the quality of their vision.[76]

Thus, peculiarly, the people, unfit to rule themselves in a radical sense, were responsible for the appointment of an enlightened lead-ership. At the same time, Babbitt wanted to deny that there had to be an expediency of choices, that is, between an imperialist like Theo-dore Roosevelt and an idealist like Wilson. "But there is no reason why one should accept either horn of this dilemma."[77] Similarly:

> Circumstances may arise when we may esteem ourselves fortu-nate it we get the American equivalent of a Mussolini; he may be

needed to save us from the American equivalent of a Lenin. Such an emergency is *not* to be anticipated, however, unless we drift even further than we have thus far from the principles that underlie our unionist tradition.[78]

But the space between a dilemma's horns tends to be a vacuum. Babbitt's inability or unwillingness to fill it with faith in someone who represented a median between apparent extremes betrayed his passivity and his obligation to make do before the faits accomplis of political realities. Rather than lionize a hero-as-politician in the manner of Carlyle, he preferred to mark vacant time. His notion of disinterested temperate leadership required no heroism at all, but instead an improbable mixture of executive ability and judicial control. Ideally he wanted a president to act like a court justice.

As a judiciary executive, this ideal leader was properly the critic of the democracy he governed. The delicacy of the matter was that in Babbitt's stern estimation democracy was almost inherently unfit for adjustment to critical constraint: "Democracy needs the critic and yet will have none of him—a fact symbolized by the Athenian condemnation. Democracy is unable to distinguish between its friends and its flatterers and yet on this very distinction hinges its only hope of survival."[79]

It was Wilson's failure to act in a judicial manner during the wartime crisis that prompted Babbitt's despair over democratic leadership. Wilson's rationales for keeping the United States out of the war and then for engaging it in the war were alike sufficiently popular to prove to Babbitt that Americans were "the most pacifistic and the least peaceful of people."[80] Opposing Wilson's crusade for international democracy, Babbitt warned that "democracy as it is now coming to be understood is itself a form of absolutism" not qualitatively different from that against which America was fighting.[81] Wilson's idealism invited an absolutism that was, in fact, hardly distinguishable from democracy.

If a direct democracy that heralded equality and fraternity usually ended in class warfare, it followed that an internationalism on the same terms would end in a war among nations. Babbitt assessed the American entry into the war as this ideological imperialism, a logical extension of the "unwarranted meddling" that had taken the United States into war with Spain in 1898 and near war with Mexico immediately prior to the World War.[82] Recalling John Woolman's imperative of "inner stillness," Babbitt took the war as ironic proof that "no one has less inner stillness in him than the American; at the same time he

looks upon it as his mission to establish peace for the world . . .
to establish his humanitarian evangel by force among the wicked Eu-
ropeans."[83]

His prescription for restoration of inner stillness was a reiteration
of the emphasis, familiar to all his other works, on "an inner working
of some kind with reference to standards."[84] Calling for a revolution
that would be limited to the dictionary, one that would correct the
humanitarian's abuse of terms such as liberty, equality, and virtue,
Babbitt conjured up a hypothetical corps of "Socratic critics": "a
dialectical scrutiny of terms," he urged, was needed to determine
whether one's idealism was "merely some windy inflation of the
spirit, or whether it has support in the facts of human experience."[85]
So adamantly was he bound to "sane moral realism" that it is difficult
to conceive what idealism, Socratically treated, would have remained
legitimate in his eyes.[86]

To exemplify the critical spirit, he applied the Christian separation
of Caesar's things and God's to the progressivism of Bryan and Wilson and found them guilty of confusing the proprieties of the two
kingdoms in presuming their campaigns were hallowed crusades. Although he loathed Wilson, Babbitt had no fondness for his chief
adversary, Roosevelt, who was similarly prone to appropriate the
kingdom of heaven. Referring to the launching of Roosevelt's "Bull
Moose" campaign in 1912, he observed, "People who turn politics
into a religious crusade like Roosevelt's Progressive Party and sing
'Onward Christian Soldiers' may turn out to be essentially mad."[87]

But Babbitt was no less guilty of a sacrosanct air in seeking to
borrow outmoded Christian doctrine and redress it in a politically
humanistic form. When his former protégé, Stuart Sherman, en-
joined him to "remember 'the tongues of men and angels'" and that
caritas was necessary if men were to "respect the function of the will,"
Babbitt attempted this transformation:[88]

> *Caritas* means traditionally . . . not the love of man but the love of
> God and of man through God. Now that we have got rid of this
> theological conception we need to retain in some positive and
> critical form the element of truth that it contains. . . . When men
> impose the yoke of the ethical will upon their ordinary selves
> they find that they are, in so far, being drawn to a common
> centre and the *caritas* follows the union and is dependent upon
> it.[89]

Sherman's criticisms were basically political and came from his
gradual departure from the austerities of his mentor's views toward a

gospel of democratic idealism. (He characterized himself as a "conservative of the future."[90]) His cooling distance from Babbitt's attitudes, though not from Babbitt personally, enabled him to perceive some shortcomings in humanistic politics. He had never shared Babbitt's covert elitism and was far more sensitive to the impress of events and circumstances upon character and will. During World War I, he had become an ardent supporter of Wilson, whose idealism Babbitt had always viewed with marked aversion. Sherman attributed urbanity and high intellectual merit to Wilson and believed the president disposed "to civilize the public mind and conscience."[91] He never embraced the instrumentalism of Dewey, but he envied the vigor of its youthful exponents, indicating to More his regretful feeling of being of a fading "sedentary" generation.[92] His compensatory show of enthusiasm for Wilson seemed to Babbitt a yielding to the shibboleths of the hour. As he told More, Sherman's

> declamations about the "plain people" and "never again" leave me very cold. I do not doubt that he will awaken an ecstatic response in many quarters. Personally I should prefer never to get any recognition at all than to get it by flattering the enormous humanitarian illusions of the age. Most of what now passes as democracy, involving as it does the class war and the confiscation of property, is an even worse menace to civilization than the Kaiser.[93]

While composing *Democracy and Leadership*, Babbitt expressed his ironic regret that Sherman had been "somewhat diverted of late by [his] desire to defend American idealism against the intelligentsia."[94] His defensive tone belied Sherman's assumption that in writing on modern democracy, Babbitt was evincing a "magnanimous concession to the times" and was thus "refusing to be maneuvered into 'uncompromising opposition.'"[95] Sherman praised what he hoped to be a positive temper in Babbitt's political opinions. He tried to prompt Babbitt obliquely to a public position by sarcastic criticism of More's increasingly valetudinarian absorption in Platonism. More, suggested Sherman, once freed from his arid scholarship, could "emerge as a living soul . . . if he would abandon himself to writing as a person instead of writing as a damned professor."[96]

Babbitt defended his old friend and strongly implied that he shared More's stance and political biases. When Sherman realized the chilling extent of Babbitt's disdain for the progressive trend of the democratic age and his silent disapproval of Sherman's own acceptance of it, he responded acidly. Babbitt "fears I am slipping into the gutter. The trouble with Babbitt is that, in the path he treads, there is only room for one; the rest *must* be in the gutter."[97] From the vantage of a humanitarian idealism, Sherman had come to a conclusion about his teacher similar to that of another quondam disciple, T. S. Eliot, from the point of religious orthodoxy. Babbitt's humanism was too narrowly based in scope to allow an appreciable corps of adherents beyond those that Eliot, with perhaps some irony but no malice, called "a few highly cultivated persons like Mr. Babbitt."[98]

To their mutual friend, Frank Mather, Sherman made points against Babbitt and More: "as leaders of the intellectual and literary movement at the present time," they were remote from "the actual conflict," too restricted in their interests, "remorselessly negative," and "dogmatic."[99] But Babbitt and More were not and could not be "leaders" of any sort, not even of those "Socratic critics" that Babbitt looked for to cure American democracy of its semantic ills. Of the two the more anxious for a following, Babbitt could not command it because his convictions were too narrowly congruent with his temperament. It was not merely his dogmas, Sherman believed, but a lack of "reasonable and humane temper" that rendered Babbitt ineffectual and nowhere more so than in his political prejudices.[100]

Were Sherman's charges just? To a telling extent, it seems they were. But he did not reflect that the inflexibility, negativity, and dogmatism in his former mentor were functions of Babbitt's lifelong sense of isolation within and through the humanist tradition he sought to enliven.

One of Babbitt's last letters to Sherman carried a tone that, though not compromising, was atypically concessive. It was, in fact, a résumé of some points that Sherman himself had made on the defects of Babbitt's position:

> Many Americans are getting shaky about their idealism of late; your eloquent defense of it should hearten them and gain you a considerable following. Men like More and myself, on the other hand, who take a frankly anti-humanitarian attitude condemn ourselves to a comparative isolation. You might, to be sure, if it came to a sharp break between the humanists and the humanitarians find yourself in the position of Mr. Pickwick when he tried to mediate between the two angry combatants. I do not, however, see many signs of any such development. What is more likely is a continuation of the present conflict between the idealists and the machiavellian realists or "hard guys" with the outlook for the idealists rather uncertain.[101]

What prompted Babbitt's admission to "comparative isolation"? Possibly he perceived in Sherman's criticism of More's hauteur and intransigence some remarks applicable to himself. Citing the example of Matthew Arnold, Sherman sought from his humanist elders a show of "passion for diffusing ideas," to make their copious transcultural knowledge, in Arnold's words, "efficient outside the clique of the cultivated and learned."[102] Sherman's urging, one that went totally unheeded, underscored Babbitt's need for a tactical indulgence toward the humanitarian's divine democratic average in order for the dissemination of humanist principles and values to be effective.

It was a chimerical front that Babbitt wanted to unite against the drift of modern American politics and the reform movements that were in its mainstream. Perhaps in conceding that he had condemned himself to "comparative isolation" and "uncompromising opposition" he recognized as well that it was absurd to discuss a saving remnant of just and temperate individuals. Whether a community of ethical will could be effected through a Socratic revision of terminology or by the election of a humanistically cultivated leadership to high offices, Babbitt did not say. It was against his character and the tenor of his views to presume for a moment anything in favor of the indolent multitude that would weaken his cherished anomaly—the aristocratic principle in America.

7. Babbitt's Halfway House
The Religion of Humanism

"Se fosse tutto pieno il mio dimando,"
    Rispuosi lui, "voi non sareste ancora
    De l' umana natura posto in bando.
Chè 'n la mente m' è fitta e or mi accora
    La cara e buon imagine paterna
    Di voi, quando nel mondo ad ora ad ora
M' insegnavate come l' uom s' etterna."

        Dante, *Inferno*

In his lectures entitled "The Varieties of Religious Experience," William James concluded:

> The God whom science recognizes must be a God of universal laws exclusively, a God who does a wholesale, not a retail business. He cannot accommodate his process to the convenience of individuals. The bubbles on the foam which coats a stormy sea are floating episodes, made and unmade by the forces of wind and water. Our private selves are like those bubbles; . . . their destinies weigh nothing and determine nothing in the world's irremediable currents of events.[1]

A few years after those 1902 lectures, James summarized the logic of his position. In a pluralistic universe, God was a part of the cosmic process, not its creator; he was a finite partner of the human being, working for good out of evil. Instead of passively accepting dogmas contrived in the name of an intellectualized external deity, people would now actively shape their religious values within the flux of experience.

Although he was on James's side of the Darwinian chasm that made earlier generations of believers seem, as James said, another race, Babbitt struggled to retain a sense of the old spirituality above the pragmatist's flux. At the same time he was aware that total affirmation of religious faith was impossible for him and perhaps for the modern age. As he remarked during a lecture tour, "I do not deny the sublimities of religion; . . . on the contrary, I suspect that religion is too sublime for the likes of us."[2]

James's *Religious Experience* won wide acclaim upon publication, perhaps not least because of its broad accommodation of testimony to a religious sense, the belief by which one identified oneself with a divine source. In his gentlemanly and scientific way, James would not exclude seeming lunacy or fanaticism from consideration as genuine religious experience. By sharpest contrast, Babbitt, seeking the severe sublimity of religion, found it credible only in a "vision . . . so difficult, so alien, one is tempted to say, to human nature, that one is not surprised to learn that Buddhas are rare, only five at the most in a kalpa or cosmic cycle, a period, according to Hindu computation, of something over four billion years."[3]

As for the Christian tradition of the West, Babbitt found reasons for commendation and rejection. He was contemptuous of church dogmas, particularly Catholic ones, so far as they immobilized reason and individual will, but he recognized that religious orthodoxy was an important, possibly essential factor in social stability. If the fate of cultures would be determined between Catholicism and Bolshevism, Babbitt knew where he would cast his lot.

Babbitt was a protestant skeptic in metaphysical matters; he skirted questions about immortality or afterlife simply because there were no conclusive data to affirm or deny. Here, as in his aesthetic criticism and in his view of the function of criticism itself, he seemed to owe a debt to Lessing, who, in Thomas Mann's words, made a religion of skepticism—not the Pyrrhonic skepticism of materialists, which is based solely on sense data, but the eschewing of merely speculative metaphysical propositions. Babbitt reverted to a position common to the English and French Enlightenments through which godhead receded to a respected but remote distance while the claims of human intellect pressed forward. But he endorsed neither mere religiosity nor atheism, for he believed that human beings should seek and worship some power above themselves. That seeking, that worship, he argued, necessitated a recognition of human limitations, including the capacity for evil. It was that awareness of the human potential for evil that he felt the deists had facilely denied. A humanistic acknowledgment of evil meant that before seeking to account for God, human beings had to account for themselves. This accounting was itself an almost religious process save that it had no fixed goal, no teleology beyond a continuous striving for self-mastery.

Babbitt did not willfully ignore the claims of religion. The mind with whom he enjoyed the deepest intellectual communion, Paul Elmer More's, ultimately avowed the need for religious orthodoxy beyond the tenets of anthropocentric humanism. In Anglicanism More found expression for his awe before cosmic mysteries that his intellect, highly Platonized, intuited but could not explain. Similarly, T. S. Eliot eventually embraced church authority as the only alternative against an atheistic humanitarianism on one side and reactionary despair on the other. After coming under the influence of T. E. Hulme, Eliot concluded that humanism would finally suffer romantic perversion. These apostasies enforced Babbitt's realization that humanism was on a historically narrowing margin between equally abhorrent extremes. He criticized Joubert for abandoning it in favor of neo-Jesuitical fanaticism. Even closer to home was Brunetière, who, in dismay and asperity, turned to Catholicism "simply because it seemed to him to hold out the hope of a better ordered social progress, of a more thoroughly disciplined collectivism."[4] Brunetière's use of Catholicism as a palliative for his despair over the inefficacy of individualism implied that humanism alone could not resist modern atheism or spiritual anarchism; it was itself a kind of spiritual anarchism.

Babbitt's rejection of More's intellectual and Brunetière's political motives for conversion was a part of his conviction that humanism was all the more necessary to affirm the individual's power to achieve ethical insight and religious idealism through unaided will. During his first sabbatical to France, in 1908, Babbitt had witnessed for himself the social pressures that had hardened Brunetière. With the erosion of Catholicism there, "a man is practically forced to be either a Rousseauist or a Jesuit, and a refusal to accept either horn of this dilemma is taken not as a proof of superior insight but as a lack of logical thoroughness."[5] He fought the dilemma by arguing that humanism rightly conceived was a precondition to any affirmation of a transcendent or supernatural realm. The nature of this realm, in turn, could not be "put in terms of the intellect," yet it was "something attained in this life."[6] He had no use for otherworldly schemes: "Perhaps from the point of view of the highest wisdom, every possible paradise is a fool's paradise."[7]

In his pungent sense of irony, Paul Elmer More once described Babbitt's life as "a steady growth, not in Grace, but in obedience to the unrelenting exactions of conscience and in the sense of the littleness of men protesting against the law of their own being."[8] More seemed to be hinting that by his own reasoning, Babbitt should have accepted "Grace"—it was the inductive certainty at which the humanist, acknowledging the limits of reason and will, was supposed to arrive. If humanism was only a preparation before admission of a religious absolute, it was transitional. Babbitt never dwelt upon the implication of his concession: it would have implied, if not required, conversion, an action the psychological legitimacy of which Babbitt followed Sainte-Beuve in doubting.

The intellectual break between Babbitt and More—that is, More's departure from humanism into Platonic and then Christian mysticism—came gradually in the years following More's resignation from the *Nation* in 1914. His *Platonism* (1917) revealed the closest affinity he had with Babbitt's humanism. Shortly after its publication, he wrote, "As you know, I owe my whole mental direction from what I have got from you in conversation, and some day, in the proper place, I shall state this in print."[9] It was a poignant admission, for More was already moving fully consciously and irresistibly away from the humanistic perspective that he had shared with Babbitt for nearly a generation.

In his memorial tribute to Babbitt, More recalled that when he met him at Harvard in 1892, in Lanman's Sanskrit class, he was outgrowing a youthful romanticism and becoming increasingly susceptible to the classicism that Babbitt, then only twenty-seven (a year younger than More) was already preaching: "The astonishing fact, as I look back over the years, is that he seems to have sprung up, like Minerva, fully grown and fully armed. No doubt he made vast additions to his knowledge and acquired by practice a deadly dexterity in wielding it, but there is something almost inhuman in the immobility of his central ideas."[10] In debates over the texts they were mastering, More even then, or so he recalled, "instinctively" tried to conceive of a monotheism such as became the central point for his disaffection from humanism. More remained far more impressionable in temperament and far more catholic in his reading (as his *Shelburne Essays* indicate) than Babbitt; in short, he was more intellectually flexible and amenable to a modification of ideas.

In his exposition of Platonism, More equated the humanist principle of restraint and the Socratic conscience:

> We may not know what this *daemonic* or, as I have elsewhere translated it, this *inner check* is; we may not know how and why it acts, or why it does not act, but we do know that the clarity of our spiritual perception and the assurance of our freedom depend on keeping this will to refrain distinct from any conception of the will as a positive force.[11]

This passage is crucial on several points. First, although Babbitt concurred with the equation, he was never so explicit as More about the quality of one's ignorance concerning the will to refrain. The inner check was for Socrates a voice, allowing More to infer that it was a "divine immanence"—two words fatefully absent from Babbitt's lexicon.[12] Second, More's dialectical application of the will to refrain, if it was not to be conceived as a positive power, was positive in its ends. Suspension of desire, that is, deliberation over the possible effects of satisfying that desire, brought, no matter what one's final decision might be, a happiness based on the sense of one's temperance. For Babbitt, who understood happiness in precisely this sense, the immediacy of temperance sufficed. More, however, took it as a Platonic Idea, and as such it involved in an intellectually literal way, an anagogy, a path leading the mind upward to the divine.[13] Babbitt refused to be carried up or away by ideas; he was content with the mundane but nebulous moral direction of the *Nicomachean Ethics* and "the workings of happiness according to virtue" (1100b). As for the vagaries of Platonism,

> Men who follow Plato have to spend an alarming amount of their time in explaining why they themselves are true disciples and others are not. When I think of you and Shelley and Bertrand Russell all setting up as Platonists I am troubled. To put the matter mildly Plato did not make it clear as he should have done that the proper basis for philosophy is not geometry or any other form of mathematics but common sense.[14]

Emphatic though the differences between More and Babbitt might have been according to their Platonic or Aristotelian lights, it was not the Greeks but a Nazarene who caused the decisive split. Criticizing More's manuscript of *The Christ of the New Testament* (significantly, the third volume of his *Greek Tradition*), Babbitt characterized Christ's incarnation as a "psychological truth" rather than an "experimental" or experientially valid one. More objected that he did not see

> how by taking [the Incarnation] as a psychological truth a man can be saved from acting merely as if it were a fact, and there is no solid ground for morality or religion on that basis. I do not see how we can avoid the dilemma of accepting it as a true objective fact or dealing with it, in the manner of Santayana, as a pretty bit of poetry. The middle ground is a quagmire.[15]

Thus More rejected Babbitt's claims for imaginative illusion or "psychological truth" as a cul-de-sac ensuring no higher level of truth. Babbitt, conversely and with a trace of disdain, pointed to More's presumption of a cosmic personality, an anthropomorphic metaphysics:

I remember remarking after reading one of James' books and noting his hostility to capitals that he seemed determined to live in a lower case universe. After scanning your pages and seeing how peppered they are with H's, I am a bit inclined to bring against you the opposite charge. I am especially inclined to query this extreme holiness in your reference to the deity of Plato.[16]

More ultimately found that the highest expression of this deity was Christian, but Babbitt wanted to remain with the pagan sources. He once remarked in an assault on romanticism, "Either the Platonic or the Aristotelian line of attack is justifiable. If I prefer personally the latter, it is because it does not lend itself to such subtle and baffling perversions."[17] But the point of this remark was distorted in Babbitt's recognition that Platonism had its own romanticisms. He concluded that the basic trouble was the questionable legitimacy of Platonic means in descerning the noumenal realm: "It is hard to discredit the shams without seeming to discredit at the same time genuine religious meditation." But he seemed almost to discredit even meditation when he proceeded to attack as a "usurpation of the intellect" the Platonic tendency "to project the idea of personality into the region of the infinite and the eternal."[18]

Babbitt's notion of religion, then, was something other than an Arminian's celebration of will, for the will, like the intellect and the imagination, was earthbound. Deity, like immortality, was a postulate beyond anyone's intellectual honesty; when one employed "sufficient psychological tact," these terms would be found "neither true nor false but meaningless or at any rate insoluble with our existing faculties."[19] By this humanist skepticism, one similar to Hume's attack upon "natural religion," Babbitt virtually dismissed the claims of faith.

But the issue was more than epistemological. Babbitt was alarmed at More's tendency "to abandon the Socratic *autarkeia* in favor of dogmatic and revealed religion." While granting somewhat gratuitously that belief in revealed religion was "an eminently respectable position," he knew that in More it meant a defection from humanism: "it seems in fact to involve a change of base line, and when a man at your age changes his base line, the effect is always a bit disquieting."[20] After thirty years of close rapport, Babbitt was so disquieted that he could reproach More only in the third person: "One is beginning at all events to abandon the positive and critical attitude toward life in favor of dogma and revealed religion. I am at least as anxious as you are to get rid of mere metaphysics but what I would substitute is not theology but psychology."[21] As so often before, there was also a tactical motif:

> As a result of your apparent refusal to recognize any valid intermediary between the crude anthropomorphism of the Nicaean and Chalcedonian formulae and mere modernism, joined to your tendency to present Aristotle as the evil genius of occidental philosophy, effective cooperation between us is going to become more difficult.[22]

It was exactly in the inconsistency between Aristotle's psychology and his theology that More rested his case. A metaphysic without purpose or personality abrogated the point of any purposeful effort by man. For his part, he could accept as compatible what Babbitt wanted to keep separate—the "mysterious background" of "central peace" and a theistic personality. "I see no profit in peering into the ultimate void; I suspect that void is a pure creation of the *intellectus sibi permissus.*"[23]

Babbitt escaped the charge by disdaining to peer into any void. In a sense, his difference with More can fairly be distinguished as one of civilization versus salvation in that Babbitt consistently maintained his focus on immediate problems and willed resolutions of them within and for human life. He vaunted the catholicity of humanism as a common ground for people of religious differences, and he even questioned the pertinence of supernatural religion to humanist culture. Although Christian ethics had much in common with humanism, "Did not the highest civilization of all time, that of Periclean Athens, develop four hundred years *before* Christian revelation?"[24] The humanist faith in the potential of great human beings had, therefore, a corollary faith in the culture they could create without theistic aids. That Babbitt sometimes obscured the boundaries of religious and cultural volition was evident when he cited More as among those who were compelled "to fall back upon the traditional evidence of The Will's existence," whereas "I have merely to look within myself to know that it is."[25]

Wherever between James's "lower case" and More's capital universe the humanist will resided, Babbitt yielded ground to More following their exchange by granting that humanism did not suffice in itself, that its position between the natural or unregenerate and the spiritually whole person was not autonomous and static but dynamic. "I admit," he wrote to More in preparing an introduction to his translation of the *Dhammapada*, "that if the mediation of the humanist is to be effective it must have a background of religious meditation."[26]

The admission rested upon his having found a religion that, unlike Platonic or Christian mysticism, did not violate humanism. Buddhism neither affirmed a deity nor promised immortality, but its ethic was rigorous and severe. Most important, it kept the human being as the measure. In stating his inability to find satisfaction in Buddhism, More put to Babbitt the very questions that Babbitt believed Buddhism obviated: "What is the permanent or is there any permanent, that Buddha offers when the impermanent is escaped? Does Buddha totally eliminate the sense of cosmic purpose?" The first question was "scarcely quieted by declaring Buddha's repudiation of metaphysical curiosity." A human spirituality void of what Christians undersood as "soul," achieving its own order in the midst of chaos, represented to More an "insistent and disquieting antinomy."[27]

It was that antinomy that facilitated Babbitt's liaison between Buddhism and Western humanism. There was a devious irony in his saying that "Buddha is so disconcerting to us because doctrinally he recalls the most extreme of our occidental philosophers of the flux, and at the same time, by the type of life at which he aims, reminds us rather of the Platonist and the Christian."[28] Far from disconcerting Babbitt, Buddhism was in his view virtually exempt from any criticism that would deny or qualify endorsement of it as humanistic.

Babbitt never referred to himself or to his humanism as Buddhistic. He may have felt that an open espousal of Buddhism would undermine, as surely as would Christianity, the integrity of humanism. Chagrined by More's and Eliot's withdrawal to religious orthodoxy, Babbitt had no taste for conversion or what he called "pistol-shot transformations of human nature."[29] Recognizing that his writing in support of Buddhism "might suggest that I am trying to convert occidentals," he trusted that in the context of his other works, "it will be seen to be a part not of a religious but of a humanistic argument."[30]

Privately he knew that he had not adequately rebutted More's queries. They had in fact come as an epilogue to a long series of discussions that Babbitt enjoyed with More when, in the spring of 1926, More lectured at Harvard in classics.[31] Babbitt's public answer came in the preface to his last book, several years later, in 1932. Many of his remarks are veiled counter-arguments to More just as "Humanism: An Essay at Definition" had a few years before been directed on significant points to T. S. Eliot. There are few passages in Babbitt's works that carry so demonstrable an expression of the isolated independence he felt. Owning that a humanism above mere reason might lead to a religious affirmation, he wrote:

> I am unable to agree with those who deny humanism independent validity, who hold that it must be *ancilla theologiae* or at least *religionis*. One has to face the fact, an unfortunate fact perhaps, that there are many men of good will for whom dogmatic and revealed religion has become impossible. Are they therefore to be banished into outer darkness where there is wailing and gnashing of teeth?[32]

Babbitt's reasoning was peculiar in that nowhere else had he ever allowed that sincerity or "good will" sufficed as justifications of or substitutions for intellectual positions. But he would not pursue a need for faith in the manner of Carlyle nor try to make humanism a surrogate for religious orthodoxy. "Even if one dispenses with absolutes, one may still retain standards," was the remark that probably best delineated his stance from More's and Eliot's.[33] Standards were, of course, not religious but cultural criteria. But Eliot denied that even with standards humanism alone was adequate as a foundation for culture and it was surely no substitute for church offices.

Apart from the matter of culture, Babbitt believed that religion often suffered most *through* its offices. His attitude may partly be traced to the influence of his father, Edwin Babbitt, a wayward epigone of American transcendentalism whose career in successive spiritualistic quackeries and faith remedies may have early informed his son's contempt for bogus religiosity. The elder Babbitt apparently inculcated into his son some common Protestant biases against Rome, so that into adulthood Irving used "Jesuit" as a synonym for fanaticism, even once accusing More, in the midst of a heated debate, of being a Jesuit in disguise.[34] Catholicism in France, Babbitt believed, had brought about its own decrepitude by failing to break the fetters of Jesuitical reaction. By contrast, as there was no strongly rooted church hegemony in America, Babbitt hoped there might be "still in the American consciousness some stirrings of genuine religious vitality."[35] This vitality, to be sure, would have to depend like humanism upon a nonorthodox but disciplinary will.

Eliot suggested that Babbitt's jealous regard for individualism even in spiritual matters was based upon his desire to make humanism supranational as an aid to civilization. Babbitt's erudition was a factor to be reckoned in the claim: "I mean that he knows too many religions and philosophies, has assimilated their spirit too thoroughly (there is probably no one in England or America who understands early Buddhism better than he) *to be able to give himself to any.* The result is humanism."[36] This logic of cancellations unduly flattered Babbitt's viewpoint and downplayed his emphasis upon a religious and humanistic interworking between the East of Buddha and Confucius and the West of Christ and Aristotle. It was Babbitt's resistance to religious dogma, his inability to "give himself," that made this humanistic conciliation an imaginative possibility.

Babbitt's disinclination to accept an anthropomorphic deity (a point Eliot ignored) and his stress upon the power of will to transcend the relativity of nature brought him into close sympathy with the Theravadin sects of early Buddhism. But it would be misleading to interpret his concentrated studies in Buddhism late in his life as an attempt to fill a void that More and Eliot had exposed in criticizing a secularly based humanism. His attraction to Buddhism had begun as early as his graduate years when he studied Sanskrit under Harvard's Charles Rockwell Lanman and Pali under Sylvain Levi. Buddhism became integral to what Eliot, in 1928, called Babbitt's "struggling to make something that will be valid for the nation, the race, the world."[37] Conceiving Woodrow Wilson's Fourteen Points for international peace as "not the remedy but a symptom of the disease" of outward force, Babbitt claimed that postwar Europe would be saved only by "a change of heart in a Buddhistic or Christian sense," and he made clear that the change of heart would have to begin with the leadership that had precipitated the war.[38] A dramatic instance of the political value of such a conversion Babbitt found in the story of the ancient Indian prince, Asoka, who, upon beginning an imperial crusade on an Alexandrian scale, was suddenly converted to Buddhism and not only learned contrition for his cruelties in war but won, allegedly, true peace, a peace internally willed and thus outwardly ensured. "A mighty emperor who not only repented of his lust of dominion but had his repentance cut into rock for the instruction of future ages—this under existing circumstances is something to ponder."[39]

"Buddha and the Occident," an essay Babbitt composed for his translation of the *Dhammapada*, was, though not an explicit credo, as close as he ever came to stating one. It was prima facie a review of Buddhist philosophy, distinguishing its major sects and examining some of its concepts. But it was also Babbitt's apologia. His idea that to be modern humanism had to have an empirical base (a notion variously stated from his earliest essays) was reformulated when he defined Buddhism as a "critical and experimental supernaturalism."

Buddhistic humanism prescribed that "one must deny oneself the luxury of certain affirmations about ultimate things and start from the immediate data of consciousness."[40] His characterizations of Buddha made clear that on several points he saw Buddhism and humanism as one: Buddha was neither a "rationalist" nor an "emotionalist" but a "religious empiricist" because he "aims at a present blessedness and does not encourage one to entertain any hope that is likely to divert one from [it] and the kind of effort by which it is attained."[41] He was referring, of course, to the penchant of Christians, particularly those prone, like More, to mysticism, for a disengagement from immediacy. Many years before, citing More's *Studies in Religious Dualism*, he had asked whether his friend had not

> insisted unduly on the sheer oppositeness of religion and ordinary life, . . . whether you have not made of religion something too mystically unreal, too infinitely remote from the "scene of our sorrow," something that does not come close enough into contact with the concrete and the human. . . . The essentially humane act after all is that of mediating between the lower and the higher natures, the many and the one.[42]

Buddhism, Babbitt realized, offered a solution to this, the oldest problem in Western philosophy.

The transformation of the historical Siddhartha into the Buddha or Enlightened One afforded Babbitt the necessary empirical evidence of human spiritual powers attained through concentrated will. He admitted that basically Buddhism was an ethic of self-love rather than of love for deity or human beings in Christian fashion. As the *Dhammapada* said, "Self is the lord of self, who else could be the lord?" and "Self is the refuge of self, therefore curb thyself," which seemed to imply in Buddhism a rejection of any godhead or earthly authority to support it. The quality of this self was not ascetic but essentially communitarian: "the self that one loves is not only a higher self but a self that one possesses in common with other men."[43] The Buddhist ethic was a cultural event.

It would seem that perhaps Buddhism was not a religion at all in Babbitt's accounting. At least, it satisfied his contention that "one may get humanistic and religious purpose into one's life without indulging in ultimates after the metaphysical fashion of Aristotle or the theological fashion of traditional Christianity."[44] Of what he termed the religious virtues—awe, reverence, and humility—only the third figured at all in humanism, and he qualified even that as Confucian, not Aristotelian. Conversely, the humanist virtues of "moderation, common sense and common decency" were integral to the empiricism that he ascribed to Buddha's "present blessedness."[45] When, in *Rousseau and Romanticism*, he identified Buddha as a "spiritual positivist" and implied that this positivism meant the opposite of dogma, he believed he had humanized Buddha and freed him from the supernatural realm of religion.[46]

But the "lower nature" required mediation, too. Instead, in Babbitt's estimation, it was being flattered, particularly by what he saw as the sickly sentimentality of Protestant Christianity epitomized in the "social gospel" of urban clerics like Walter Rauschenbusch. Charity of this melioristic sort was as remote from Babbitt's comprehension as was the evangelism of Billy Sunday or Aimee Semple McPherson.

In his intense disdain for a debauched Christianity and in his allegiance to Buddhism, Babbitt offers comparison with strikingly similar views held by a man he reviled as a decadent, Friedrich Nietzsche. As Nietzsche praised it in *Der Antichrist* (1888), Buddhism served as a precious foil to the religion he despised. Although his attraction to Buddhism may have been part of Schopenhauer's legacy, Nietzsche had his own reasons for admiring it. Buddhism was, he wrote, "hundertmal realistischer als das Christentum," so far as it was the only positivistic religion in world history. Free of the spurious metaphysics of faith, grace, and redemption, it offered instead a challenge to self-perfection. It prescribed a perfecting attention to "das Gütigsein als gesundheit-fördernd" (goodness as health-furthering), thus setting Buddhism in sharpest contrast to the putatively sickly consciousness in Christian virtues.[47]

Not the least factor in drawing Babbitt as well as Nietzsche to Buddhism was this stimulation in mental discipline as an affirmation of individual will. Neither the calisthenics of a Loyola nor the therapeutics of a Wesley but logically consistent argumentation was the means for saving oneself. Buddhism was less a religion than an attitude toward the will and what it might achieve of itself. Buddha, claimed Babbitt, "has worked out his ideas to the ultimate degree of clarity, a clarity that is found not merely in separate propositions but in the way they are woven into an orderly whole."[48] Christianity had historically precluded intellectual rigor apart from church dogma and was, according to Nietzsche's characterization by contrast to Buddhism, outwardly hostile to knowledge: "The elevation over other men through logical training and schooling of thought became among the Buddhists a signification of holiness and was accordingly furthered, just as the same qualities were scorned and persecuted in the Christian world as a signification of unholiness."[49] If, though tacitly sharing Nietzsche's contempt for Christianity's seemingly preposterous metaphysics and its decline into the fanatical and sentimental, Babbitt did not come anywhere near to the German's furious, hyperbolical and rebarbative style, it was because he perceived the need for an alliance between humanism and Christianity, whatever the faults of church orthodoxy, against an increasing social and political degeneracy. "In the dark situation that is growing up in the Occident," he noted in the aftermath of the World War, "though religion can get along without humanism, humanism cannot get along without religion."[50] It was a tactical or political rather than philosophical concession. He knew as well that, however intellectually attractive, Buddhism was likely to remain too esoteric to find a place within Western societies, even though it had been fashionable among European intellectuals at the turn of the century. It behooved him, therefore, to be conciliatory to Christians by emphasizing that "humanism should have in it an element of religious insight: it is possible to be a humble and meditative humanist" and that "in a genuinely spiritual enthusiasm the inner light and the inner check are practically identical."[51]

Yet, as Babbitt must have known, despite the convenience of such word play and loose equation, Christianity and humanism could form only a *misalliance*. A religion the chief predicate of which is, as Kierkegaard insisted, a dying to this world would be ill-fitted to any compromise or conjunction with a secular philosophy.

Babbitt never regarded Christianity as the bane of Western civilization, nor, though a learned student of pagan classicism, did he uphold Greece and Rome against Christendom in the manner of d'Holbach, Gibbon, and Nietzsche. But clearly Christianity was, in comparison with Buddhism, inadequate for a psychological rapprochement with humanism. The most convincing reasons for this inadequacy were to be found in the Christian apologists, in the "tremendous spiritual romanticism" of Saint Augustine, in Pascal's "*cilice* and like austerities," and in the obscurantism of Luther and Calvin, who destroyed the "critical" potential of the Protestant Reformation by their fanatical reliance upon the doctrine of grace at the expense of human will.[52] Although Babbitt once generalized that "what is true of Buddhism is at least equally true of Christianity," his own criticisms of the intellectual failures of Christian thinkers belied this statement.[53] It would be difficult to deny that the summary of Babbitt's notes on Buddhism and Christianity, whatever strategic motives he entertained toward the latter, accorded with Nietzsche's incisive words on their fundamental difference: "Buddhism promises nothing, but contains; Christianity promises everything, but contains nothing."[54]

Keenly aware that Buddhism had been adulterated over the centuries, largely by the Madyamikan transformations of Buddha into a deity, Babbitt, as a native of the West, did not feel this degradation as acutely as that of Christianity. Although his private note that "Buddhas themselves can only be teachers but men want scapegoats and saviours" seemed to slight the soteriology of Christianity, Babbitt was incensed over the Protestant debasement of Christ into "the humanitarian phantom that has for several generations past tended to usurp his place."[55] Between this phantom of the "lower nature" and the trinitarian view of Christ as divine, Babbitt conceived a Christ of the middle way, a personified principle of humanistic will: "Theologically the office of Christ is to mediate between God and man but from the point of view of cool psychological analysis his chief office has been to mediate between man and man. Men cannot meet on the level of their ordinary selves, they meet only in a third."[56] This third was none other than the "higher self." But however convincingly Christ may have appeared to him as its exemplar, Babbitt could not overcome his revulsion at the perverse image of a savior on one hand and a political or social subversive on the other. Either a divine or a romantic Jesus nullified the importance of a higher will that one might achieve in oneself.

If the ethics of Christ were obscured by all too human transfigurations of his personality, no such problem attended Buddha. Instead of offering vicarious atonement, Buddha exemplified the attainment of a "super-rational perception, . . . the presence in man of a restraining, informing and centralizing power that is anterior to both intellect and emotion." Babbitt believed that in this moral positivism he had found a humanistic equivalent of Christian grace on the ground that the Buddhistic power of will or "vital control . . . is not present equally in all persons; in some it seems scarcely to exist at all."[57] As to the implications of an absence of this grace in human nature, Babbitt had to go no further than the hellishness on earth that resulted from individually or collectively unbridled temperaments, of which the World War was an almost apocalyptic instance.

Babbitt's quasi-religious humanism of a higher self, as formulated in his "Essay at Definition" in 1930, seemed to abandon his long-affirmed scheme of the Aristotelian mean, or balanced temper of classical humanism. To understand how and why this transition came about, it is necessary to consider the nature of Aristotle's influence upon Babbitt. Aristotle's method of inquiry had been a prototype of the humanist's critical spirit, combining "hard consecutive thinking in working out principles" with the "utmost flexibility in the application of them."[58] Such was the basis for the kind of insight by which one rose from the humanistic to the religious level. Babbitt went so far as to claim that in the *Nicomachean Ethics* "uncompromising analysis kindles into religious insight."[59] In *Rousseau and Romanticism* the practices of Buddha and the humanism of Aristotle were defined as in some aspects complementary. Although Babbitt avoided absolutes and denied any need for them, he made a consciousness of Aristotle's "unmoved mover" essential to the ethical task of opposing "a definite aim or purpose to the indefinite expansion of desires." But what he granted in one tenet he seemed to negate in another, stating rather ambiguously that an ethical goal was not "to any fixed centre but to an ever increasing centrality."[60] If humanism made the human its ultimate measure, it could claim no higher spirituality than what could be attained by human effort.

Short of religious conviction or conversion, Aristotelian humanism "as an attempt however imperfect to give an account of actual experience" nonetheless suggested "the inner and human infinite [that] cannot be formulated intellectually, [but] can be known practically in its effect on life and conduct."[61] This unclarified human infinite in which purposeful effort was carried out proved a convenient ground for linking Aristotle to Buddha. Having sought in his writings up to 1919 to make the humanistic Aristotle a figure of spirituality, Babbitt subsequently reversed his approach by making Buddha a humanist. The necessity for this alteration came simultaneously with Babbitt's admission that religion was indispensable to humanism. "I am struck by the danger of leaving the humanistic life without any support in religion," he wrote in 1919, but by 1930, when he conceded to Eliot that "it is an error to hold that humanism can take the place of religion," he felt he had settled the matter to his own satisfaction.[62]

The defect in Aristotelian humanism had been that its mechanistic notions of control did not provide for a transcendent will. So far as Aristotle did suggest that mind was divine in furnishing the human being with ideas of divinity and that it was thereby the agent for human assumption of immortality as much as was possible, he had passed from humanistic mediation to religious meditation.[63] The difficulty for Babbitt was that even with Aristotle, there could be no extrication of the religious sense from human craving for immortality or likeness to divinity. The passage to a higher plane of being seemed invariably to include a baggage of absolutes for human self-ingratiation.

To dispense with these absolutes yet retain standards, Babbitt, despite his own insistence upon Socratic precision in terms, depended upon an equation of Buddhism with humanism by giving the "higher will" a participation in "higher immediacy," the Buddhistic "present blessedness." He excused his imprecision—perhaps remembering that Matthew Arnold, too, was a practitioner of it—by arguing that such terms connoted "a mystery that may be studied in its practical effects, but that, in its ultimate nature, is incapable of formulation."[64] So far as this language, in his 1930 essay, was virtually the same as in his reference to the "human infinite" in *Rousseau and Romanticism*, Babbitt was removing the "mysterious background" of religion into the mundane sphere of the humanistic will. The revelation in Buddhism was that the human being could achieve a religious experience, with no arguable claim to soul, to immortality, or to divinity.

"Present blessedness" was something other than Babbitt's humanism of mediation; rather, it was the religious aspect of humanism, as he suggested in his private notes:

> The very quality of working on which Buddha puts main emphasis implies an intensely dualistic position—good is conceived negatively inasmuch as [it is] the result of the higher working, [and] is *not merely the limiting but the renunciation of expansive desires*. . . . What supervenes? what then? [It] cannot be put in terms of intellect—most important to remember [it is] something attained in this life.[65]

The strenuousness of will that Buddhism and humanism alike demanded tended to obscure the critical difference between them: one was a transcendent experience, while the other was a secular one. Meditation, unlike mediation, involved a terminus. In Buddhism there was the very opposite of the Christian Victorian's supposition of a "far off divine event to which all creation moves"; instead, as Babbitt somewhat inelegantly put it, there was "a remarkable tendency to take the cash and let the credit go, the cash being not immediate pleasure but immediate peace, the rest that comes through striving."[66]

More, who had found Babbitt's arguments and terms comprehensible when sifted out in conversation, urged him to make some clarification of them in print. Privately, Babbitt confessed himself "a sort of pragmatist of the higher will" arguing that this will was subject neither to imagination nor reason, nor even to a higher illusion such as Christian mystics might claim.[67] Of one thing More was sure: Babbitt had so convinced himself that Buddhism was compatible with humanism that any real accord between Buddhism and Christianity was impossible. The irreconcilability had been evident all along, insofar as Buddhism was essentially atheistic: "Certainly if Buddha is right then Christ's doctrine of God is an illusion, if not a ghastly one. You must take your choice," More concluded.[68]

In one of his last notes to Babbitt, he reiterated Eliot's charge that only a few men could live up to the rigors of the humanistic will, which, even in its loftiest spiritual form, left the mind in the peculiarly dignified posture of a godless elevation. "We are something more than bare will," pleaded More, "we must reckon with the desires, with those of both orders."[69] But Babbitt seemed at no time able to appreciate fully the point of More's insistence nor to see how total was his own doctrinal isolation. It is illuminating that he had persuaded himself that More's "total position" "not only implies a high type of religion but carries with it a high type of humanism," since Babbitt believed that he himself had achieved this levitation with the help of Buddhism.[70]

More was perhaps franker than Babbitt in facing the fact that their religious differences were irreconcilable. He rejected Buddhism because of the psychological obscurities of its terms, particularly its implied dissolution of dualism (as dear to the humanist as to the Christian) in the state of Nirvana, and because he found that Christianity, "better in logic," had "produced a richer life than Buddhism."[71] Babbitt's most damaging charge as a "pragmatist" against More was that dualism was immediate to experiential consciousness but could not be justifiably projected "into the mysterious Beyond . . . to endure *in saecula saeculorum*."[72] In fine, all that More had was faith.

But the character of Babbitt's own faith, one that rested entirely upon "present blessedness," had its confusions, too. According to More, Babbitt was trying to conceptualize a supernaturalism above humanism while reducing it within humanism to a quality of will: "It is just impossible to get the psychological benefits of Christianity while rejecting the Christian and Platonic conception of the supernatural as a reality."[73] Neither Buddha nor Aristotle served Babbitt in that stratagem. It is strange that, defending Buddhism on the tactical ground that "it should be used to give psychological support to Christianity," Babbitt failed to realize or at least to admit that it was humanism, not Christianity, to which he tried to give that support.[74]

Perhaps weary from his metaphysical jousts with More, Babbitt, in the last year of his life, mellowed to an unusual stance of *laisser aller*. His private differences with More, far more important to both than the public images they presented to the "New Humanist Controversy," may finally have appeared too scholastic even to such inveterate academicians as Babbitt and More had always been. As Babbitt pithily concluded,

I should regard it as arrogant to make what I am myself capable of achieving in the way of belief the measure of what is desirable or attainable. There is a side of Christianity for which I do feel a real antipathy—namely the fanaticism and intolerance it has so often displayed as a historical religion, so much so that you yourself would have been persecuted for certain statements in your last volume during the genuine ages of faith.[75]

As for the image and influence of humanism among the learned public, Babbitt, who had spent most of his life attempting to create a united front against the utilitarians and the sentimentalists, found himself no longer so zealous for combat. He wanted to understate More's breach with him as "a matter of regret":

My regret would be still greater if my temper were primarily that of the crusader, something that in spite of all appearances to the contrary, it is not. I shall of course continue to do all I can to oppose the naturalistic deliquescence and to cooperate with those who are making a similar effort, even though on postulates very different from my own. I am not sure that any of us can accomplish very much. The anti-naturalist who wishes to preserve his peace of mind these days would do well to recall the Hindu maxim and, while working to the utmost, to be not unduly attached to the fruits of his working.[76]

Having held tenaciously and unyieldingly to a small body of ideas, Babbitt had to face the consequences of his rigidity: he could appreciate another's understanding of his position only as an endorsement. More's failure to follow his refinement of humanism through Buddhism meant that More no longer understood him.

Babbitt had made the rapprochement between humanism and the Orient convincing only to himself, but he seemed loath to recognize that his singular success made him more remote from his hope of integrating humanism into the broad stream of American thought. Just as Stuart Sherman had complained that the humanists kept themselves at a lofty remove from the national life, it was for More and Eliot to complain that Babbitt had individualized a spirituality for humanism beyond the bounds of even their narrow sympathy.

Babbitt's measure of religious belief extended only halfway up the mountain of faith. It presupposed an almost divine capacity in human beings to elevate their minds above contingency and flux, but it ensured no theistic aids. Babbitt wanted to dispense with the old terrors of orthodoxy and yet keep the sublimity of the religious sense, but his aristocratic view of the "higher will," abstractly excluding most people from either the exercise or the possession of it, left humankind to what for Babbitt was the hellishness of its "lower nature." The sublimity of belief he may well have found but it was too private for words. In its final formulation, Babbitt's humanism was more than an ethic but less than a religion, and so it was fit to satisfy neither the secular nor the spiritual temperaments. Having eradicated the claims of fear, hope, desire, and other emotive elements common to most religions, Babbitt was ineluctably drawn to Buddhism because it too had denied those claims.

It is not surprising, then, that in Henri Bergson's attack upon certain inadequacies in Buddhism there may be found insight into some of the defects of Babbitt's humanistic faith. In the midst of his attempt to conceive an *élan moral et mystique*, Bergson wrote of Buddhism as "arrested halfway, detached from human life but not attaining the divine life, suspended between two activities in the vertigo of nothingness."[77] It was without action, creation, or love; it held neither belief nor confidence in the efficacy of human action. Babbitt might well have agreed with all of Bergson's points except the last. He savored the paradox that in the seeming inaction that the meditative *samadhi* or utter tranquillity of the Buddhist achieved in the exercise of the humanistic inner check, there was the highest activity of which people, not saints, might be capable.

8. Conclusions

It is characteristic of the most interesting heretics, in the context in which I use the term, that they have an exceptionally acute perception, or profound insight, of some part of the truth; an insight more important often than the inferences of those who are aware of more but less acutely aware of anything. So far as we are able to redress the balance, effect the compensation ourselves, we may find such authors of the greatest value. If we value them as they value themselves we shall go astray.

T. S. Eliot, *After Strange Gods*

In his 1911 obituary, "The Genteel Tradition in American Philosophy," George Santayana commended his late colleague at Harvard, William James, for having served as its mortician. For James had wedded intellect to experience and had formed the peculiarly American synthesis of will and energy, which had banished all the static and abstract notions of human character and human fate that genteel arbiters since Puritan days had imposed upon the American mind. It was an imaginative more than intellectual reaction: "Nothing will have been disproved, but everything will have been abandoned," thus leaving the individual to a future of indeterminate variety, "to salute the wild, indifferent, non-censorious infinity of nature."[1]

Santayana characterized this emancipation as a romantic attack upon the genteel mentality in that James had set its staid assumptions upside down. The human species and nature exchanged their master-servant roles; human centrality in the universal scheme and the authority of human will were displaced by impermanence and relativity. James was, moreover, the liberator of his most eminent precursors in subjectivism—the New England transcendentalists, particularly Emerson. Their romantic autonomy of self, while pointing in James's direction, had not found escape from the mere indulgence of private fancies: "It was a play of intra-mental rhymes.... These fancies expressed their personal genius sincerely, as dreams may; but they were arbitrary fancies.... In their own persons they escaped the mediocrity of the genteel tradition, but they supplied nothing to supplant it in other minds."[2]

By Santayana's time, the stamp of philosophical genius in America was granted validity, if it was recognized at all, only so far as its perspective included an expansive embrace of the American chaos as patented, though hardly invented, by men such as Emerson, Whitman, and James. There had to be acknowledged a multiplicity of character and will so wide that any thinker's effort to set it in an order of postulates or imperatives would be a pretense somewhat reminiscent of Old World ways. America was now the community of experiment and, hence, in the word of its master logician, Charles Peirce, unlimited. To such an optimist as he, this experiment was a logical continuum sure to work itself out to an increasing reasonableness.

But the national experience bore ineradicably within its executors some vague compulsion, often grudging, of homage to the Old World, and in no better way could metaphysical debts be paid than in the European coin of inexperiential abstractions, preferably Germanic ones. For, just as the American temper shared with the German a Protestant pietism, so, secularly, both had an insatiable zeal for investigatory sciences and their efficient uses. An adjunct of both the spiritual and mundane facets was the penchant for transcendental schemes. No other people had ever fused idealism and materialism so successfully as had Americans, and at no time in their history was Germanic character as manifest as in the late nineteenth century. It was evident in positivists like Herbert Baxter Adams, in entrepreneurs like Mary Baker Eddy, and in philosophers like Peirce, Royce, and, at least in training, James. In contrast, not the least element in the disembodiment and aloneness of Irving Babbitt was that the fulcrum of his thought and much of his writing was Gallic.

Santayana's grotesque image of America as a child with an old head did not include a depiction of how the child and the head would get along, but he did suggest that the child would develop a mentality of its own. William James gave the formulation: any experience would be valuatively admissible as such, and any philosopher, taking the proper scientific stance, would sanction that experience. There was too much within and behind the continuum of experiential data to justify any dogmatizing about it. One had to learn to rationalize spontaneity and to justify—indeed, to mystify—the plays of impulse and unreason. *Spieltrieb* and *strengwissenschaftliche Methode* were complementary. James liked to quote a poet's "There shall be news in heaven," and his own news to genteel Charles Eliot Norton that "mere sanity is philistine" must have struck his friend like a thunderbolt.[3]

If this congeries of poet's play and philosopher's license, subsumed in the religion of science, was one academic sort of American experience at the turn of the century, Irving Babbitt was wholly alien to it. Babbitt had grown up, outwardly rootless and unfettered, in the frontier experience that might have been called classical if it had not included unmistakably romantic qualities. He had never assimilated the complacent, self-inhibiting proprieties of genteel manners. On the other hand, he was indifferent to the materialistic individualism typified by the industrial epoch in which he had matured, but he was no less hostile to the communitarianism that was a reaction to it and that his friend Royce consecrated toward an absolute. As for James's laboratorial hegemony of experience over moralistic will, it was plainly anathema.

Babbitt's humanism was a sturdily individual experiment against experimentation. In an age increasingly hostile to dogma, at least of the nonscientific sort, he characterized this experiment only as a "quality" of will. He reacted in a void between the credos of a listless Victorian faith and the vagaries of an unsounded scientism. Like Santayana's Emerson, he was consigned to a play of intramental rhymes, but he conceived the play not to subvert an exhausted intellectual tradition but to revitalize it. He had seen, as Emerson could not, how far a romantic reaction to old pieties, spurred on by scientific inquiry and a moral relativism, threatened to go. The consequences were as portentous to the broader culture as to its servants. Babbitt deplored Emerson's congratulating the potentials of American character, for Emerson's own skepticism and sobriety did not seem to offer adequate counterpoise to it. Even more he despised, as only one could who had overcome his commoner's origins, the egalitarian afflatus epitomized in Whitman. Babbitt addressed himself neither to a collective nor a personal egoism. That in his works he excoriated the surface flatteries of both and lacked a meliorist's eye for either made clear that he was foreign to the time and the culture in which he worked.[4]

His one-time friend and devotee, Stuart Sherman, once attempted to locate Babbitt within a dualistic literary construct of theocratic Puritanism and radical democracy, the two predominant strains of the native temper. He failed, as Babbitt knew he had to. Indeed, Babbitt's position within American letters is difficult to fix. It would have been no easier for Sherman to have accommodated him between, say, Royce's idealism and Dewey's materialism. Although it is possible to argue that his humanism had philosophical antecedents—Platonic, Aristotelian, or Thomist—such tags ill fit him because they ignore his own aversion to ratiocination, especially of the metaphysical kind. That aversion he reflected in a vague use of abstractions, much in the manner of Matthew Arnold, and in an adherence, by repetition of idiosyncratic formulas, to a small cluster of terms that served at best to indicate his desire for an elevation free of religious dogma yet somehow supranaturalistic.

Babbitt was a moralist, but he left the antinomies of right and wrong, good and evil, to be inferred from his arguments rather than directly derived. More important, perhaps, his premises and terms were outside the American legacy of Judaeo-Christian ethics: not sin but error of judgment was his bane. His stress upon will, attended by its helpmate the rational intellect, might have given him a basis for rapport with dominant philosophical trends of his time, notably those influenced by Dewey. But Babbitt's focus was defiantly internal and individual. He scorned the problem-solving techniques of the sciences while he dreaded their inroads into humane values. He regarded the optimism of a generation of "instrumentalists" and engineers as ill-founded and misdirected, because no society, however adroitly planned or subjected to experiment, would ever escape the human frailties documented in the works of Sophocles, Dante, and Goethe, and revealed to the wisdom of the humanely balanced individual.

Babbitt's conception of human will was essentially tragic in that the will's effort toward internal peace had to be unremitting; it could never be relieved by any outer agency, human or divine. He declined to accept either the vague theism of the gloomy past or the pragmatist's optimism toward the future. Lacking communion with a native tradition and unsympathetic to the vitalistic trends of his age, Babbitt had to improvise his own sense of human worth. But he refused to admit or even to consider meaninglessness in human activity whereby human efforts would become merely material and mechanical, pathetic and absurd. He shared Pascal's assumption of misery and grandeur as inextricable parts of human nature. What Babbitt believed in he called classical and what he despised or distrusted he called romantic. At a time when such a dualism might have appeared even to academicians as outmoded and artificial, classicism and romanticism were internalized, dramatic contraries so alive to Babbitt's temper that he may never have sensed that they were not at all alive or even appreciable to others. Besides, to comprehend this dualism required one's exposure to and understanding of worlds of intellect and will far too exotic for the American proneness to bounteous, reciprocal immediacy.

In spirit, Babbitt was a peripheral American. The Hellenic notion of failure or blunder, ἁμάρτημα, complemented perfectly his dualism of centripetal and centrifugal aspects of will. Likewise, the negativity of Socrates' internal monitor bore far closer resemblance to *le frein vital* than did the admonitions of Christian conscience. So Babbitt's private, wistful love of pagan antiquity, for the loftiness of Aeschylus and the earthy sense of Aristotle, not to include his attraction to the East, made him eccentric, and yet by such allegiances he believed he was attentive to a permanently valuable human character. In an era whose better minds perceived and resolved problems according to mechanistic or communitarian assumptions, he maintained rigid attention to the single self as the ultimate repository of good and ill.

Babbitt's use of literature to espouse this moralism was part of the genteel legacy he took up at Harvard. He was no critic by the orthodox journalistic or academic modes. His fastidiously held literary priorities, largely European, were joined to a conviction that modern literature was *eo ipso* defective, sickly, and scarcely deserving reading. It may fairly be charged that he lacked the flexible receptivity essential to judicious criticism. His precocious ripening to a humanism of discipline and decorum firmly held and (against his own prescription) narrowly applied no doubt aborted his capacity to respond and furthered his polemical prejudices. Although he made occasional forays into the journalistic haunts of adversaries, his polemics were exercised mainly in the lecture room. There, with his advocacies and challenges being unmet and unrefuted save by the most audacious students, his one-sidedness resonated into an inclusive dogma as self-sustained and as certain, it must have seemed, as the verities he had gathered from literary masterworks.

Babbitt's mind was not adaptive but appropriative; like a kernel or seed, it built around it successive reinforcements. It was as though within him certain premises had appeared sui generis; all subsequent mental endeavor became a deductive underpinning of those premises. His thought was so consistently and totally self-contained and self-justified that it was without the dross of intellectual waywardness, waste, digression, or even self-deceit that makes most thinkers humanly interesting.

One may grant, therefore, that Babbitt never seemed to have entered the house of literature. He was always outside of it making sure that a work's foundations, its ethical properties, were incontestably sound, for only then would the inner rooms and stories hold up. Ideas or "first principles" as the moral substructure made literature a conveyor of spiritual insight as well as aesthetic pleasure: "Art only fulfills a high function when it is used to throw a veil of divine illusion over some essential truth," he generalized, and he gave his own attention undividedly to seeing through that veil.[5] Divinity, even in the allurement of illusory art, failed to carry him from the claims of a moralistic will.

When he spoke of one's "literary conscience," Babbitt closely approximated the genteel recourse to taste as the arbiter of values. But he knew himself to be without any recourse except to a particular individuality that by implication denied collective supports. T. S. Eliot's contention, a seeming mixture of castigation and commendation, that Babbitt's humanism was possible only for a few select individuals, was a corollary that ran throughout Babbitt's demand for closely maintained standards of taste, belief, and conduct. He himself perhaps never fully acknowledged that corollary. Jesting that one day he would write the confessions of a worst seller, he assumed that his failure to win recognition was due to the prevalence of humanitarian "uplift" in contemporary letters and thought rather than to an exclusiveness inherent in his own views.

Perhaps as much as any collation of his major tenets, a parenthetic remark reveals Babbitt's isolation and the narrowness of the margin on which he stood, the margin that he considered the essential controlling power of every human will: "I am sorry that I need so many 'pseudos' in describing our modern activities."[6] We may accept this statement as more genuine than gratuitous, for Babbitt believed his age to be almost entirely alien and irreconcilable to what he intuited and affirmed as the true, enduring values of civilized life. Probably few men in the history of the intellect in America ever willed themselves so much as he to be a crucible for the values of cultures that America, especially in its extroverted and sanguinely "progressive" epoch, had no inclination to receive.

Babbitt wrote as though the hierarchism of Confucius, the metron of Aristotle, and the renunciation of selfhood in Buddhism were verities as immanent to the American mentality as to those born into the cultures that Confucius, Aristotle, and Buddha shaped. He universalized the personalities of Socrates and Rousseau, Pascal and Goethe into aspects of human behavior, norms of sense and of nonsense, and from that arbitrary symbolization he deduced their applicability to every cultural context. It is not surprising, then, that Babbitt willed himself into an aspect of temperamental imbalance as an antidote to the imbalance he regarded as the great disease of his age. The will to refrain—the vital check—was itself never to be restrained. The dangers of a time that he could see only as reckless and confused were too mighty to be risked. Against the "pseudos" of transience and superficiality, the Rousseauist impulse, and the Bergsonian flux, Babbitt's will to refrain was covertly a stopgap by which to maintain a somewhat divine illusion of what endures in human character, that sense by which the Greek tragedians, as he said, "seem to sound the very depth of human destiny."[7]

Although no one factor in Babbitt's personality and doctrine can be used exclusively to account for his influence, undoubtedly his forceful, highly dramatized appeal to what he believed to be abiding in human nature—a sane and sober judicial sense—must be a principal element for consideration. His influence has extended variously to some of the best critical minds of the past two generations, to T. S. Eliot, Newton Arvin, Allen Tate, Yvor Winters, Harry Levin, and David Riesman. Among educators his influence has reached as far as Harvard where, in 1960, its president, Nathan Pusey, created the Irving Babbitt Chair of Comparative Literature. It was appropriate that when, in the last year of his life, Babbitt sought a more positive definition of "higher will" than he had yet given, he borrowed some words from a former student: "One cannot perhaps hit upon a better phrase than that devised by Mr. Walter Lippmann to describe the belief that the modern man has tended to lose—the belief, namely, that 'there is an immortal essence presiding like a king over his appetites.'"[8]

The extremity of will that Babbitt manifested in affirming that "immortal essence" might be likened to that of characters in the dramas of Goethe, who, imposing and self-consistent, seem dangerously partial and incomplete. The stringent, lofty Iphigenia accords with the temper of his humanism as Tasso's romantic egoism serves as its antonym. But it was the ever-negating spirit of Faust's Mephistopheles that most warranted Babbitt's concern: Why, he wondered, did Goethe attribute negation and denial to the demonic aspect of man? Without probing toward a satisfactory answer such as might have helped him to become as resilient and as confident a modern as Goethe, Babbitt undertook to validate the claims of a humanistic denial of the natural self and to make that denial a spiritual force. But, as a creed that joined to secular discipline and temperance a humility and reverence before divine unknowables, Babbitt's humanism lay within the dead god's shadow that Nietzsche said it was now incumbent upon humanity to vanquish.

Notes

Chapter 1

1. James Russell Lowell, "Emerson the Philosopher," in *The Literary Criticism of James Russell Lowell*, ed. Herbert Smith (Lincoln, 1969), pp. 208, 213, 214.
2. Ralph Waldo Emerson, "Self Reliance," in *Selections from Ralph Waldo Emerson*, ed. Stephen Whicher (Boston, 1957), p. 147.
3. Emerson, "Fate," in *Emerson*, ed. Whicher, p. 346.
4. Josiah Royce, *The Philosophy of Loyalty* (New York, 1908), p. 241.
5. Paul Elmer More, in *Irving Babbitt, Man and Teacher*, ed. Frederick Manchester and Odell Shepard (New York, 1941), p. 324.
6. George Santayana, *Character and Opinion in the United States* (New York, 1921), p. 50.
7. William Giese, in *Irving Babbitt*, ed. Manchester and Shepard, pp. 7–8.
8. Irving Babbitt, conclusion of an undated address, Irving Babbitt Papers, Harvard University Archives, Harvard University, Cambridge, Mass. (hereafter cited as Babbitt Papers).
9. Irving Babbitt, *Literature and the American College* (Boston, 1908), p. vii.
10. G. R. Elliott, in *Irving Babbitt*, ed. Manchester and Shepard, p. 162.
11. T. S. Eliot, in *Irving Babbitt*, ed. Manchester and Shepard, pp. 103, 104.

Chapter 2

1. Paul Elmer More, in *Irving Babbitt, Man and Teacher*, ed. Frederick Manchester and Odell Shepard (New York, 1941), p. 329.
2. William Giese, in *Irving Babbitt*, ed. Manchester and Shepard, p. 4.
3. Paul Elmer More to Charles Eliot Norton, May 6, 1898, Charles Eliot Norton Papers, Houghton Library, Harvard University, Cambridge, Mass. (hereafter cited as Norton Papers).
4. Irving Babbitt to Paul Elmer More, December 23, 1895, in the correspondence between Irving Babbitt and Paul Elmer More, privately held by Mrs. Esther Babbitt Howe, Washington, D.C. (hereafter cited as the Babbitt-More Correspondence).
5. Babbitt to More, March 5, 1896, Babbitt-More Correspondence.
6. Ibid.
7. Charles Grandgent, in *The Development of Harvard University*, ed. Samuel Eliot Morison (Cambridge, Mass., 1930), p. 88.
8. Quoted by Alan Heimert in the introduction to *Cotton Mather: The Puritan Priest* by Barrett Wendell (1891; reprint, New York, 1963), p. xv.

9. Irving Babbitt, *Literature and the American College* (Boston, 1908), p. 8. Here and elsewhere, as will be noted subsequently, Babbitt's perspective is essentially Platonic, resting upon the assumption that the strengths and weaknesses of a society, as reflected in its politics and its arts, are chiefly those of the individual writ large. Hence, the whole pedagogy of Babbitt's humanism addresses the moral and intellectual training of the individual and ignores any inclusive scheme or system aimed at social reform.

10. See the "Ode to W. H. Channing," ll. 52–57, in *Selections from Ralph Waldo Emerson*, ed. Stephen Whicher (Boston, 1957), pp. 440–41.

11. Babbitt, *Literature*, p. 178. Unfortunately for Babbitt's political calculation, the United States had long been passing from a republic to an empire. But that transition did not, for Babbitt, invalidate—indeed, it necessitated—a Ciceronian perspective, that of cultivating the minds proven best for training in leadership.

12. Ibid., p. 152.

13. Ibid., p. 145.

14. Babbitt to More, April 1, 1906, Babbitt-More Correspondence.

15. Ibid.

16. Most of the information in this paragraph is based upon an interview with the late Harry Hayden Clark, May 6, 1971. Clark, who was one of Babbitt's teaching assistants in the 1920s, visited Mrs. Babbitt a few years after her husband's death in 1933. His extensive notes taken from Babbitt's lectures in comparative literature, now deposited in the University of Wisconsin Archives, provide a valuable source in determining the content of the lectures.

17. Babbitt to Norton, November 19, 1907, Norton Papers.

18. Irving Babbitt, "Matthew Arnold," *Nation*, August 2, 1917, p. 118.

19. Ibid.

20. Babbitt, *Literature*, p. 99.

21. Ibid., pp. 9, 10.

22. Ibid., pp. 94, 95.

23. Irving Babbitt, undated lecture notes, Babbitt Papers. His stress upon will sets Babbitt apart from Hellenic rationalism, yet he shares implicitly with Plato the assumption that the emotive Many may be selectively subordinated as the strictly controlled effect of reason. At least, Plato acknowledges the legitimacy of pleasureful emotions when they are the product of rational endeavor. See *Philebus* 63d–e.

24. Babbitt, *Literature*, p. 44.

25. Charles William Eliot, "The New Education," *Atlantic Monthly*, February, 1869, p. 206.

26. Charles William Eliot, "Inaugural Address," in *Development*, ed. Morison, p. lxvi.

27. Irving Babbitt, "President Eliot and American Education," *Forum*, January, 1929, pp. 9, 1.

28. Babbitt, *Literature*, p. 75.

29. Ibid., p. 108.

30. Ibid., pp. 259, 174.

31. Ibid., p. 180. The motifs of escape and initiation for the few suggest the Platonic prescriptions that derive from the famous cave metaphor in the *Republic* 514a–517e.

32. Ibid., p. 145.

33. Paul Shorey, review of *Literature and the American College, Nation,* April 30, 1908, p. 403. Having Jeremiah Ford in mind, Babbitt remarked, "One would suppose that Shorey had never heard of the combination which has boosted the author of a treatise on the Spanish sibilant into the Smith professorship as the successor of James Russell Lowell (to take only one example in a hundred)." Babbitt to More, May 17, 1908, Babbitt-More Correspondence.

34. Babbitt to More, May 17, 1908, Babbitt-More Correspondence.

35. Ibid.

36. Quoted by K. T. Mei in *Irving Babbitt,* ed. Manchester and Shepard, p. 123.

37. Babbitt to More, May 17, 1908, Babbitt-More Correspondence.

38. Evarts Greene to Babbitt, February 24, 1911, Babbitt Papers.

39. Babbitt to More, February 3, 1912, Babbitt-More Correspondence.

40. Babbitt to More, April 17, 1912, Babbitt-More Correspondence.

41. Babbitt to More, March 5, 1896, Babbitt-More Correspondence.

42. Van Wyck Brooks, *An Autobiography* (New York, 1965), p. 123. The remark about the cudgel refers to a Spanish proverb, *Hay gustos que merecen palos.*

43. T. S. Eliot, in *Irving Babbitt,* ed. Manchester and Shepard, p. 102.

44. Irving Babbitt, *Democracy and Leadership* (Boston, 1924), p. 242.

45. Irving Babbitt, *On Being Creative and Other Essays* (Boston, 1932), p. 148.

46. Austin Warren, in *Irving Babbitt,* ed. Manchester and Shepard, p. 215.

47. Harry Hayden Clark, lecture notes for Comparative Literature 11, Harry Hayden Clark Papers, University of Wisconsin Archives, University of Wisconsin, Madison, Wisc.

48. Quoted by Henry William Taeusch in *Irving Babbitt,* ed. Manchester and Shepard, p. 173.

49. Babbitt to More, September 19, 1913, Babbitt-More Correspondence.

50. Irving Babbitt, undated lecture notes, Babbitt Papers.

51. Irving Babbitt, *Rousseau and Romanticism* (Boston, 1919), p. 157.

52. Irving Babbitt, *The New Laokoon: An Essay on the Confusion of the Arts* (Boston, 1910), p. 36. Babbitt may have derived the comparison with Luther from Heinrich Heine's *Zur Geschichte der Religion und Philosophie in Deutschland* (1834).

53. Harry Hayden Clark, lecture notes, Clark Papers.

54. Quoted by Gordon Keith Chalmers in *Irving Babbitt,* ed. Manchester and Shepard, p. 243.

55. See Stuart P. Sherman, "Professor Kittredge and the Teaching of English," *Nation,* September 11, 1913, p. 227.

56. Babbitt to More, April 1, 1906, Babbitt-More Correspondence.
57. Babbitt, *Literature*, p. 95.
58. Quoted by Henry William Taeusch in *Irving Babbitt*, ed. Manchester and Shepard, p. 174.
59. T. S. Eliot, "Tradition and the Individual Talent," in *T. S. Eliot: Selected Essays*, ed. John Hayward (London, 1963), pp. 22, 23.
60. Babbitt, *Rousseau and Romanticism*, p. 206.

Chapter 3

1. Irving Babbitt, miscellaneous notes for French 17, Babbitt Papers.
2. Irving Babbitt, "Are the English Critical?," *Nation*, March 21, 1912, p. 283. Similarly applicable is Babbitt's suggestion that "Johnson the moralist often prevails too completely over Johnson the critic" (p. 284).
3. Babbitt to More, July 27, 1909, Babbitt-More Correspondence.
4. Irving Babbitt, *The New Laokoon: An Essay on the Confusion of the Arts* (Boston, 1910), p. 45.
5. Irving Babbitt, undated lecture notes, Babbitt Papers. It is unlikely that by this teleology Babbitt intended anything more specific than the higher sort of meditation Aristotle vaguely described in the *Nicomachean Ethics*. As to how the greatest of Christian poets could inspire a humanist, Babbitt once noted: "The poetry of Dante has flashes of supernatural light and hints of things far beyond the reach of the senses such as hardly exist in other poets. Carlyle has said the right thing for once when he remarks that Dante is not world wide but world deep. His dominant note is intensity. He sings the triumphant grappling of the free individual will with sin and evil. This is inspiriting even though the terms in which he states the problem have become obsolete." Babbitt to More, April 10, 1902, Babbitt-More Correspondence.
6. Irving Babbitt, *The Masters of Modern French Criticism* (Boston, 1912), p. 53.
7. Babbitt to More, July 27, 1909, Babbitt-More Correspondence.
8. Babbitt to More, May 6, 1897, Babbitt-More Correspondence.
9. Babbitt to More, July 3, 1907, Babbitt-More Correspondence.
10. Babbitt to More, December 6, 1905, Babbitt-More Correspondence. He defined gusto as a vitality of expression that in the romantic imagination became unrestrained and impassioned.
11. Babbitt to More, September 28, 1905, Babbitt-More Correspondence.
12. More to Babbitt, October 31, 1907, Babbitt-More Correspondence.
13. Babbitt to More, October 31, 1908, Babbitt-More Correspondence.
14. Babbitt to More, June 11, 1908, Babbitt-More Correspondence.
15. Ibid.
16. Babbitt to Norton, November 19, 1907, Norton Papers.
17. Babbitt to More, July 3, 1907, Babbitt-More Correspondence.
18. Babbitt to More, October 9, 1910, Babbitt-More Correspondence.

19. Babbitt to More, November 16, 1897, Babbitt-More Correspondence.

20. More's letters to Norton denoted his sense of an inbuilt doom in man's cultural destiny. The Greeks themselves, he observed, splendid as they were, had been unable to maintain the inner poise they achieved between belief and action. Their Delphic injunction—know thyself—had tragically ironic implications: "It requires the fullness of self-consciousness. Now this complete self-consciousness means that the individual has learned to distinguish clearly his own interest from the general good, and this, as I take it, is the inevitable and infallible sign of over-ripeness, the beginning of ruin. And in this fatal course the human race seems to revolve from doom to doom. . . . Perhaps after all, the true philosophers, as you intimate, will be diffident in theorizing on such complex phenomena as the fate of nations and choose rather to ascribe their decay to the mysterious agency of fate." More to Norton, May 6, 1898, Norton Papers.

21. Babbitt identified this withdrawal as a part of More's abstruse metaphysics, which made his *Studies in Religious Dualism* "too aridly erudite" and his aphorisms "hard and close reading even for those who have some philosophical training." Babbitt to More, April 19, 1909, and September 26, 1911, Babbitt-More Correspondence.

22. Babbitt, *Laokoon*, p. xiv.

23. Ibid., p. 184.

24. Ibid., p. 250.

25. Irving Babbitt, *Literature and the American College* (Boston, 1908), p. 135. However felicitous this paradoxical phrase in balancing the tradition of the One and the originality of the Many, it invites the sort of charge Hoeveler makes against Babbitt and More, that they "tried too much to contain art in a formula. Their demand that art reflect an interplay of the individual and the universal, the permanent and the flux (*sic*), could indeed serve as a useful standard for the critic but it was not much help to the artist." J. David Hoeveler, *The New Humanism: A Critique of Modern America, 1900–1940* (Charlottesville, 1977), p. 77.

26. Babbitt to More, February 13, 1916, Babbitt-More Correspondence.

27. More to Babbitt, March 6, 1916, Babbitt-More Correspondence.

28. Babbitt to More, February 13, 1916, Babbitt-More Correspondence.

29. Babbitt, *Laokoon*, p. 185.

30. Ibid., p. 186. This passage gives an instance of Babbitt's inexactness in terms. He undoubtedly meant "delusion" as in the following: "Life is at best a series of illusions; the whole office of philosophy is to keep it from degenerating into a series of delusions." Irving Babbitt, *Rousseau and Romanticism* (Boston, 1919), p. 259.

31. Babbitt, *Laokoon*, p. xiii.

32. Ibid., p. 226.

33. Ibid., p. 231. Some of Babbitt's critics have placed him at one or the other of these extremes. Arthur Lovejoy, in his review of *Rousseau and Romanticism* in *Modern Language Notes* 35 (May 1920): 302–7, and Frances Russell, in "The Romanticism of Irving Babbitt," *South Atlantic Quarterly* 32 (Oc-

tober 1933): 399–411, fault him for romantic excesses in his very assault upon romanticism, while Wylie Sypher's "Irving Babbitt: A Reappraisal," *New England Quarterly* 14 (March 1941): 64–76, charges him with pseudo-classical narrowness and dogmatism.

34. Babbitt, *Laokoon*, p. 28. Sensitive to the desiccation of imagination under pseudoclassical formalism, Babbitt said that ethical purpose in aesthetics was not an issue of imagination. Everything depended upon *how* the imagination was used, on whether it was disciplined to standards above the individual's creative sensibility. Neither was imagination an exclusively romantic property: "A man may have very little imagination and yet be wildly romantic; he may have any amount of imagination and yet be classical." Irving Babbitt, undated lecture notes, Babbitt Papers.

35. Babbitt, *Laokoon*, p. 65.

36. Ibid., p. 81.

37. Ibid., p. 145.

38. Ibid., p. 148.

39. Ibid., p. 147. Citing Shelley's ecstatic identification of self with an external beauty, Hoeveler alleges that "the Humanists' fear of expansive emotionalism surely blinded them to the ego-restraining aspects of romanticism." Hoeveler, *New Humanism*, p. 65. As will be noted presently, Babbitt did acquiesce to a species of expansive romanticism, in the England of Sidney and Shakespeare. It would, however, be difficult to discern in romantic ecstasy any restriction of the ego. What Babbitt did fail to acknowledge in Shelley was the poet's own acute perception of the pathology of romantic egotism as revealed, for example, in "The Triumph of Life."

40. Argumentative incongruities resulted. For example, Babbitt could excuse the "eleutheromania" of Byron and Shelley as "a protest against a counter-excess of Toryism in the society of their time," yet he failed to allow such a factor in his attack upon Schiller, who endured a far more stifling ancien régime. Similarly, Babbitt failed to detect an oppressive Toryism in late Victorian middle-class conventions against which the decadents revolted. See Babbitt, *Laokoon*, p. 197.

41. Ibid., pp. 128, 130. It was Winckelmann's confusion of the provinces of the arts through a nostalgic revery over antiquity that prompted Lessing to redraw aesthetic boundaries in his *Laokoon*.

42. Ibid., p. 113.

43. Ibid., p. 73. On this ground, it is easy to understand how Babbitt failed to appreciate the foremost poet of his generation, William Butler Yeats, who is the revivalist of whom Babbitt was thinking. One might incautiously presume that Babbitt was approximating Schiller's distinction between naive and sentimental poets, which is that the naive poet is in harmony with nature, whereas the sentimental poet suffers in sickly elegiac longing for or pretentious celebration of nature. But Babbitt rejected Schiller's distinction exactly because it was conceived from the viewpoint of sentimentalism.

44. Babbitt, *Rousseau and Romanticism*, p. 366. This sense of a void, "the ef-

fect on a mature observer of an age so entirely turned from the One to the Many as that in which we are living," enforced Babbitt's tacit alliance with Plato. Although he expressly denied any pursuit of a Platonic metaphysics that would transcend the phenomenal, there remains a substantial and unrecognized Platonic legacy in Babbitt's aesthetic. The artistry of Plato's myths served Babbitt's argument as exemplifications of a spontaneous imagination complementing reason so as to achieve "that vital fusing of illusion and insight with the accompanying infinitude that is found in the true symbol." Babbitt, *Laokoon*, p. 101.

45. Heinrich Heine, *Die Romantische Schule* (1836) (Munich, 1964), p. 24.

46. Babbitt, *Laokoon*, p. 204. Novelists were sparsely represented in Babbitt's library: Fielding, Balzac, Chateaubriand, Goethe, Thackeray, and Meredith; from the twentieth century, only Aldous Huxley. On the almost willful indifference of Babbitt and More to contemporary fiction, to, for example, the works of Norris, Dreiser, Dos Passos, Anderson, and Lewis, Hoeveler suggests, "Had the Humanists looked closer they might have found elements there of the spiritual struggle and the search for self-perfection that they themselves endorsed." Hoeveler, *New Humanism*, p. 106.

47. Irving Babbitt, *On Being Creative and Other Essays* (Boston, 1932), pp. 111, 112. Keats was Babbitt's frequent example of a legitimate poet of revery, free of sophistical pretensions. Shelley's poetry, he felt, was revery with the pretensions. "I do not wish to be too absolute. Shelley has passages especially in his 'Adonais' that are on a high level. Yet nothing is more certain than that the quality of his imagination is on the whole not ethical but Arcadian or pastoral. The imagination wanders irresponsibly in a region quite outside of normal human experience." Babbitt, *Rousseau and Romanticism*, p. 358.

48. Babbitt, *On Being Creative*, p. 216.

49. Irving Babbitt, miscellaneous notes, Babbitt Papers. In the delineation of an aesthetic dualism, these terms recall Sophocles' alleged distinction of his own work from that of Euripides, that the One is prescriptive; the Many, descriptive.

50. Babbitt found in the eighteenth-century bourgeois dramas of France and Germany some antecedents for the modern novel. In those lachrymose spectacles of domestic sentimentality "no one wills either his goodness or badness, but appears more or less as the creature of accident or fate (in a very un-Greek sense) or of a defective social order." Babbitt, *Rousseau and Romanticism*, pp. 124–25.

51. Babbitt, *On Being Creative*, p. 204. He declined to vote on Mencken's nomination to the National Institute of Arts and Letters, feeling Mencken intellectually unfit but assuming that a negative vote would be construed as personal spite. "I regard him as, on the whole, an evil influence on our contemporary life and literature," he wrote to the institute's secretary. Irving Babbitt to Robert Underwood Johnson, October 27, 1925, Papers of the American Academy of Arts and Letters, New York, N.Y.

52. Babbitt, *On Being Creative*, p. 222.

53. Ibid., p. 212.

54. Ibid., p. 219. The reference to "sociological documents" is pejorative, an echo of More's lament that the modern student is perforce "dragged through the slums of sociology" rather than being made resident "in the society of the noble dead." Paul Elmer More, *Aristocracy and Justice: Shelburne Essays, Ninth Series* (New York, 1915), pp. 36–37.

55. Babbitt, *On Being Creative*, p. 216.

56. Ibid., p. 220.

57. Babbitt, *Literature*, pp. 194–95.

58. Babbitt, *Laokoon*, p. 161.

59. Ibid., p. 166.

60. Ibid., p. 106. A sophisticated explanation of Wagner's terms may be found in Thomas Mann's *Richard Wagner und 'Der Ring'* in his *Rede und Aufsätze* (Oldenburg, 1965), vol. 1. Nothing is more Wagnerian, claims Mann, than the mixture of mythic origins and modern psychology. Thus, Wagner consecrated nineteenth-century naturalism through myth. Had Babbitt read Wagner's libretti, he would have discovered that Wagner's almost exclusive central theme was not expansive sympathy of will but its annihilation in what Schopenhauer called tragic atonement for the guilt of existence itself.

61. Ibid., p. 107.

62. Babbitt, *Rousseau and Romanticism*, p. 203.

63. Babbitt, *Laokoon*, pp. 196, 202.

64. Babbitt, *On Being Creative*, p. 173.

65. Babbitt, *Laokoon*, p. 225.

66. Irving Babbitt, "Croce and the Philosophy of the Flux," *Yale Review* 14 (January 1925): 381.

67. Hoeveler notes that if Babbitt and More "were sensitive to the depths of the romantic movement in modern culture, they were less sensitive to the reasons why it occurred or why it had to occur in the manner it did." Hoeveler, *The New Humanism*, p. 67.

68. Arthur Lovejoy, "Reply to Professor Babbitt," *Modern Language Notes* 37 (May 1922): 272. Babbitt's answer to Lovejoy's initial criticism immediately precedes this reply.

69. Babbitt, *Rousseau and Romanticism*, p. 90. A superb interpretation of the divided consciousness in Schiller is Georg Lukacs's *Goethe and His Age*, trans. Robert Anchor (London, 1968). As a Marxist, Lukacs views the division of the artist within himself as an inevitable facet of bourgeois art, a conflict between appearance and essence that capitalism creates and which must make its negation in an idealized antiquity. Babbitt's view of the novel as generically decadent adumbrates Lukacs's discussion of the novel (Goethe's *Wilhelm Meister*) as a problematic depiction of the ugliness of (bourgeois) life which the artist overcomes in expressing an awareness of that ugliness. But that awareness necessitates idealistic illusions of escape. Babbitt's discussion of romantic melancholy in *Rousseau and Romanticism* is particularly apposite to Lukacs's thesis.

70. Babbitt, *Laokoon*, pp. 226, 228.
71. Babbitt to More, September 22, 1927, Babbitt-More Correspondence.

Chapter 4

1. Quoted by William Giese in *Irving Babbitt, Man and Teacher*, ed. Frederick Manchester and Odell Shepard (New York, 1941), p. 5.
2. Babbitt to More, April 17, 1908, Babbitt-More Correspondence.
3. Irving Babbitt, miscellaneous lecture notes, Babbitt Papers.
4. Michel de Montaigne, *Essais*, 2 vols. (Paris, 1962), 2:577. As Montaigne's statement epitomizes humanist decorum, it deserves quotation in full: "Les plus belles vies sont, à mon gré, celles qui se rangent au modelle commun et humain, avec ordre, mais sans miracle et sans extravagance."
5. Irving Babbitt, miscellaneous lecture notes, Babbitt Papers.
6. Quoted by Johann Peter Eckermann, *Gespräche mit Goethe* (1836), for November 24, 1824. Babbitt's views of French literary culture accord well with Goethe's and so differ markedly from those of Matthew Arnold, who, in "The Literary Influence of Academies," celebrates the keen intellectual freedom of the French, a freedom he judges to be admirably tempered by the severe standards of the academy.
7. Irving Babbitt, *Literature and the American College* (Boston, 1908), p. 37.
8. Irving Babbitt, "Are the English Critical?," *Nation*, March 28, 1912, p. 310.
9. Irving Babbitt, lecture dated October 26, 1902, Babbitt Papers.
10. Babbitt, *Literature*, pp. 16, 20.
11. Van Wyck Brooks, *An Autobiography* (New York, 1965), p. 123.
12. Babbitt, "Are the English Critical?," p. 283. Babbitt's antinomy might suggest qualification of Hoeveler's claim that "whereas the impressionist looked for creative reenactment on the part of the critic, the Humanist sought the incorporation of the critical fusion into the creative process." J. David Hoeveler, *The New Humanism: A Critique of Modern America, 1900–1940* (Charlottesville, 1977), p. 67. Yet, Babbitt did contend that true art is an indeterminable fusion of imaginative and rational faculties, and the effect of it is almost mystically elusive and never the product of mechanical or formulaic processes.
13. Friedrich Nietzsche, *Götzendämmerung* (1889) (Stuttgart, 1964), p. 131.
14. Quoted by Irving Babbitt, undated lecture, Babbitt Papers. I have been unable to find the source of this remark.
15. Irving Babbitt, Notes on French Classicism, Babbitt Papers.
16. Irving Babbitt, *The New Laokoon: An Essay on the Confusion of the Arts* (Boston, 1910), pp. 40, 41.
17. Irving Babbitt, *The Masters of Modern French Criticism* (Boston, 1912), p. 380; *Laokoon*, p. 41.
18. Babbitt, *Masters*, pp. 380–81.

19. Ibid., p. 239; Irving Babbitt, *Rousseau and Romanticism* (Boston, 1919), p. 29.

20. Babbitt, *Masters*, p. 115.

21. It made perfect sense to Babbitt during his first sabbatical to France, in 1907–8, to find that there was a Pascal revival concurrent with one for Rousseau and that the former was or seemed as exclusively French and reactionary in tone as the latter was cosmopolitan.

22. Babbitt, *Masters*, p. 240.

23. Ibid., pp. 127, 174.

24. Charles Augustin Sainte-Beuve, *Portraits contemporains*, 5 vols. (Paris, 1881), 5:222–23.

25. Irving Babbitt, "Pascal," *Nation*, November 17, 1910, p. 469. My italics.

26. Blaise Pascal, *Pensées* (Paris, 1962), p. 187.

27. Babbitt, *Rousseau and Romanticism*, p. 24. Pascal's perception of the humanist thus anticipates the final judgment of T. S. Eliot, who was to claim that between naturalism and supernaturalism, Babbitt's humanism could not stand autonomously, it being rather a disguised or self-exalted naturalism. See Chapter 7.

28. Irving Babbitt, Notes on Pascal, Babbitt Papers.

29. Irving Babbitt, *Democracy and Leadership* (Boston, 1924), p. 12.

30. Babbitt used Pascal himself as plaintiff against Rousseau in determining the "higher" and "lower" senses of *coeur* to designate respectively "the illumination of grace" and "expansive feeling." Babbitt, *Masters*, p. 53; Irving Babbitt, *On Being Creative and Other Essays* (Boston, 1932), p. xxxix.

31. Babbitt, "Pascal," p. 467. Cassirer contends that Voltaire neither fully sounded Pascal's thought nor escaped Pascal's own philosophical skepticism. See Ernst Cassirer, *The Philosophy of the Enlightenment*, trans. Fritz Koelln and James Pettegrove (Boston, 1955), pp. 144–46.

32. Babbitt, *Rousseau and Romanticism*, pp. 32–33.

33. Ibid., p. 32. Joubert, who anticipated Babbitt's view on many points, wrote of Voltaire: "He is a writer whose extreme elegance one must carefully avoid or one will never take anything seriously again." Joseph Joubert, *Pensées, Essais et Maximes*, 2 vols. (Paris, 1842), 1:178.

34. Joubert, *Pensées*, 1:385.

35. Babbitt, *Masters*, p. 40.

36. Ibid., p. 37.

37. Ibid., p. 53.

38. For example, Joubert contended that it is a hundred times better to harmonize a work of art to the abiding nature of man than to what is called the state of society. Each man, says one maxim, has within him a power to shape his conduct by a norm and must be his own magistrate and judge. These presuppositions accord with Babbitt's in his belief in a "vital check" as the innate centripetal control mechanism of the human will. See Joubert, *Pensées*, 1:129, 271.

39. Ibid., 2:182, 183.

40. Ibid., 2:151–52.

41. Babbitt to More, December 7, 1912, Babbitt-More Correspondence. Babbitt's weightiest charge against Platonism was that it could be readily distorted to romantic ends, as the fifth chapter of *The New Laokoon* documents.

42. Joubert, *Pensées*, 2:182.

43. Babbitt, *Masters*, p. 41.

44. Ibid., pp. 148, 149.

45. Ibid., p. 131.

46. Ibid., p. 138.

47. Irving Babbitt, Notes on Sainte-Beuve, Babbitt Papers.

48. Babbitt, *Masters*, p. 160.

49. Ibid., p. 187.

50. Babbitt, Notes on Sainte-Beuve, Babbitt Papers.

51. Babbitt, *Masters*, p. 188. A positive turn to this thought came in the introduction to *Rousseau and Romanticism*: "In a sense one may say with Goethe that the excellences are of the individual, the defects of the age" (p. xvii). It might be more accurate in the case of Rousseau, according to Babbitt's own analysis, to say that the excellences are of the individual but that his defects become magnified in the age that follows him.

52. Babbitt, *Masters*, pp.112–13.

53. Ibid., p. 193.

54. Ibid., p. 196.

55. Irving Babbitt to Horace Scudder, December 27, 1896, in the correspondence between Irving Babbitt and the Houghton Mifflin Company, Houghton Library, Harvard University, Cambridge, Mass. (hereafter cited as Babbitt–Houghton Mifflin Correspondence).

56. Babbitt, *Masters*, p. 304.

57. Ibid., p. 331.

58. Quoted by Irving Babbitt, "Bergson and Rousseau," *Nation*, November 14, 1912, p. 453. Against "intellectualism," James described his own and Bergson's philosophies as "tychism," or reality viewed as in a constantly changing organic continuum. See William James to Henri Bergson, June 13, 1907, quoted by Gay Wilson Allen in his *William James* (New York, 1967), p. 459.

59. Babbitt to More, February 17, 1912, Babbitt-More Correspondence.

60. The Protagorean maxim that makes the individual the measure of all things signifies as well that "each man's sensations are true for him and no one else." Each one of us, in Bergsonian terms, has a *moi profond* as uniquely one's own as one's particular experiences. Bergson was not a Heraclitean because Heraclitus posited an outward world of contraries and made exhortations to a cogitated or intuited Logos. See W. K. C. Guthrie, *A History of Greek Philosophy*, 5 vols. (Cambridge, 1967), 1:401, 431.

61. One of Bergson's defenders writes that he "loved Jean-Jacques for his call to intuition, to feeling according to depth of consciousness." Madeleine Barthelemy Madaule, *Bergson* (Paris, 1969), p. 174. Bergson himself said

that the greatest influence on the human spirit since Descartes was incontestably Rousseau: "It works upon us still." Henri Bergson, *Écrits et Paroles*, ed. Rosa Mosse-Bastide (Paris, 1957), p. 420.

62. Babbitt, *Rousseau and Romanticism*, p. 147.

63. Babbitt, "Bergson," p. 454.

64. Irving Babbitt, Notes on Bergson, Babbitt Papers.

65. See Plato, *Gorgias* 506c.

66. Walter Pater, *The Renaissance* (1873) (New York, 1959), p. 158.

67. Ibid., p. 157.

68. Irving Babbitt, lecture of May 26, 1913, Babbitt Papers.

69. Santayana assessed Bergson's works as "a brilliant attempt to confuse the lessons of experience . . . to make us halt, for the love of primitive illusions, in the path of discipline and reason." These words might well have been Babbitt's. Like him, Santayana did not underestimate the basis of Bergson's appeal, for his philosophy "tells us that nothing is truer and more precious than our rudimentary consciousness, with its vague instincts and premonitions . . . that the universe is as palpitating and irrational as ourselves." George Santayana, *The Winds of Doctrine* (1913; reprint, New York, 1957), pp. 107, 108.

70. Babbitt, *Masters*, p. 362.

71. He contended that "the French romanticists in inner and spiritual remoteness from normal human experience . . . can scarcely vie with the early German romanticists." Babbitt, *Rousseau and Romanticism*, p. 61.

72. Babbitt, *Democracy*, p. 242; Babbitt, *Masters*, p. 364.

73. Quoted by Warner Rice in *Irving Babbitt*, ed. Manchester and Shepard, p. 243.

74. Babbitt, *Laokoon*, p. 193.

75. Quoted by Gordon Keith Chalmers in *Irving Babbitt*, ed. Manchester and Shepard, p. 297.

76. Irving Babbitt, "The Breakdown of Internationalism," *Nation*, June 17, 1915, p. 678.

77. Babbitt, *Rousseau and Romanticism*, p. 361.

78. Like many other nineteenth-century writers, including Sainte-Beuve, Goethe subscribed to the notion of a master or ruling passion, which he defined as "the manly in man": "For indeed such passions propel man to one side and push him on a consistent track with no need of reflection, conviction, purpose or will power, and sustain him in continual life and motion." Johann Wolfgang von Goethe, *Werke*, 14 vols. (Hamburg, 1967), 12:346. It is striking that Goethe's remarks on this romantic fallacy date from what Babbitt presumed to be his classical or humanistic period, 1827.

79. Quoted by Eckermann in his *Gespräche*, January 18, 1827.

80. Babbitt, *Masters*, p. 366. The phrase is Emerson's, whom Babbitt described as "a true sage who must yet be numbered among the sycophants of human nature." Ibid., p. 361.

81. Babbitt, *Literature*, p. 194.

Chapter 5

1. Charles Eliot Norton to Horace Howard Furness, May 5, 1908, in *The Letters of Charles Eliot Norton*, ed. Sara Norton and M. A. DeWolfe Howe, 2 vols. (Boston, 1913), 2:401.

2. Charles Eliot Norton, "The Paradise of Mediocrities," *Nation*, July 13, 1865, pp. 43, 44.

3. Ibid., p. 44.

4. Irving Babbitt, *Literature and the American College* (Boston, 1908), p. 8.

5. Babbitt to More, August 5, 1906, Babbitt-More Correspondence. It is safe to assume that he took "first principles" from the opening statement of Aristotle's *Poetics*: "Let us speak commencing as is natural first from first things."

6. Babbitt, *Literature*, p. 43. Complementing here the dualism of the higher and lower aspects of human nature is the Aristotelian notion of a mean or *metron*, which reconciles opposites, as defined in the *Nicomachean Ethics* 1106a–1109b.

7. Irving Babbitt, *Democracy and Leadership* (Boston, 1924), p. 273.

8. I borrow the term from Karl Jaspers who applies it to Nietzsche.

9. Babbitt, *Literature*, pp. 60, 61.

10. Ibid., p. 70.

11. Ibid., p. 173. Babbitt was fond of quoting James Russell Lowell's remark, "Oblivion looks in the face of the Grecian Muse only to forget her errand" (p. 179). But it is not wholly within the classical context that Hoeveler's criticism of Babbitt and More must be weighed: "They looked to books to find what life could not give, and in books they sought the realization of their highest aspirations for man. . . . The Humanists too often confused literature and life. If the real world did not reflect the highest human promise then literature, they felt, must." J. David Hoeveler, *The New Humanism: A Critique of Modern America, 1900–1940* (Charlottesville, 1977), p. 25. Babbitt and More indeed believed that the standards that the best of the Greeks had achieved were imperishable, yet they felt that literature reflected not only moral values (those which pointed to the One) but also the hazards of their abandonment. The writings of Rousseau, for example, or Bergson, documented the pathology of the Many.

12. Babbitt to More, April 10, 1902, Babbitt-More Correspondence.

13. Ibid.

14. Babbitt, *Literature*, p. 115.

15. Matthew Arnold, *Culture and Anarchy* (1869), ed. J. Dover Wilson (Cambridge, 1966), p. 109.

16. Ibid., pp. 55, 46.

17. Babbitt, *Literature*, p. 27.

18. John Henry Newman, *The Idea of a University* (1856), ed. Charles Frederick Harrold (New York, 1947), pp. 106–7.

19. Irving Babbitt, *Rousseau and Romanticism* (Boston, 1919), p. 265.

20. Quoted by Irving Babbitt in his miscellaneous notes, Babbitt Papers. See Chapter 4, n. 4.

21. Irving Babbitt, lecture notes dated May 1918, Babbitt Papers.

22. Babbitt, *Literature*, p. 89.

23. Ibid., p. 84. The reference is to Plato's *Laws* 819a. Babbitt distorts the context and the key terms within it. Plato's point is that knowledge coming from a bad teacher is more harmful to a student than his own ignorance. It is difficult to see how "encyclopaedic smattering" and "miscellaneous experiment" can be derived from πολυπειρία καὶ πολυμαθία, which, literally rendered, mean almost the opposite, much experience and much learning.

24. Samuel Eliot Morison, *The Development of Harvard University*, ed. Samuel Eliot Morison (Cambridge, Mass., 1930), pp. xlii–xlvi.

25. Babbitt, *Literature*, p. 52.

26. Ibid., p. 105.

27. Ibid., p. 84.

28. Ibid., p. 131.

29. Ibid., p. 102. Babbitt was specifically addressing Hugo Münsterberg, professor of abnormal psychology at Harvard. Münsterberg, who had come to Cambridge from Germany in 1892 to replace William James as head of laboratory research in psychology, called upon American professors to rival their German counterparts in "productive" scholarship.

30. Ibid., p. 47.

31. Ibid., pp. 147, 142.

32. Ibid., p. 259.

33. Ibid., p. 243. In 1930, Babbitt headed an interdepartmental committee that submitted a prospectus for an honors degree. Its argument came directly from his educational essays of nearly twenty-five years before. Placing emphasis upon "assimilative reading," it was to immunize doctoral candidates against "premature specialization." Honors candidates were urged to "build up a classical background"; examinations were to include a general comprehension of literature from medieval to modern times. "Program for Honors," Babbitt Papers.

34. Irving Babbitt, lecture notes of June 1, 1920, Babbitt Papers.

35. Irving Babbitt, "President Eliot and American Education," *Forum*, January, 1929, p. 9.

36. Ibid., p. 9.

37. Irving Babbitt, "Pascal," *Nation*, November 17, 1910, p. 468.

38. Babbitt, *Literature*, p. 247. "In this country the productive scholar often has to teach or lecture from nine to eighteen hours a week; in addition he is likely to be burdened with administrative duties, not to speak of the pot-boiling devices to which he sometimes resorts to eke out an insufficient salary. This state of affairs is . . . contrary to common sense, and will no doubt gradually be remedied" (p. 247). Babbitt's own pot-boiling included editions of Voltaire's *Zadig* (1905) and Racine's *Phèdre* (1910).

39. Babbitt, *Literature*, p. 262.

40. James's stress upon unreflected action is effectually the antithesis of Babbitt's prescription of leisure. To relieve anxiety and tension, James suggested that "when a decision is reached and execution is the order of the day, dismiss absolutely all responsibility and care about the outcome. Unclamp, in a word, your intellectual and practical machinery, and let it run free; and the service it will do you will be twice as good." William James, *Talks to Teachers* (New York, 1962), p. 109.

41. Interview with Harry Hayden Clark, Madison, Wisconsin, May 6, 1971.

42. Irving Babbitt, "The Problem of Style in a Democracy," an address to the American Academy of Arts and Letters, November 10, 1932, reprinted in Irving Babbitt, *Spanish Character and Other Essays*, ed. Frederick Manchester, Rachel Giese, and William Giese (Boston, 1940), pp. 178–79.

43. Charles Sanders Peirce, "The Marriage of Religion and Science," in *Charles S. Peirce: Selected Writings*, ed. Philip P. Wiener (New York, 1966), p. 352.

44. John Dewey, *A Common Faith* (New Haven, 1934), pp. 131–32. In the same passage, Dewey writes: "The new methods of inquiry and reflection have become for the educated man today the final arbiter of all questions of fact, existence and intellectual assent" (p. 131).

45. Irving Babbitt, *On Being Creative and Other Essays* (Boston, 1932), p. xxxviii.

46. Irving Babbitt, "What I Believe," *Forum*, February 1930, p. 80.

47. Ibid., p. 87.

48. Babbitt, *On Being Creative*, p. xxxv.

49. Babbitt to More, September 17, 1923, Babbitt-More Correspondence.

50. Irving Babbitt, "Matthew Arnold," *Nation*, August 2, 1917, p. 121. Although scorning "Menckenism" as "the current form of bad taste and false smartness," Babbitt found Mencken's ridicule of educators justified in that Mencken's leadership as a critic "would have been impossible if the professors, especially those of ancient and modern humanities, had been at all equal to their tasks." Irving Babbitt, lecture notes of May 6, 1929, Babbitt Papers.

51. Irving Babbitt, "Genius and Taste," in *Criticism in America*, ed. Joel Spingarn (New York, 1924), p. 172.

52. Irving Babbitt, miscellaneous notes, Babbitt Papers.

53. Babbitt, *On Being Creative*, p. 240.

54. Babbitt, *Democracy*, p. 146; Babbitt, review of Paul Elmer More's *A Century of Indian Epigrams*, *Atlantic Monthly*, October 1899, p. 576.

55. Babbitt, review of More's *A Century of Indian Epigrams*, p. 576.

56. Babbitt, *Democracy*, p. 273.

57. Ibid., p. 309.

58. Ibid., p. 261.

59. On Babbitt's election to the National Institute of Arts and Letters, he told More, one of his sponsors, "I approve on principle of an organization

of this kind though to be very effective it would have to be better known. A French writer describes it as a 'vague imitation' of the French Institute. The vagueness is, I fear, in the minds of the public." Babbitt to More, April 5, 1920, Babbitt-More Correspondence. In an address to the American Academy of Arts and Letters he urged fellow members to follow the French example and survey contemporary literature even at the risk of notoriety and ridicule, to "take any measures that seem likely to extend the Academy's influence." But he was not "oversanguine" about that influence "in a country so vast and decentralized." Babbitt, *Spanish Character*, pp. 180, 181.

60. Babbitt, *On Being Creative*, p. 197.

61. Randolph Bourne, "The War and the Intellectuals," in *Collected Essays, 1915–1919*, ed. Carl Resek (New York, 1964), p. 7.

62. Ibid., p. 14.

63. Amid his lecture and reading notes Babbitt kept a trove of newspaper and magazine reports, reviews, and editorials at the heads of which he scrawled the ominous rubrics of his scorn: "romantic morality," "imperialism," "confusion of genres," etc.

64. Babbitt, *On Being Creative*, p. 5.

65. Irving Babbitt, "The Breakdown of Internationalism," *Nation*, June 24, 1915, p. 706.

66. Babbitt, *Rousseau and Romanticism*, p. 348.

67. Babbitt, *On Being Creative*, p. 197. Emphasis mine.

68. Irving Babbitt, miscellaneous notes, Babbitt Papers.

69. Irving Babbitt, "Humanism: An Essay at Definition," in *Humanism and America*, ed. Norman Foerster (New York, 1930), p. 49. Privately he wrote, "Whether a sufficiently large international remnant can get together on essentials at present to stay the main trend of Occidental society—that is a question on which I do not care to hazard an opinion." Irving Babbitt, miscellaneous notes, Babbitt Papers.

70. Babbitt, *On Being Creative*, p. 199.

71. Babbitt to More, June 12, 1932, Babbitt-More Correspondence.

72. Babbitt, *On Being Creative*, p. xix.

73. Babbitt, "What I Believe," p. 86.

74. Babbitt, *Democracy*, pp. 325, 326.

75. Charles Sanders Peirce, "Some Consequences of Four Incapacities," in *Charles S. Peirce: Selected Writings*, ed. Philip P. Wiener, pp. 40, 41.

76. Babbitt, *Democracy*, p. 322.

77. Babbitt, *On Being Creative*, p. 261.

78. Babbitt, *Democracy*, pp. 165, 161.

79. Irving Babbitt, Notes on Buddhism, Babbitt Papers. Among these papers he wrote that to "help [the] Chinese in working to a sound individualism of a humanistic kind—this even more than religion perhaps might be made the basis of a rapprochement between China and the Occident."

80. Ibid.

Chapter 6

1. Oliver Wendell Holmes, Jr., *Collected Legal Papers* (New York, 1921), pp. 38, 47.

2. Irving Babbitt, Notes on Democracy and Imperialism, Babbitt Papers.

3. Babbitt to More, April 10, 1902, Babbitt-More Correspondence.

4. Henry James, *The American Scene* (1907; reprint, New York, 1967), p. 58.

5. Irving Babbitt, miscellaneous notes, Babbitt Papers.

6. Friedrich Nietzsche, *Jenseits von Gut und Böse* (1886) (Munich, 1964), p. 95. In philosophy's awkward accommodation of modern science, "der rechte Philosoph . . . riskiert sich beständig, er spielt das schlimme Spiel."

7. Irving Babbitt, *On Being Creative and Other Essays* (Boston, 1932), p. 206.

8. Irving Babbitt, undated lecture, Babbitt Papers. Hoeveler observes that Babbitt, More, and their supporters "had no program for society; in application, theirs was a program for individuals only" in that they were "far more concerned with the art and science of governing oneself." J. David Hoeveler, *The New Humanism: A Critique of Modern America, 1900–1940* (Charlottesville, 1977), p. 125. The absence of any humanistic platform was correlative to the Platonic focus upon leadership, that is, on the temperament and the training of a fit few. What Babbitt seems never appreciably to have grasped was that however well-trained an elite could be, there is no means in a democratic polity to ensure its acceptance or even its recognition.

9. Irving Babbitt, *Rousseau and Romanticism* (Boston, 1919), p. 156.

10. Irving Babbitt, lecture at Radcliffe College, November, 1932, Babbitt Papers.

11. Babbitt to More, December 23, 1895, Babbitt-More Correspondence. As in other contexts, Babbitt did not make a blanket condemnation of Rousseau as a political thinker. He noted that Rousseau's private correspondence often revealed shrewdness and insight. "Rousseau's head could on occasion stand aloof and deal rather Socratically with his heart. It is not, however, this self-critical Rousseau . . . that need concern us, for the simple reason that it is not this Rousseau who has moved the world." Irving Babbitt, *Democracy and Leadership* (Boston, 1924), p. 85. Ernst Cassirer's Kantian view of Rousseau's "pure ethics of obligation" underscores Babbitt's attack. See Ernst Cassirer, *The Question of Jean-Jacques Rousseau*, trans. Peter Gay (Bloomington, 1963), esp. pp. 36 and 96.

12. "In effect, what is generosity, clemency, humanity if not pity given to the weak, the guilty or to the human race in general? Kindness and friendship, too, are products of a continual pity fixed upon a particular object. . . . Pity is a natural sentiment, which, moderating in each person the actions of his love of self, works for the mutual preservation of the race." Jean-Jacques Rousseau, *Discours sur l'origine de l'inégalité* (1755) (Paris, 1962), pp. 59, 60.

13. Ibid., p. 72.

14. Babbitt, *Democracy*, p. 15. While Babbitt has often been charged with distortions or misrepresentations of Rousseau, it should be noted that he omitted a great deal that might have served his indictment had he been concerned not with the essential character of Rousseau's ideas and their influence but with mere ad hominem defamation. The sustained sociopathy of *Rousseau, Juge de Jean-Jacques,* in which Rousseau accuses d'Alembert, Voltaire, and others of homicidal intent against him and his reputation, might have been adduced to reveal the darker aspects of romantic enthusiasm, but Babbitt made no apparent use of this bizarre work.

15. "The social order is a sacred right which serves as the basis for all the others." Jean-Jacques Rousseau, *Du Contrat social* (1762) (Paris, 1962), p. 236.

16. Many passages in Rousseau's confessional works indicate not only escapism but clinical paranoia: "I am only myself when I am alone; beyond that I am the laughing-stock (jouet) of all those who surround me." Jean-Jacques Rousseau, *Rêveries du promeneur solitaire* (1777–78) (Paris, 1965), p. 160.

17. Babbitt, *Rousseau and Romanticism*, p. 156.

18. Rousseau, *Rêveries*, pp. 70, 74; Babbitt, *Democracy*, pp. 70–96. "The profession of truthfulness which I have made has its foundation more in feelings of uprightness and equity than in the reality of things and in practice I have followed the moral directions of my conscience more than abstract notions of the true and false." Rousseau, *Rêveries*, pp. 86–87.

19. See Karl Jaspers, *Socrates, Buddha, Confucius, Jesus,* ed. Hannah Arendt and trans. Karl Manheim (New York, 1962), pp. 87–96.

20. Babbitt contended that "if there is such a thing as the wisdom of the ages, a central core of normal human experience, it is this wisdom, on the religious level, found in Buddha and Christ and, on the humanistic level, in Confucius and Aristotle. These teachers may be regarded both in themselves and in their influence as the four outstanding figures in the spiritual history of mankind." Babbitt, *Democracy*, p. 163. T. S. Eliot challenged Babbitt's understanding of "normal" in "Second Thoughts about Humanism," in his *Selected Essays* (New York, 1950), pp. 429–38; see esp. p. 437.

21. Irving Babbitt, miscellaneous notes, Babbitt Papers.

22. Irving Babbitt, undated lecture, Babbitt Papers.

23. Babbitt, *Democracy*, p. 5. He considered initiative, referendum, and recall among the most dire tools of popular will. Socrates and Jesus, he claimed, were victims of "solemn" referenda.

24. Babbitt to More, April 27, 1932, Babbitt-More Correspondence.

25. See Plato, *The Apology* 40a, 4–6: ἡ γὰρ εἰωθυῖά μοι μαντικὴ ἡ τοῦ δαιμονίου. In the *Republic* 496c, Socrates emphasizes the uniqueness of the *daimon* to himself.

26. Heeding "the admonitions of the inner monitor" would bring "two of the most positive of all things: character and happiness." Babbitt, *Democracy*, p. 24.

27. Ibid., p. 61.

28. Ibid., pp. 308, 309. While the Platonic notion of the just man as one who "does his own things" (τὸ τὰ αὑτου πράττειν, *Republic* 433b) is in itself unobjectionably humanistic, as is Plato's definition of temperance (*Republic* 432a), Babbitt recoiled from the appeal to fear as an incentive to justice as found in the eschatological myth of Er, which concludes the *Republic*.

29. Babbitt, *Democracy*, p. 261.

30. Ibid., p. 34.

31. Irving Babbitt to Stuart Sherman, June 28, 1918, Stuart Sherman Papers, University Archives, University of Illinois, Urbana, Ill. (hereafter cited as Sherman Papers). It is peculiar that nowhere did Babbitt acknowledge the damaging effects of the 1911 revolution in China and the collapse of the Ch'ing Dynasty upon Confucianism as a social dogma.

32. Babbitt, *Democracy*, p. 35.

33. Ibid., p. 150. Yet, Aristotle was far more willing than either Plato or Babbitt to concede sense and merit to collective opinion. See Aristotle, *Politics* 1281b, 1282a, 1283b.

34. Babbitt, *Democracy*, p. 103. Babbitt considered Samuel Johnson no less worthy a conservative, but he found that Johnson was also a Tory too reactionary to be accounted a humanist of true critical spirit. Babbitt's reading notes on Horace Walpole suggest that he formed a composite view of eighteenth-century British decorum from which he defined Burke's "moral imagination."

35. Irving Babbitt, "What I Believe," *Forum*, February 1930, p. 81.

36. Ibid. In *Politics* 1294a, Aristotle makes excellence in virtue the guiding principle of aristocracy, as freedom is the guide of a democracy. Mere wealth would not provide rule by the best but only rule by the few, that is, an oligarchy.

37. Babbitt, *Democracy*, p. 114. It could fairly be charged, as Hoeveler has, that Babbitt himself was "largely ignorant of the demands of a technologically advanced society." Concern with the higher self of the cherished dualism made him indifferent or blind to "the value of studying human nature in its social, economic and political interactions with the world." Hoeveler, *New Humanism*, pp. 122, 123. One critic, however, has suggested that Babbitt's humanism could be an important champion of the individual's worth in the face of the modern world's technologically imposed conformities. See Henry S. Kariel, "Democracy Limited: Irving Babbitt's Classicism," *Review of Politics* 13 (October 1951): 440.

38. Basil Willey finds Burke "in many ways a spiritual progenitor of the nineteenth century" so far as "the attempts of Coleridge, Carlyle, Green and Ruskin to reintroduce a conception of the state as a spiritual and not merely an economic partnership derive in part from him." *Eighteenth-Century Background* (London, 1965), p. 237.

39. Babbitt, *Democracy*, p. 115.

40. Irving Babbitt, miscellaneous notes, Babbitt Papers.

41. His British sources formed a Burkean continuum of a sort conforming to his biases. According to Babbitt's reading notes, Fitz-James Stephens,

in *Liberty, Equality, Fraternity* (London, 1874), found enthusiasm for liberty "hardly compatible" with the "virtues" of obedience and discipline. About American democracy he asked whether "the rapid production of an immense multitude of commonplace self-satisfied essentially slight people is an exploit which the whole world need fall down and worship" (pp. 189, 271). Another source, W. H. Lecky's *Democracy and Liberty* (London, 1896), was no less stringent in deriding "blind worship of mere numbers." Of particular interest to Babbitt was Lecky's praise of the English tradition by which offices still went only to educated gentlemen. It had saved England from some of the consequences of direct democracy (pp. 223, 140). Irving Babbitt, Reading Notes for "Democracy and Imperialism," Babbitt Papers.

42. Babbitt to More, August 7, 1919, Babbitt-More Correspondence.

43. Babbitt, Notes on Democracy and Imperialism, Babbitt Papers.

44. Ibid.; see also Babbitt, *Democracy*, p. 242.

45. Henry Adams, *History of the United States* (1909), 2 vols. (Englewood Cliffs, N.J., 1963), 1:105, 107.

46. Irving Babbitt, *Literature and the American College* (Boston, 1908), pp. 42–43.

47. Quoted by Babbitt from Robert L. Morse, *Thomas Jefferson* (Boston, 1897), pp. 13, 52, 48, 148, in Notes on Democracy and Imperialism, Babbitt Papers.

48. Babbitt, *Democracy*, p. 247.

49. Ibid., p. 110.

50. Irving Babbitt, "Humanism: An Essay at Definition," in *Humanism and America*, ed. Norman Foerster (New York, 1930), p. 35.

51. Babbitt, Notes on Democracy and Imperialism, Babbitt Papers. He had in mind Bryan's Populist movement of 1896. A stern opponent of bimetallism, Babbitt viewed its inflationary tendencies as a kind of fraud.

52. Babbitt, *Democracy*, p. 249. He was apparently ignorant of how cavalier Lincoln could sometimes be in his attitude toward officers of government, including Supreme Court justices and members of his own cabinet.

53. Ibid., p. 307.

54. Ibid., p. 305.

55. Quoted by Babbitt from A. Lawrence Lowell, *Essays on Government* (Boston, 1890), p. 125, in Notes on Democracy and Imperialism, Babbitt Papers.

56. Ibid., p. 127; Babbitt to More, August 7, 1919, Babbitt-More Correspondence.

57. Irving Babbitt, undated lecture, Babbitt Papers.

58. Quoted by Babbitt in *Literature*, p. 68. This may be a reference to the anarchist, Alexander Berkmann, who attempted an assassination of the industrialist, Henry Clay Frick, during the 1892 Homestead strike against Carnegie.

59. Babbitt refers to the following passage: the rich, Rousseau writes, are "like famished wolves that, having once tasted human flesh, reject all other nourishment and want only to devour men." *Discours*, p. 77.

60. A lecture in which Babbitt depicted modern socialists as offspring of Rousseau brought a unique and formal rebuttal from a precocious student. Besides indicating something of Babbitt's own position, it is a well-argued defense and deserves lengthy citation:

> I am a member of your course in Comparative Literature. I was present at the lecture on Rousseau in which you had a fling at socialism. Looking at your attitude as impartially as possible, I cannot feel that your views on socialism are associated with anything more modern than the Utopists of the first half of the century, unless it be the daily newspapers. For, if you will pardon me for saying it, no man with any grasp of modern socialist philosophy, as expounded by the English Fabians for example, would ever have made the mistake of associating Rousseauistic humanitarianism with scientific socialism based on a larger social consciousness. And further, a moderate knowledge of economics shows that the direct outcome of Rousseauism was the Manchester School of Economics. These men, the devotees of laissez-faire and "the rights of the individual" are the direct descendants of Rousseau in the industrial field. Taking the cue from Rousseau, they proceeded on the Anarchistic assumption, alias Jeffersonian Democracy, that you had only to leave the individual to run things by the dictates of his own sweet will, and all things would be "for the best in this best of all possible worlds."
>
> As has been statistically proved, this philosophy landed us in modern conditions where drink, vice, crime, prostitution, riches and poverty are prevailing factors. Socialism rises straight out of a criticism of this anarchistic philosophy. It repudiates "the natural goodness of man" as absurd; but it repudiates the "natural badness of man" with equal gusto. Its position is based on modern biological investigation into the formative influences of environment. It does not say, as you assumed it did, that human nature is naturally good; it assumes that with the exception of rare hereditary influences human nature is moulded by its surroundings.
>
> Therefore, your attempt to associate socialism of the twentieth century with Rousseauism is misleading. It hardly seems fair to use your position of authority to stimulate in the minds of college men prejudice against a body of thought, which may be right or wrong, but which at least demands the most fair minded consideration. . . .
>
> My objection to your attitude is illustrated in your treatment of Proudhon. Certainly on the face of it a bold statement that property is theft is a startling one to a set of men nourished on the belief that private property is a sacred thing. It is quite as startling as the notion that kings are not divinely ordained must have been when it was first expounded. . . . The point is that Proudhon's statement, which you tossed off as the vagary of a mind obsessed with logic, made an impression on modern thought which it will never shake off. It is extremely unfair to treat his

work as a piece of pure foolishness. I submit that unless you are prepared to value his influence you ought not to stir up a laugh at his expense. [Walter Lippmann to Irving Babbitt, October 7, 1908, Babbitt
Papers]

Support for Lippmann on the crucial import of environment can be found
in a lengthy argument for behaviorism in Book 5, Letter 3 of *La Nouvelle
Héloïse* by Jean-Jacques Rousseau.

61. Irving Babbitt, miscellaneous notes, Babbitt Papers; see also *Democracy*,
p. 193.

62. Babbitt, *Democracy*, p. 193.

63. Babbitt, Notes on Democracy and Imperialism, Babbitt Papers.

64. Babbitt, *Democracy*, p. 288. He was referring specifically to Wilson's
signing the Adamson Act, which reduced hours for railroad workingmen.

65. Ibid., pp. 307, 232.

66. Babbitt to More, August 7, 1919, Babbitt-More Correspondence.

67. Babbitt, *Democracy*, p. 193. "The type of efficiency that our master
commercialists pursue requires that a multitude of men should be deprived
of their specifically human attributes and become mere cogs in some vast
machine" (p. 255). He drew from this concession no implications that might
have justified, to him, labor's political organization.

68. Babbitt, *Literature*, p. 71.

69. Irving Babbitt, "The Breakdown of Internationalism," *Nation*, June
24, 1915, p. 706.

70. Babbitt, *Democracy*, p. 205. Finding that mercantile contests for hegemony spawned "a raw plutocracy" and "monstrous inequalities," Babbitt further objected to capitalism on cultural grounds, that it defrauded men of
true leisure: "Commercialism is laying its great greasy paws upon everything (including the irresponsible quest of thrills); so that, whatever democracy may be theoretically, one is sometimes tempted to define it practically
as standardized and commercialized melodrama" (pp. 204, 242).

71. Ibid., p. 272. Babbitt was genuinely alarmed over what he felt to be
the threat of property confiscation by radicals of every ilk. This fear is directly related to his own constant financial worries. He felt that his income
from teaching, writing, and lecturing on tour was never enough; he was a
moderate investor in stocks and kept extensive longhand accounts of his
earnings.

72. Ibid., p. 297.

73. Ibid., p. 104.

74. The static quality of Babbitt's attitude has its inevitable antecedent in
Aristotle's *Politics*. His defense of property took its cue from Aristotle, who
rejected Plato's quasi-socialism of public ownership for the ruling class, arguing that private property furthered liberality among individuals. Aristotle
also rejected the idea that property was responsible for social evils, claiming
that such evils were due to fundamental defects of human character. "Regu-

lations about property are no substitute for the training of the character and intellect or for using the laws and customs of the community to that end." *The Politics*, trans. J. A. Sinclair (Baltimore, 1962), pp. 64–65.

75. Babbitt to Sherman, April 8, 1913, Sherman Papers.

76. Babbitt, *Democracy*, p. 16.

77. Ibid., p. 294.

78. Ibid., p. 312. Italics mine. It must be noted that in the early 1920s Mussolini enjoyed, thanks to assiduous propaganda, a generally favorable reputation outside of Italy for having apparently restored order out of postwar economic and parliamentary chaos. Babbitt was undoubtedly ignorant of Trotsky's remark that "il Duce" was Bolshevism's best student. Indeed, authoritarianism or "puritan" elements of restraint have been too facilely imputed to Babbitt, as in David Spitz's *Patterns of Anti-Democratic Thought* (New York, 1965), pp. 265–93. What Spitz terms Babbitt's "restrictive way of life" was a universe apart from the modern forms of dictatorship with which Spitz implicitly associates it; that is, he confuses Babbitt's insistence upon self-control in leadership with control over the masses.

79. Babbitt, Notes on Democracy and Imperialism, Babbitt Papers.

80. Ibid.

81. Irving Babbitt, undated lecture, Babbitt Papers.

82. Babbitt, *Democracy*, p. 268.

83. Irving Babbitt, miscellaneous notes, Babbitt Papers.

84. Babbitt, *Democracy*, p. 255. Although this elusive phrase might suggest the Platonic guardian of the *Republic* in contemplation of transcendent forms, Babbitt's dualism here likely refers only to the embodiment of political ideals in constitutional tradition.

85. Ibid., p. 282.

86. Ibid., p. 269.

87. Babbitt, Notes on Democracy and Imperialism, Babbitt Papers.

88. Sherman to Babbitt, March 24, 1922, Sherman Papers.

89. Babbitt to Sherman, April 5, 1922, Sherman Papers.

90. Jacob Zeitlin and Homer Woodbridge, *The Life and Letters of Stuart P. Sherman*, 2 vols. (New York, 1929), 2:680.

91. Ibid., 1:302.

92. Sherman to More, January 20, 1919, Sherman Papers.

93. Babbitt to More, November 21, 1917, Babbitt-More Correspondence.

94. Babbitt to Sherman, March 18, 1922, Sherman Papers.

95. Sherman to Babbitt, undated letter, Sherman Papers.

96. Ibid.

97. Sherman to Mather, January 13, 1923, Sherman Papers.

98. T. S. Eliot, "The Humanism of Irving Babbitt," in his *Selected Essays*, p. 420.

99. Sherman to Mather, January 13, 1923, Sherman Papers.

100. Ibid. "Babbitt erects his *chevaux-de-frise* of arbitrary 'definitions' warranted to eviscerate every gizzard and break every neck born into this disas-

trous world since Aristotle; while More retreats into a blinding white mist of
Platonism, where God himself would think twice before pursuing." Ibid.

101. Babbitt to Sherman, February 18, 1923, Sherman Papers.

102. Stuart Sherman, *Americans* (New York, 1922), p. 332.

Chapter 7

1. William James, *The Varieties of Religious Experience* (London, 1902),
pp. 493–95.

2. Irving Babbitt, undated lecture marked "Indiana" (probably Bloomington, in June of 1919), Babbitt Papers.

3. Irving Babbitt, "Buddha and the Occident," in *The Dhammapada*, trans.
Irving Babbitt (New York, 1965), p. 71.

4. Irving Babbitt, *The Masters of Modern French Criticism* (Boston, 1912),
p. 330.

5. Babbitt to More, May 17, 1908, Babbitt-More Correspondence.

6. Irving Babbitt, Notes on Buddhism, Babbitt Papers.

7. Irving Babbitt, miscellaneous notes, Babbitt Papers. In this regard, his
position approximates Greek humanism as one classical scholar has recently
defined it. The Greeks "found grief, defect and mortality, when faced with
gallantry of mind, to be better than unearthly states of blessed existence."
Emily Vermeule, *Aspects of Death in Early Greek Art and Poetry* (Berkeley,
1979), p. 123.

8. Paul Elmer More, in *Irving Babbitt, Man and Teacher*, ed. Frederick Manchester and Odell Shepard (New York, 1941), p. 336.

9. More to Babbitt, September 14, 1917, Babbitt-More Correspondence.

10. Paul Elmer More, in *Irving Babbitt*, ed. Manchester and Shepard,
p. 325. More continues: "He has been criticized for this and ridiculed for
harping everlastingly on the same thoughts, as if he lacked the faculty of assimilation and growth. On the contrary, I am inclined to believe that the
weight of his influence can be attributed in large measure to just this tenac-
ity of mind. In a world visibly shifting from opinion to opinion and, as it
were, rocking on its foundation, here was one who never changed or fal-
tered in his grasp of principles, whose latest word can be set beside his earliest with no apology for inconsistency, who could always be depended on"
(p. 325).

11. Paul Elmer More, *Platonism* (Princeton, 1917), p. 146.

12. Ibid., p. 143.

13. He characterized "real Platonism" as "not a metaphysic but a discipline, an ἀναγωγή." Paul Elmer More, *Shelburne Essays, Sixth Series: Studies of
Religious Dualism* (New York, 1909), p. 346.

14. Babbitt to More, February 12, 1915, Babbitt-More Correspondence.

15. More to Babbitt, December 26, 1923, Babbitt-More Correspondence.
Having defined religion as a balance of "otherworldliness and morality,"

More described the philosophical imagination of Platonism and its Forms as "the beginning of religion, its anchor, its hope, its last refuge of assurance," but over it he exalted the mythological imagination embodied in Christianity, "the revelation of a personal God through the historic event." Paul Elmer More, *The Christ of the New Testament* (Princeton, 1924), pp. 23, 24.

16. Babbitt to More, August 10, 1921, Babbitt-More Correspondence.

17. Babbitt to More, December 7, 1912, Babbitt-More Correspondence.

18. Babbitt to More, May 14, 1924, Babbitt-More Correspondence. Babbitt never allowed that Platonic meditation might be termed a higher romanticism, distinct from the putative "sham" or bogus spirituality he broadly attacked. A friendly critic has noted that insofar as he discerned a pseudoclassicism apart from classicism (and, in *The New Laokoon*, a pseudo-Platonism), Babbitt should have discerned a pseudoromanticism apart from a legitimate and healthy romanticism. See Lynn Harold Hough, "Dr. Babbitt and Vital Control," *London Quarterly Review* 147 (January 1927): 1–15. (As Babbitt never attained the doctoral degree, the article is mistakenly titled. It was corrected in a reprint as "Professor Babbitt and Vital Control," in Hough's *Vital Control*, Forest Essays, 1st ser. [New York, 1934].)

19. Babbitt to More, May 14, 1924, Babbitt-More Correspondence.

20. Ibid.

21. Babbitt to More, July 9, 1924, Babbitt-More Correspondence. Babbitt found that More's "distinction between the self-moved and the unmoved mover" came "very near to overpassing the bounds of human faculty. The Aristotelian phrase, by the way, has always seemed to me to correspond to certain primary intuitions regarding the mysterious background of our conscious life." Further, "to project the idea of personality into the central element of calm that is, as I take it, a matter of primary intuition, is to depart from the Socratic reserve at the very point it may be most needed." Ibid. Babbitt's primary intuitions were those of the intellect unaided either by spiritual dogma or the sentimental naturalism of Rousseau and Bergson. Ever prone to hierarchical categories, he designated the "intuitions" of Christianity and romanticism as "higher" and "lower," but charged that both had made historic incursions upon the autonomy and validity of intellectual insight.

22. Babbitt to More, May 14, 1924, Babbitt-More Correspondence. More had attacked the mysticism of Plotinus and the gnostics as based upon an absolute derived from Aristotle. Babbitt upheld his master as wholly foreign to mysticism "in his total temper," because of his mundane attention to "purposeful effort, which is the most Aristotelian thing in the world."

23. More to Babbitt, May 24, 1924, Babbitt-More Correspondence.

24. Quoted by Harry Hayden Clark in *Irving Babbitt*, ed. Manchester and Shepard, p. 265.

25. Quoted by G. K. Chalmers in *Irving Babbitt*, ed. Manchester and Shepard, p. 296. Chalmers construed this utterance (wrongly, I feel) as a statement of religious faith.

26. Babbitt to More, September 22, 1927, Babbitt-More Correspondence.

27. More to Babbitt, October 12, 1927, Babbitt-More Correspondence. More's criticism of Buddhism, complementing Bergson's, is cited at the conclusion of this chapter.

28. Babbitt, "Buddha and the Occident," pp. 77–78.

29. Irving Babbitt, "What I Believe," *Forum*, February 1930, p. 86.

30. Babbitt to More, September 22, 1927, Babbitt-More Correspondence.

31. Babbitt was as lonely as ever, particularly so after his sister, to whom he was always intellectually and temperamentally close, was killed in an automobile accident in November 1925. As More recalled their discussions, he and Babbitt occupied much the same ground as in the 1890s. "Babbitt's fundamental ideas had not changed by a jot, though they were now reinforced by an appalling mass of erudition at the service of an unhesitating, unfailing, unerring memory." *Irving Babbitt*, ed. Manchester and Shepard, p. 330.

32. Irving Babbitt, *On Being Creative and Other Essays* (Boston, 1932), pp. xvii–xviii.

33. Ibid., p. xxii.

34. Paul Elmer More in *Irving Babbitt*, ed. Manchester and Shepard, p. 324.

35. Babbitt to More, May 17, 1908, Babbitt-More Correspondence.

36. T. S. Eliot, "The Humanism of Irving Babbitt," in his *Selected Essays, 1917–1932* (New York, 1950), p. 428. Italics mine.

37. Ibid., p. 424.

38. Irving Babbitt, Notes on Democracy and Imperialism, Babbitt Papers. His remark in the same note that "an idyllic dreamer may have his uses but not in the White House" was the sum of his opinion of Woodrow Wilson.

39. Babbitt, "Buddha," p. 111.

40. Ibid., p. 80.

41. Ibid., pp. 85, 97.

42. Babbitt to More, April 19, 1909, Babbitt-More Correspondence. More himself underscored Babbitt's criticism in depicting humanism as "the way of the world and of humanity caught in the web of ever-changing needs" and dependent upon compromise and mediation, whereas Christianity offers an imaginative refuge for "those who at times must fret under the bondage of compromise." More, *Christ*, pp. 136, 141. Babbitt's retention to the end of his life of this dualism and his no less insistent atheism disqualify him from the company of "the Humanist theology" as caricatured by Mencken: "The hot sun is too much for them: they want an asylum that is reassuringly dark and damp, with incense burning and the organ playing soft and delicate hymns." H. L. Mencken, "Pedagogues Aflutter," *American Mercury*, May 1930, p. 127.

43. Babbitt, "Buddha," p. 113.

44. Babbitt, *On Being Creative*, p. xxxv. Thus, Hoeveler overstates Babbitt's position on religious faith in claiming that he "while always averse to the in-

stitutional church, personally respected religious faith as a force that lifted man above the natural plane of existence through its imaginative and spiritual qualities." J. David Hoeveler, *The New Humanism: A Critique of Modern America, 1900–1940* (Charlottesville, 1977), p. 153. One can as readily argue the reverse, that Babbitt, like Cicero, saw formal religion as a bulwark for social order, yet he was also suspicious of the religious temperament, as his essay "Pascal" indicates.

45. Babbitt, *On Being Creative*, p. xxx.

46. Irving Babbitt, *Rousseau and Romanticism* (Boston, 1919), p. 154.

47. Friedrich Nietzsche, *Der Antichrist* (1895) (Munich, 1964), pp. 21, 22. Nietzsche's position on this subject, as on many others, was not consistent. He did class Buddhism with Christianity as a decadent religion, that is, a manifestation of a decrepit, collapsed civilization, but he conceived it as fundamentally opposite to the subversive *ressentiment* of Pauline Christianity. He makes abundant reference to Buddhism in his notebooks, *Der Wille zur Macht*. In *Fröhliche Wissenschaft* (1882) (Munich, 1964), pp. 278–82, he charges Buddhism with pessimism and "Willenserkränkung."

48. Babbitt, "Buddha," p. 72.

49. Friedrich Nietzsche, *Menschliches, Allzumenschliches* (1878, 1879), 2 vols. (Munich, 1964), 1:143. "Die Erhebung über die andern Menschen durch die logische Zucht und Schulung des Denkens wurde bei den Buddhisten als ein Kennzeichen der Heiligkeit ebenso gefordert, wie dieselben Eigenschaften in der christlichen Welt als Kennzeichen der Unheiligkeit abgelehnt und verketzert werden."

50. Babbitt, *Rousseau and Romanticism*, p. 379.

51. Ibid., pp. 380, 258.

52. Babbitt, *Masters*, p. 367. Babbitt to More, April 19, 1909, Babbitt-More Correspondence; Irving Babbitt, *Democracy and Leadership* (Boston, 1924), p. 188. A substantial shortcoming in Mercier's characterization of Babbitt's humanism as implicitly religious or "supercosmic" is that he ignores Babbitt's atheism, the crucial sticking point for the theists, More and Eliot. Babbitt never accepted a revealed religion or a personal deity. Mercier does not make clear that Babbitt's support of Catholicism was tactical, that he perceived it as a historical buttress of civilization against the impending chaos of socialism. See Louis Mercier's "The Legacy of Irving Babbitt" in his *American Humanism and the New Age* (Milwaukee, 1948), pp. 9–33.

53. Babbitt, *Masters*, p. 311.

54. Nietzsche, *Antichrist*, p. 44: "Der Buddhismus verspricht nicht sondern hält, das Christentum verspricht alles, aber hält nichts."

55. Babbitt, Notes on Buddhism, Babbitt Papers.

56. Babbitt, Notes on Democracy and Imperialism, Babbitt Papers. The remark seems to suggest Josiah Royce's triadic view of Christian ethics, but Babbitt would have been highly suspicious of Royce's communitarian idealism. Rather, the mediation of a disinterested good between two people suggests Plato's norm for ideal friendship as described in the *Lysis* 221e.

57. Babbitt, *Rousseau and Romanticism*, p. 156. The austerity of what Babbitt called "Buddha's tillage of the spirit" contrasted sharply with the dogmatic austerity of Christianity as reflected in a mind like Pascal's. Babbitt's private notes underscore this contrast. According to early Buddhism, he wrote, "no one else can do the work for you; no one can purify another; no grace such as developed in later Buddhism; no good works in [the] sense of performance of rites and ceremonies; nothing is of avail save work upon oneself . . . strenuousness, not love, [is] central." Babbitt, Notes on Buddhism, Babbitt Papers.

58. Irving Babbitt, "Matthew Arnold," *Nation*, August 2, 1917, pp. 118–19.

59. Ibid., p. 119. The probable reference is to Book 10, in which meditation is defined as the activity most likely to bring happiness as it is akin to the activity of the unmoved mover.

60. Babbitt, *Rousseau and Romanticism*, pp. 161, 250. The "escape from impermanence" that Hoeveler finds to be the keynote of Babbitt's interest in Buddhism suggests, if not a frigid Eleatic One, a kind of Neoplatonic mysticism. Babbitt did not, perhaps, realize how much of the Greek tradition he carried over to Buddhism. In a late essay, reviewing the aesthetic of Croce, Babbitt was still appealing to a metaphysic of the One and the Many, the unchanging as an aesthetic reference against unchecked expansive impulse. For Babbitt, as for Plato, art was inextricably involved in both political and religious issues. See Hoeveler, *New Humanism*, p. 60.

61. Babbitt, *Rousseau and Romanticism*, pp. 202, 252.

62. Ibid., p. 270; Irving Babbitt, "Humanism: An Essay at Definition," in *Humanism and America*, ed. Norman Foerster (New York, 1930), p. 43.

63. According to Aristotle, *aretē* or virtue in the sense of excellence is the exercise of a mean between extremes of excess (ὑπερβολή) and deficiency (ἔλλειψις). But by possessing an excess of virtue man becomes godlike: ἐξ ἀνθρώπων γίνονται θεοὶ δι᾽ ἀρετῆς ὑπερβολήν (*Nicomachean Ethics* 1145a 22–24). Mind becomes the agent for man's divinization: ὅσον ἐνδέχεται ἀθανατίζειν (1177b 33). Babbitt cited the latter passage as evidence of Aristotle's religious enthusiasm. But, as several of Aristotle's commentators note, his metaphysics of divinity remains problematic, if not obscure. The issue is treated with admirable lucidity in Sir David Ross, *Aristotle* (London, 1949), pp. 79, 126, 179–86, and in Werner Jaeger's *Aristotle* (Oxford, 1948), esp. p. 243, where Jaeger's discussion of Book 10 of the *Nicomachean Ethics* includes a description strikingly pertinent to the nature of Paul Elmer More's religious conversion.

64. Babbitt, "Humanism," p. 40.

65. Babbitt, Notes on Buddhism, Babbitt Papers.

66. Ibid.

67. Babbitt to More, June 12, 1932, Babbitt-More Correspondence.

68. More to Babbitt, August 2, 1931, Babbitt-More Correspondence.

69. More to Babbitt, June 16, 1932, Babbitt-More Correspondence.

70. Babbitt to More, April 17, 1932, Babbitt-More Correspondence.

71. More to Babbitt, August 12, 1931, Babbitt-More Correspondence.
72. Babbitt to More, April 17, 1932, Babbitt-More Correspondence.
73. More to Babbitt, May 17, 1932, Babbitt-More Correspondence.
74. Babbitt to More, August 6, 1931, Babbitt-More Correspondence.
75. Babbitt to More, June 12, 1932, Babbitt-More Correspondence.
76. Ibid.
77. Henri Bergson, *Les Deux Sources de la morale et de la religion* (Paris, 1932), pp. 240, 241.

Chapter 8

1. George Santayana, "The Genteel Tradition in American Philosophy," in his *Winds of Doctrine* (1913; reprint, New York, 1957), pp. 211, 214.
2. Ibid., pp. 192–93.
3. Quoted by Santayana in "The Genteel Tradition," p. 208; William James to Charles Eliot Norton, June 30, 1904, *The Letters of Charles Eliot Norton*, ed. Sara Norton and M. A. DeWolfe Howe, 2 vols. (Boston, 1913), 2:348.
4. Babbitt referred to an "ethical self" that one shares with others, one like Royce's ideal self to which a seeking self is directed, but his pronouncement in favor of individual over social redemption was his most characteristic emphasis. A Roycean community was expressly humanitarian; a humanistic one was a contradiction in terms. Irving Babbitt, *Rousseau and Romanticism* (Boston, 1919), p. 348.
5. Babbitt to More, October 19, 1896, Babbitt-More Correspondence.
6. Irving Babbitt, *The Masters of Modern French Criticism* (Boston, 1912), p. 352.
7. Irving Babbitt, "Racine and the Anti-Romantic Reaction," *Nation*, November 18, 1909, p. 480.
8. Irving Babbitt, *On Being Creative and Other Essays* (Boston, 1932), p. xix.

Bibliographical Essay

Unpublished Materials

The two essential collections of Irving Babbitt's papers are his forty years of correspondence with Paul Elmer More (referred to in the text as the Babbitt-More Correspondence), privately held by Babbitt's daughter, Mrs. Esther Babbitt Howe, in Washington, D.C., and his lecture and reading notes in the Harvard University Archives, Harvard University, Cambridge, Massachusetts. The latter, comprising some nine boxes, are loosely arranged by subject but in reading through the notes one has the sustained impression of a vast, chaotic miscellany. Babbitt's widow made a valiant attempt to sort the materials, but many are little more than fragments and most have neither dates nor headings.

The Harvard Archives also contain the manuscript of Babbitt's translation of the *Dhammapada* and a file of his financial records. A box of letters to him has only isolated items of interest, among which are letters from some of his devoted Oriental students who had returned to the East. Babbitt was a poor correspondent. Excepting More, only Stuart Sherman managed to elicit responses from him with any consistency. Their exchange, from 1910 to 1923, is in the Stuart Sherman Papers at the University of Illinois Archives at Urbana, where there are twenty-one letters from Babbitt, a few of which can be found in *The Life and Letters of Stuart Sherman*, edited by Jacob Zeitlin and Homer Woodbridge (New York, 1929). Other Babbitt materials are in the Papers of the American Academy of Arts and Letters in New York City, and in his voluminous exchange with his publishers, the Houghton Mifflin Company (referred to in the text as the Babbitt–Houghton Mifflin Correspondence), housed at the Houghton Library, Harvard University.

The Charles Eliot Norton Papers, at the Houghton Library, Harvard University, form an inestimably rich collection, notable in the humanist context mainly for Paul Elmer More's letters to Norton in the 1890s. Finally, the Harry Hayden Clark Papers at the University of Wisconsin Archives at Madison include his extensive lecture notes as Babbitt's student assistant in comparative literature.

Published Primary Materials

From 1908 to 1932, Babbitt published five books and a collection of essays. The first, *Literature and the American College* (Boston, 1908), is one of his best and contains, at least in abbreviated form, most of the arguments of his later works. It has little that is dated; a change of some terms and names would give it striking pertinence to educational issues some four generations after its publication. *The New Laokoon: An Essay on the Confusion of the Arts* (Boston, 1910) is Babbitt's least successful polemic; its aesthetic materials seem at times beyond his grasp and there is a noticeable lack of the aggressive vigor of its predecessor. It has long been out of print and is not likely to enjoy a new edition. By contrast, *The Masters of Modern French Criticism* (Boston, 1912), although academic in nature, affords many instances of Babbitt's talent for imaginative characterization. Much in his personality and bias is reflected in his portraits, but the harshness of his more explicit polemics is not so evident here. The conclusion is perhaps his most lucid exposition of the humanistic function of criticism. Although many critics regard *Rousseau and Romanticism* (Boston, 1919) as Babbitt's chef d'oeuvre, it is diffuse and repetitious. It does contain many of his most inflammatory generalities and a good deal of his damning epithets so that it has become a kind of documentation of Babbitt as a reactionary. Yet it also contains some of his most important formulations of humanism vis-à-vis religion. *Democracy and Leadership* (Boston, 1924) is an Arnoldian application of the humanist's "critical spirit" to the broader problems of society and politics. One might say that it has the virtues of his first book and the vices of his fourth, that is, some amazingly modern criticism is combined with a relentless conservatism. *On Being Creative and Other Essays* (Boston, 1932) is a cross section of arguments, largely regarding literature and criticism, that can be found in his earlier books. Among the essays, the introduction, the title essay, and "The Critic and American Life" are best written, each of them having Babbitt's typically spirited bite.

Babbitt's translation of the *Dhammapada* was published three years after his death, in 1936. The 1965 edition includes his most important essay on religion, "Buddha and the Occident." A second collection of his essays, principally articles that had appeared in the *Nation*, was edited by his friends, Frederick Manchester, Rachel Giese, and William Giese. *Spanish Character and Other Essays* (Boston, 1940) is curiously mistitled since the bulk of the topics is French. This volume, however, has two special merits: a chronological bibliography of all of Babbitt's publications, including anonymous reviews, and an index of nearly one hundred pages, covering each book.

A recent collection of some of Babbitt's essays and selections from his books is *Irving Babbitt: Representative Writings*, edited by George Panichas (Lincoln, 1981). In addition to a bibliography, the editor supplies an extensive index of names with brief identifications, a helpful resource for readers who might be unfamiliar with some, if not most, of the multitude of authors upon whom Babbitt drew. The introduction is a slightly enlarged version of Panichas's "The Critical Mission of Irving Babbitt" (see *Published Secondary Materials: A Selection of Criticism*).

Unlike Babbitt, More has been well served by biographers. In his *Paul Elmer More* (Princeton, 1960), Arthur Dakin has drawn extensively from More's vast correspondence. Francis Duggan's study with the same title (New Haven, 1966) is an admirable review of More's intellectual development as revealed in his massive publications. A sympathetic summary of More's life and thought can be found in Austin Warren's "Paul Elmer More: A Critic in Search of Wisdom," *Southern Review* (Autumn 1969): 1091–1111. For a penetrating and refined study that places More within the dualism of the modern as well as the classical philosophical tradition, see Paul Grimley Kuntz, "The Dualism of Paul Elmer More," *Religious Studies* 16 (1980): 389–411.

Published Secondary Materials:
A Background for Babbitt's Humanism

An understanding of Babbitt's humanism requires some acquaintance with writers to whose works he gave particular attention. A thorough review of these sources would prove an encyclopedic task. I have preferred a highly selective listing of the most important works.

Aristotle's *Politics*, *Poetics*, and *Nicomachean Ethics* had a canonical status for Babbitt: Aristotle was a synonym for common sense of the sort that Babbitt claimed as a basic humanistic virtue. Conversely, he consulted Plato only with great caution; yet, as this study argues, the influence of Plato is pronounced in Babbitt's aesthetics and politics. Hence the *Republic* serves as an indispensable background. Most important to Babbitt was the image of Socrates that emerged from the "Socratic" dialogues, particularly the *Apology*. Among other Greeks, Aeschylus and Sophocles ranked highest. Homer, like the Old Testament, was apparently short of ideas, but he was the epitome of what Babbitt called "recreative" reading. It may be noted parenthetically that Babbitt read the Greeks in their language, but, in the midst of a "progressive" trend in education, he knew better than to insist that students read in foreign languages. At the same time, he was sure that no one ignorant of Greek and Roman culture and history could pass for an educated person and that the learning of Greek and Latin was the proper disciplinary means to the appreciation of those civilizations. They provided, in fact, the primary touchstones for the classical aspects of humanism.

When we consider Babbitt's wide reading in Latin and the Roman quality of his stress upon social order and hierarchic models of authority, it is surprising how little he referred even to his favorites, Horace and Cicero. As the German humanist, Werner Jaeger, has remarked, Rome, not Athens, is the model of humanist culture so far as it required an imaginative assimilation of another culture, the creation of a more than parochial tradition.

Oriental humanism reached its acme in the *Analects* of Confucius and the *Sayings* of Mencius, his foremost disciple. These were the only texts that Babbitt had to consult in translation. He once remarked in middle age that if he were thirty years younger, he would undertake to learn Chinese. Buddhism as the spiritual complement to Confucianism was best represented, Babbitt thought, in its early works, especially the *Dhammapada*. Babbitt's labor of years in translating this work, which is shorter than any of the synoptic gospels, reflected his scholarly concern for as much accuracy in terms as could be kept in passing from one language and cultural context to another.

Among medieval writers, Dante looms far above all others. He is an example of a basically religious artist transformed by Babbitt into a proponent of humanistic will. Dante's mysticism was the only kind for which Babbitt ever stated that he could feel a possible sympathy. *De Monarchia* is included in Babbitt's bibliographical notes for *Democracy and Leadership.*

By nationality, the French comprised the largest literary culture for Babbitt, even though they provided him with none of the highest models of humanism. Pascal came closest. His *Pensées*—fragments far less stylistically accomplished than his *Lettres provinciales*—convinced Babbitt that Pascal was the man of faith most necessary to the twentieth century if it was to find its way out of its humanitarian delusions. In this sense, Pascal was, on the spiritual plane, like Montaigne on the humanistic, the ideal foil of Rousseau.

Babbitt's reading of his principal antagonist was literal. What Rousseau wrote was either sensible or it was not; usually, not. Babbitt showed little awareness of Rousseau's sophisticated talent in masking, stylizing, and even satirizing his own views. The Protean nature of Rousseau's sensibility is evident in all of his major works, but nowhere is it better revealed than in the adroitly misnamed *Confessions* (1770), the major text for most of Babbitt's citations against him. A sequel to this apologia is *Rousseau, Juge de Jean-Jacques* (1772–76), in which the clinical nature of his temperament becomes increasingly evident. The last of the autobiographical works are the *Rêveries du promeneur solitaire* (1777–78); absolute solitude enabled Rousseau to attain a style of lyric serenity to be found almost nowhere else in his works.

Rousseau's *Discours sur l'origine de l'inégalité* (1755) served Babbitt as the principal source of Rousseau's bias against (Parisian) civilization. The ablest refutation of Babbitt's conception of primitivism remains Arthur Lovejoy's "The Supposed Primitivism of Rousseau's *Discourse on Inequality*," *Modern Philology* 21 (1923): 165–86. Babbitt used the *Contrat social* (1762) mainly to weigh Rousseau's *volonté générale* against Hobbes's *Leviathan* and to indict both as harbingers of modern totalitarian thought. Far richer than either discourse, Rousseau's *Émile ou de l'éducation* (1762) spans nearly every important theme of its author and includes acute criticisms of English and French rationalism. *Le Profession de foi du Vicaire Savoyard* in the fourth book is a virtual anatomy of Rousseau's romantic religiosity. This work abounds in statements that had such revolutionary significance for Babbitt that he overlooked the character of Rousseau's frequently iterated skepticism. *Julie ou La Nouvelle Héloïse* (1761) complements *Émile* on many points. Although both books run to an exhausting length (each is about six hundred pages of close print in the Garnier editions), they are indispensable aids in giving one a sense of Rousseau's extraordinarily elusive genius. *Julie* is particularly subtle, for in its many philosophical arguments, Rousseau seems to take each side as though it were his own. Although he professed to be scandalized by the effeminacy of Parisian culture, Rousseau in *Julie* might be said to have made woman the measure of all things.

The sharpest opposition to Babbitt's case against Rousseau comes from Ernst Cassirer in *The Question of Jean-Jacques Rousseau*, translated by Peter

Gay (Bloomington, 1967). Less pertinent but also provocative is Cassirer's *Rousseau, Kant, Goethe,* translated by James Gutmann, Paul Kristeller, and John Hermann Randall, Jr. (Princeton, 1945).

For the critics he reviewed in *The Masters of Modern French Criticism* Babbitt supplied a lengthy appendix of biographical and bibliographical data. Sainte-Beuve was without question the most prominent among these figures. Apart from his *Portraits littéraires* (1862–64) and *Portraits contemporains* (1869–71), *Chateaubriand et son groupe littéraire* (1860) holds primary importance as a document of Sainte-Beuve's romantic criticism and his romantic view of the imagination. Babbitt's friend William Giese in *Sainte-Beuve* (New York, 1932) made a thorough study of his subject's psychology; Giese's viewpoint suggests a strong influence from Babbitt and More. "The Centenary of Sainte-Beuve" in More's *Shelburne Essays, Third Series* (Boston, 1905) points to his importance for the humanist critics.

Goethe, as Babbitt's favorite among the moderns, won his high status from Johann Peter Eckermann's *Gespräche mit Goethe* (1836), which covered the last decade of Goethe's life. (Nietzsche called this work the finest book in the German language.) As this study has noted, *Faust* (1808) remained problematic for Babbitt because he could not accept Goethe's quite humanistic reconciliation of romantic striving and classical sobriety. *Dichtung und Wahrheit* (1811) was especially valuable to Babbitt in exposing the powerful influence of Rousseau and romanticism upon German letters during Goethe's youth. Some of the most penetrating criticisms of Goethe occur in Heinrich Heine's *Die Romantische Schule* (1836). This shrewd, often hilariously witty critic deserves mention with Goethe because for Babbitt he was the model of the intellectual German in whom irony and sentimentality were uneasily blended. An excellent discussion of romantic Hellenism in Goethe, Schiller, Heine, and others is E. M. Butler's *The Tyranny of Greece over Germany* (Cambridge, Eng., 1935). Georg Lukacs's *Goethe and His Age,* translated by Robert Anchor (London, 1968) rivals Butler for wealth of insights, many of which can be taken without one's sharing Lukacs's Marxist view of literary creativity. For a factual account of Goethe's life, Richard Friedenthal's *Goethe: Sein Leben und Seine Zeit* (Munich, 1968), while short on analysis, provides a helpful review of Goethe's relations with many of his illustrious contemporaries.

Highly suggestive though *Culture and Anarchy* (1869) was to Babbitt's political and cultural views, Matthew Arnold's literary essays are more relevant to humanism, particularly in supplying many key terms and definitions that Babbitt either appropriated or transformed for his own uses. "The Function of Criticism at the Present Time" (1864) is a defense that Babbitt never tired of making though he dodged Arnold's case against partisanship in criticism. "The Literary Influence of Academies" (1864) anticipates Babbitt's own tribute to French literary convention as the genius of its culture. "On the Modern Element in Literature" (1869) refers to the "critical spirit" and puts the tellingly apposite question to Babbitt: "How can a man interpret the activity of his age when he is not in sympathy with it?" Finally, and to come full circle, Warren Anderson's *Matthew Arnold and the Classical Tradition* (Ann Arbor, 1971), in discussing Arnold's substantial debts to Plato and Aristotle, among numerous ancients, provides many points for comparison, and some for contrast, with Babbitt's own.

Published Secondary Materials: A Selection of Criticism

Enumeration of every work in which Babbitt has received critical attention, positive or negative, would amount to another book. The following selection has been based upon the substance of the argument, often polemical; in some instances, it refers to the broader context in which Babbitt is placed.

Barzun, Jacques. *Romanticism and the Modern Ego* (New York, 1934). Claims Rousseau has yet to receive intelligent abuse; attempts a correlation between Babbitt's humanism and Allen Tate's favorable remarks on fascism (in his *Reason and Madness*).

Blackmur, R. P. "Humanism and the Symbolic Imagination: Notes on Re-reading Irving Babbitt," in his *The Lion and the Honeycomb* (New York, 1955). Charges Babbitt with excessive intellectualism and a correspondingly deficient imaginative sense; a perceptive, restrained criticism, answered by Panichas (see below).

Eliot, T. S. "The Humanism of Irving Babbitt," in his *Selected Essays, 1917–1932* (New York, 1950). One of Babbitt's most sympathetic critics finds humanism an inadequate substitute for religious orthodoxy. Favorable remarks on Babbitt appear in Eliot's essay on Francis Herbert Bradley in the same volume.

Fausset, Hugh I'Anson. "The New Humanism Refuted," in his *The Proving of Psyche* (London, 1929). The most extensive criticism of Babbitt and a defense of neoromantic Christianity.

Grattan, C. Hartley, ed. *The Critique of Humanism* (New York, 1930). Styled by its editor "an experiment in pamphleteering," this volume was conceived in response to the brief vogue that Babbitt, More, and their supporters enjoyed as the "New Humanists." Several distinguished literary critics contributed, including Allen Tate, Malcolm Cowley, and Edmund Wilson, but the tone and content of the essays vary greatly; some are vituperative and caustic, others urbane and insightful. The contributions of Kenneth Burke and Yvor Winters are among the more judicious, as well as sophisticated, in scope.

Grosselin, Dom Oliver. *The Intuitive Voluntarism of Irving Babbitt* (Latrobe, Pa., 1951). This work is chiefly a series of metaphysical inferences from Babbitt's humanism with little or no use made of his published views and no reference whatever to his unpublished materials. Arguments made to join humanism to Catholicism, however sincere or legitimate, tend to obscure the central importance of Buddhism to Babbitt's thought.

Guttmann, Allen. *The Conservative Tradition in America* (New York, 1967). Situated suggestively between the obscurantism of Henry Adams and the Southern Agrarians of the 1930s, Babbitt and, to some greater length, More here receive their due as spiritual aliens: Babbitt, in his isolation from the Christianity to which other humanists at least nominally deferred; More, in his gradual withdrawal into jeremiads against America's social and political realities.

Hsin-Hai, Chang. "Irving Babbitt and Oriental Thought," *Michigan Quarterly Review* 4 (October 1965): 234–44. One of Babbitt's many admiring Chinese students defends his fusion of humanism with Buddhist and Confucian ethics.

Hoeveler, J. David. *The New Humanism: A Critique of Modern America, 1900–1940* (Charlottesville, 1977). Particularly valuable for its overview of the proponents of the New Humanism, including sketches of secondary figures such as Stuart Sherman, Norman Foerster, and Gorham Munson. Hoeveler characterizes at length the competing academic ideologies of Babbitt's time, chiefly pragmatism, but his awareness of the European antecedents of Babbitt's humanism depends upon secondary sources.

Hough, Lynn Harold. "Dr. Babbitt and Vital Control," *London Quarterly Review* 147 (January 1927): 1–15. Primarily panegyric, this essay is composed of quotations as epigrammatic *aperçus* that Hough uses to summarize Babbitt's politics. He faults Babbitt only for his failure to discern the benefits of humanitarianism.

Kariel, Henry S. "Democracy Limited: Irving Babbitt's Classicism," *Review of Politics* 13 (October 1951): 430–40. A fair canvass of Babbitt's political arguments, this essay nonetheless fails to identify the Platonic assumptions from which Babbitt's "classicism" derived.

Kazin, Alfred. "Liberals and New Humanists," in his *On Native Grounds* (New York, 1942). The classically romantic portrait of Babbitt and More alternates between shrewd perceptions of Babbitt and some inaccuracies bordering upon caricature. For example, Kazin asserts that Babbitt "liked to think of himself as another Dr. Johnson" (p. 296); "fancied himself a Savonarola" (p. 304); "led some of his followers to Fascism" (p. 302).

Kirk, Russell. "Critical Conservatism," in his *The Conservative Mind* (Chicago, 1953). An excellent though brief review of Babbitt's politics by one of his most vigorous defenders, the essay is cast polemically against the Rousseauist naturalism that Kirk sees as pervasive in mid-twentieth-century America. Many lengthy but unattributed quotations.

Levin, Harry. "Irving Babbitt and the Teaching of Literature," in his *Re-*

fractions (New York, 1966). Except for More's memorial tribute, this remains the finest essay on Babbitt, sympathetic but unbiased. One might infer that some personal acquaintance with Babbitt was almost a sine qua non for any judicious appreciation of him such as Levin evinces.

Lora, Ronald. "The New Humanism of Irving Babbitt and Paul Elmer More," in his *Conservative Minds in America* (Chicago, 1972). A reliable survey of the political and religous tenets of Babbitt, contrasted with those of More; helpful in recasting the intellectual milieux within and against which they worked, but neither Babbitt nor More was programmatic enough to propose "a puritanical revolution in literature" as Lora claims. No sources given for quotations.

Lovejoy, Arthur. Review of *Rousseau and Romanticism* in *Modern Language Notes* 35 (May 1920): 302–7. Parodies the extremist bias in Babbitt's style and makes the famous charge that Babbitt's temperamental reaction to romanticism is itself romantic. Lovejoy's attack is one of the few that Babbitt deigned to answer. "In ingenious and complicated misapprehension of my point of view," wrote Babbitt, "he has easily outdone all my other reviewers."

Manchester, Frederick, and Shepard, Odell, eds. *Irving Babbitt, Man and Teacher* (New York, 1941). An invaluable collection of tributes, with an amplitude of panegyrics and anecdotes from former students, this volume contains many insightful contributions including More's, which remains the best essay on Babbitt. The distinguished writers include T. S. Eliot, Merritt Hughes, Austin Warren, Brooks Otis, and Theodore Spencer.

Matthiessen, F. O. "Irving Babbitt," in his *The Responsibilities of the Critic* (New York, 1952). A guarded sympathy for Babbitt as a critic seems to derive from Matthiessen's deference to Eliot's high estimation of Babbitt.

Mercier, Louis. *The Challenge of Humanism* (New York, 1933). A learned exposition of Babbitt's humanism in relation to the European humanistic tradition. Although at times unduly schematic, Mercier could claim Babbitt's imprimatur for the paraphrases of his views.

_____. "The Legacy of Irving Babbitt," in his *American Humanism and the New Age* (Milwaukee, 1948). Mercier's attempt to construct a metaphysics of humanism based upon Babbitt's interpretation of Buddhism fails in his underestimation of the central position of the classical tradition in Babbitt's thought.

Nash, George. *The Conservative Intellectual Movement in America since 1945* (New York, 1976). Charting the several avenues conservatism has taken in the past generation, Nash provides a useful and thorough overview from which to assess the Burkean continuum of which Babbitt was a part. He gives lengthy review to two of Babbitt's most influential admirers, Russell Kirk and Peter Viereck.

Panichas, George. "The Critical Mission of Irving Babbitt," *Modern Age* 20 (1976): 242–53. A strongly sympathetic view of Babbitt's critical principles; reprinted with some revisions as the introduction to *Irving Babbitt: Representative Writings* (see above).

———. "Irving Babbitt and Simone Weil," *Comparative Literature Studies* 15 (1978): 177–92. An original, insightful, and well-argued study conjoining two prophetically isolated thinkers, widely different in temperament yet, as Panichas indicates, in accord on first principles.

Russell, Frances. "The Romanticism of Irving Babbitt," *South Atlantic Quarterly* 32 (October 1933): 399–411. Satirically charges Babbitt with intemperance, nominalism, and straw-man arguments; a skillful exposure of Babbitt's misreading of a poem by Browning and not the first condemnation of him as a Dr. Johnson *redivivus*.

Ryn, Claes. "The Humanism of Irving Babbitt Revisited," *Modern Age* 21 (1977): 251–62. An articulate exposition and defense of Babbitt's "inner check" and "higher will" against the objections of his critics, chiefly Eliot; very helpful in clarifying the relation of Babbitt's secular emphases to religious orthodoxy.

Spitz, David. "The Undesirability of Democracy," in his *Patterns of Anti-Democratic Thought* (New York, 1965). Many incisive criticisms, judiciously posed, of Babbitt's opposition to democracy; argues that Babbitt's hierarchic values are impracticable; his notions of leadership, in a void; his reasoning, circular.

Sypher, Wylie. "Irving Babbitt: A Reappraisal," *New England Quarterly* 14 (March 1941): 64–76. An assessment purportedly sympathetic to humanism but censorious of Babbitt's failure to reconcile his "critical practice," which Sypher finds narrow and dogmatic, with his "critical theory."

Wilson, Edmund. "Notes on Babbitt and More," in his *The Shores of Light* (New York, 1952). One of the sharpest attacks upon Babbitt by a critic who viewed him as a fanatic. The article is interesting largely for Wilson's citations and corrections of Babbitt's use of Greek. Wilson descends to ridicule of Babbitt in his account of a visit with More in the company of Christian Gauss, in "Paul Elmer More and the Mithraic Bull," in his *The Triple Thinkers* (New York, 1938).

Index

Adams, Henry, 39, 43, 88, 102, 112, 118
Adams, Herbert Baxter, 145
Aristotle, 19, 43, 47, 77, 99, 102, 103, 109, 117, 131, 135, 141, 148, 149, 163 (n. 5), 169 (n. 33), 172–73 (n. 74), 173–74 (n. 100), 175 (n. 22), 178 (n. 63); importance of his *Ethics* for humanism, 18–19, 129, 139, 154 (n. 5), 163 (n. 6), 178 (n. 63); quoted, 33; metron of, 50, 149; on the higher self, 88; conjoined by Babbitt to Confucius, 90, 93, 108, 134, 168 (n. 20); on aristocracy, 118, 169 (n. 36); influence on Babbitt, 138–39. *See also* Greece, ancient
Arnold, Matthew, 6, 14, 35, 58, 63, 64, 66, 87–88, 124, 140, 159 (n. 6); influence on Babbitt, 18, 81–82; Babbitt compared to, 91, 98, 147
Asoka, 134
Augustine, Saint, 137

Babbitt, Dora Drew, 13, 17
Babbitt, Edward, 13
Babbitt, Edwin, 5, 133
Babbitt, Esther, 13
Babbitt, Irving: birth and early years, 5; education at Harvard, 5; on American Puritanism, 8; as teacher at Harvard, 9–32 passim; attacks philology, 14–32 passim; contrasts humanism and humanitarianism, 15; on himself, 24, 123, 142; his style as lecturer, 25–32; on American journalism, 36–37, 91; on Greek culture, 39; on historical method, 43, 81; critical method of, 54, 59, 62–63, 65, 68, 93, 104, 107; on French character, 54–56; on German character, 86; on American character, 91, 93, 95, 114–15, 117, 120–21; on democracy, 100–124 passim; on Catholicism, 126, 133; contrasts Buddhism and Christianity, 134–41
Bacon, Francis, 20–21, 64, 74, 84, 99
Baudelaire, Charles, 25, 49
Benda, Julien, 91, 94–95
Bergson, Henri, 43–44, 50, 55, 63, 71–73, 150, 161 (nn. 58, 60, 61), 162 (n. 69), 163 (n. 11), 175 (n. 21), 176

(n. 27); compared by Babbitt to Rousseau, 43; *élan vital* of, 72; criticism of Buddhism, 143
Berkmann, Alexander, 170 (n. 58)
Berlioz, Hector, 48
Blake, William, 26
Bôcher, Ferdinand, 14
Boileau, Nicolas, 11, 59, 62–63
Bourne, Randolph, 94–95
Brooks, Van Wyck, 25, 29, 32, 57
Brownell, William Crary, 37
Brunetière, Ferdinand, 69–71, 91, 127
Bryan, William Jennings, 103, 113, 121, 170 (n. 51)
Buddha, 8, 76, 99, 107, 168 (n. 20), 178 (n. 57)
Buddhism, 50, 92–93, 98, 108, 126, 149, 176 (n. 27), 178 (n. 60); compared to Christianity, 132–43 passim. *See also* Christianity
Burke, Edmund, 108, 110, 111, 112, 113, 169 (nn. 34, 38)
Burns, Robert, 29
Byron, George Gordon, Lord, 75, 156 (n. 40)

Calvin, John, 137
Carlyle, Thomas, 120, 133, 154 (n. 5), 169 (n.38)
Cassirer, Ernst, 160 (n. 31), 167 (n. 11)
Chalmers, Gordon Keith, 175 (n. 25)
Chapman, John Jay, 14, 75
Chateaubriand, François-René, 30, 43, 63
Child, Francis J., 14
Christianity, 8, 20, 28, 45, 60, 63, 93, 109, 121, 168 (n. 20), 174–75 (n. 15), 175 (n. 21), 176 (n. 42), 177 (n. 56); Babbitt and More on, 126–32; compared to Buddhism, 135–38, 140–42, 177 (n. 47), 178 (n. 57). *See also* Buddhism
Cicero, 6, 15, 26, 100, 152 (n. 11), 176–77 (n. 44)
Clark, Harry Hayden, 152 (n. 16)
Classicism. *See* Humanism, classical
Cleveland, Grover, 114
Colebrooke, Edward, Lord, 50
Confucius, 8, 90, 93, 99, 134, 135, 149, 168 (n. 20); exemplar of humanist tra-